3 9351 00039672 3

1-24870

Date Due

RESERVED		
		3/9/99
APR 7 1980		
APR 1 1 1980		

W/D

A Transformational Approach to
English Syntax

Root, Structure-Preserving, and Local Transformations

A Transformational Approach to English Syntax
Root, Structure-Preserving, and Local Transformations

JOSEPH E. EMONDS

Department of Linguistics
University of California, Los Angeles
Los Angeles, California

ACADEMIC PRESS   New York   San Francisco   London

A Subsidiary of Harcourt Brace Jovanovich, Publishers

ACADEMIC PRESS, INC.
111 Fifth Avenue, New York, New York 10003

United Kingdom Edition published by
ACADEMIC PRESS, INC. (LONDON) LTD.
24/28 Oval Road, London NW1

Library of Congress Cataloging in Publication Data

Emonds, Joseph E.
    A transformational approach to English syntax.

    Bibliography: p.
    Includes index.
    1.   English language--Syntax.   2.   English
language--Grammar, Generative.   3.   Generative
grammar.   4.   Grammar, Comparative and
general--Syntax.   I.   Title.
PE1380.E6   425   75-28019
ISBN 0-12-238550-0

Contents

Preface

For those working in generative syntactic theory, it has long been recognized that any formally manageable and empirically significant generative
model must drastically reduce the expressive power of grammatical transformations; this book attempts to make a significant step toward this goal by justifying
the imposition of a "structure-preserving constraint" on transformations.

The nature of this formal constraint is such, moreover, that it can be fully
justified relative to a particular language only by examination and analysis of
every transformational syntactic process, excepting those which involve deletion
under identity. Thus, since the concentration here is on English (and, to a
lesser extent, on French), most of the syntactic transformations that have been
proposed for these languages are systematically examined, except those that are
principally deletions under identity. In particular, pronominalization and other
anaphora, coordination, and comparatives are not treated here.

As a result, with the exceptions noted, the book is a fairly systematic
investigation of the current "transformational approach to English syntax"
within the general theoretical framework advanced over the past 20 years by
Noam Chomsky. A comprehensive treatment of this sort has previously appeared
only once (Stockwell, Schachter, & Partee, 1968). It is therefore hoped that
this book can serve also as a sort of "handbook of (English and French based)
syntactic theory," even beyond the period of its theoretical immediacy.

Ideally, then, both the theoretical and practical aspects of the book will
make ALL OF IT of use to anyone interested in thorough and formal syntactic
investigation. Beyond this, however, particular aspects of the book should render
it useful for many others who wish to APPLY the results of syntactic investigation to another discipline. The general import of establishing the structure-
preserving constraint for philosophy of language and for developing theories of
language acquisition, syntactic change, and mathematical linguistics should be

apparent from Chapter I alone (with Sections III.7 and VI.5 added for completeness). It is especially hoped that the formal restrictions on transformations imposed here may inspire greater interest in the mathematical treatment of transformational grammars — e.g., along the lines of a recent monograph by Hamburger and Wexler (1973).

Teachers of English as a foreign language (or English teachers more generally) will probably, on the other hand, want to concentrate on sections that treat systematically various aspects of syntax particular to English. In this regard, the following sections are recommended:

Section II.9.1	Parentheticals
Section III.3	Interplay of indirect objects and post-verbal particles
Section III.6.1	Existential *there is/are* construction
Section IV.2.4	Systematic differences between gerunds and infinitives
Section IV.3.1	"Cleft" sentences
Section V.2	Placement of adverbials
Section V.8	Some restrictions on WH fronting
Section V.9	The grammar of "*for—to*" infinitives
Section VI.2.3	Dual verb—auxiliary character of *be*

Since these sections were not written to be read in isolation or apart from the development of the theory presented, they contain much material that can be understood only by reference to the previous sections. However, the regularities exemplified by the data in these sections can perhaps be understood without a full command of the theoretical exposition.

The general organization of the book is as follows: In Chapter I, three types of grammatical transformations (root, structure-preserving, and local) and certain other basic concepts are defined and exemplified. The hypothesis is made that transformational operations (except deletions) must be of these types ("the structure-preserving constraint"). This imposes strong limits on the expressive power of transformations, and in large part solves the question: What kind of derived constituent structure may transformations produce? So as to give content to the notion "structure-preserving transformation," a set of constraints on base rules (an adaptation of Chomsky's "bar notation") is also proposed.

In Chapter II, the root transformations (roughly, main clause rules) of English are formulated and discussed. In Chapters III–V, it is argued that the rest of the major syntactic processes of English must be formulated as structure-preserving rules — that is, their outputs must essentially be configurations generated either by the base or by local rules. Totally new analyses of extraposition (Chapter IV) and WH fronting (Chapter V) are shown to crucially support the structure-preserving constraint.

In Chapter VI, transformations that have essentially to do with nonphrasal categories are discussed, and shown to fall into the three classes of transformations when correctly formulated. In particular, a detailed analysis of French clitics with no positive output constraints and an analysis of the English auxiliary are presented. It is proposed at the end of the chapter that deletions of specified formatives must be root or local transformations, and certain speculations on deletions under identity are offered.

Acknowledgments

This book is, in the first place, an extension and refinement of the linguistic theory created by Noam Chomsky. The method and the kind of results obtained are, I believe, strictly within the paradigm of language investigation that he has introduced into the domain of science. Moreover, he has had a direct, positive influence on a very large percentage of the particular analyses presented here, as well as on the general design of the work as a whole. For all these things, I am extremely grateful.

This book is also in large part the result of cooperative effort with other students of language and linguistics. I cannot here list all those who have made important contributions to my thinking on various points, although I think the bibliography turns out to be a fairly good approximation of such a list. Two people, however, deserve special mention here because conversations I had with them and with others about our similar ideas on certain points while in graduate school played a role in my initial attempts to use the base rules of the grammar to constrain transformations. They are John Kimball and Stephen Anderson.

I think it might be more appropriate here to list those "linguistic friends" to whom I owe a large personal debt, because of their constant intellectual interest in and personal encouragement of my work. Even in this case, the list can only be partial: Ann Banfield, Michael Brame, Noam Chomsky, Peter Culicover, Morris Halle, Michael Helke, Ray Jackendoff, Yuki Kuroda, Jean-Claude Milner, Frederick Newmeyer, Carlos Otero, Henk van Riemsdijk, Mitsou Ronat, Nicolas Ruwet, Jilali Saib, Arthur Schwartz.

I wish to thank William Moulton for making possible a year at Princeton University as a visiting lecturer which was absolutely indispensable in the preparation of this book. The situation he arranged and maintained made possible a great amount of productive and innovative work that otherwise could have easily never been done, and I am only one of many who he has benefited in this way.

In a similar way, the research year I spent earlier at the Center for Advanced Study at the University of Illinois was absolutely necessary for the preparation of much of this material.

I am in great intellectual debt to those friends who are active socialist militants. In general they, much more than the "academic milieu," provide me with constant motivation to search for explanations and coherent theories, which I have tried to exploit in this technical work.

I owe much gratitude also to my parents, Joseph and Margaret Emonds, who steadfastly encouraged and developed my "intellectual bent" from my earliest years. My interest in formal linguistics can be directly traced to the special interest of my father in mathematics and of my mother in grammar. It is hoped that this book will be a source of considerable satisfaction to them in these years when, because of illness, their satisfactions are quite limited.

In preparing this book, I did not have the opportunity to consult two important but as yet unpublished dissertations (John Bowers, MIT, and Carlos Quicoli, SUNY, Buffalo). These studies share the theoretical assumptions of the present work and apply them creatively; they will certainly be most important for any continuing research in the framework presented here.

The generally apolitical atmosphere of the American university tends to mask the sharp political questions involved in publishing highly technical, theoretical work in a society in which access to intellectual achievement is restricted to a handful of atomized and politically fragmented specialists. An intellectual cannot in fact really "make public" such work; one can at best hope that the ruler-owners of society derive simply profit out of one's labor, and not political or technical capital (advantage) as well. True publication of research will occur only when the divisive and restrictive social structures and ideologies of the present order are overcome. To all the socialist militants who will participate in this task, I express my gratitude in advance.

I

Constraints on Phrase Structure Configurations[1]

I.1 The Structure-Preserving Constraint

The central problem considered in this study—the problem of imposing constraints on grammatical transformations—has long preoccupied students of transformational grammar. The first proposals are in Chomsky (1964). Much important recent work has been motivated by the same problem, for example (Bresnan, 1972a; Chomsky, 1973; Ross, 1967a; Schwartz, 1972). With these investigators, I start from the premise that various conditions and restrictions on applying transformations are not ad hoc specifications on the individual rules but, rather, reflections of some deeper grammatical principles that define the formal framework in which transformational rules operate.

The purpose of this first chapter is (i) to define my claims and (ii) to define constraints on base rules that are crucial for a constraint on transformations that depends on the form of base rules.

Constraints on grammatical transformations can be defined and classified in various ways (see, in particular, Chomsky, 1973, pp. 1—3); for our purposes it may be helpful to consider the following subdivision. Certain constraints, including some proposed by Bresnan, Chomsky, Ross, and Schwartz, essentially specify that constituents CANNOT BE MOVED OUT OF CERTAIN STRUCTURAL CONFIGURATIONS, even though these configurations satisfy the structural description of a transformation that would otherwise move these constituents.

On the other hand, certain constraints proposed by Chomsky and Schwartz, for example, attempt to define what conditions are necessary in order for the

---

[1]This study is a revision of my doctoral dissertation (Emonds, 1970), supplemented by articles that have appeared elsewhere (Emonds, 1972a, 1973c). There are of course changes from what appeared in the dissertation and in the other articles. This first chapter is a revision (in places extensive) of Emonds (1973b) and is reprinted with permission.

structural change of a transformation to apply. The constraints defined in this study are of the same type; that is, they essentially specify that constituents CANNOT BE MOVED INTO CERTAIN STRUCTURAL CONFIGURATIONS.

From a study of English transformations, and some consideration of French syntactic processes (which has been greatly aided by the work of Kayne, 1970; Milner, 1973; Ruwet, 1972), I have arrived at a hypothesis for a general constraint on grammatical transformations, which may be termed the STRUCTURE-PRESERVING CONSTRAINT. Of course this constraint is subject to testing, refinement, and perhaps drastic modifications on the basis of other languages, as we cannot automatically expect inductions made on the basis of a few languages to survive in unmodified form when applied to a wide range of languages.

Some preliminary definitions are necessary for a succinct statement of the constraint.

(1)   **Root Sentence:** *A root* S *("sentence") is an* S *that is not dominated by a node other than* S.[2]

In general, the notion of root S and the notion of independent clause, taken from traditional grammar, are closely related. However, there are cases where a root S apparently is derived by transformation from a clause that may be dependent or even nonexistent in deep structure. Some examples of such root S's (boldface) follow:

(2)   **Had John arrived earlier**, *everyone would have been less upset.*
        The first chapter had been censured, **as had the introduction.**
        Will we be welcome, *do you think?*
        The table goes with the lamp, **doesn't it**?
        I guess the table goes with the lamp all right, **doesn't it**?

It would seem that the notion "independent clause" is therefore more closely related to the generative notion "DEEP STRUCTURE root S" than to the more general "root S."

It might be thought that special provision must be made in the definition of root S for the S nodes of direct quotation, which, as we will see, have all the properties of a root S. However, the most enlightening treatments of direct quotation are in my opinion those that, for reasons independent of those of interest here, treat the S nodes of direct quotation as separate sentences of discourse in deep structure (cf. Partee, 1973; Banfield, 1973a). These authors

---

[2]If there is a nonrecursive initial symbol in the grammar (see Section II.9.2), the definition of a root S can be amended so that a root S is an S that is not dominated by any node that S can dominate, other than S.

In Section II.9.3, we will see that a root S should probably be defined slightly differently: S_i is a root S if and only if, for any noninitial node B $\neq$ S such that B $= WS_iX$, then $W = X = \emptyset$. This refinement was suggested by N. Chomsky.

claim that a direct quotation is an independent sentence of discourse, so that the sentence *Bill said, "I am tired"* is derived from the discourse *Bill said this: "I am tired."* In this two-sentence discourse, when *this* is anaphoric (i.e., does not refer to something outside the discourse, such as some writing on a paper held by the speaker), it unambiguously refers to the sentence following. Of course in such an analysis a rule is required that deletes *this*, and perhaps also attaches the quoted S as a sister to the introductory S, but I see no reason to assume that the quoted S is transformationally subordinated to (made a part of) the introductory clause. See Section II.9.2 for further discussion.

(3) **Root Transformation:** *A transformation (or a transformational operation, in the case of a transformation performing several operations) that moves, copies, or inserts a node C into a position in which C is immediately dominated by a root S in derived structure is a "root transformation" (or a root transformational operation).*

(4) **Structure-Preserving Transformation:** *A transformation (or a transformational operation, in the case of a transformation performing several operations) that introduces or substitutes a constituent C into a position in a phrase marker held by a node C is called "structure-preserving."*

That is, a transformational operation is structure-preserving if it moves, copies, or inserts a node C into some position where C can be otherwise generated by the grammar. I leave open for the moment the question of whether any other transformational operations are or are not structure-preserving. In Section III.7 I propose a slight extension of the class of structure-preserving movement rules, and in Section VI.5 I tentatively propose that certain general classes of deletion rules must be considered non-structure-preserving, and hence prohibited in the same contexts as non-structure-preserving movement rules (see later discussion).

Some generally accepted transformational operations that at first glance seem to have the structure-preserving property are (i) the postposing of the subject noun phrase (NP) into a verb-phrase-final prepositional phrase (PP) of the passive construction, (ii) the preposing of the object NP into the subject NP position in the passive, (iii) the "raising" of various dependent clause NPs into subject or object NP positions of a containing clause, (iv) the extraposition of various S constituents into a VP-final S position, and (v) the transformational movement of various adverbial phrases into positions where other adverbials of the same syntactic category can be generated in deep structure. In Chapters III—V ample justification for a structure-preserving formulation of these and other transformational processes will be given.

(5)   **Local Transformation:** *A transformation or a transformational operation that affects only an input sequence of a single nonphrase node* C *and of one adjacent constituent* C' *that is specified without a variable, such that the operation is not subject to any condition* **exterior** *to* C *and* C', *is called a "local transformation" (or a local transformational operation).*[3]

Nonlocal transformational operations will be called MAJOR TRANSFORMA-TIONAL OPERATIONS. I place no special restriction on how a local transformation may "affect" the sequence C—C' (or C'—C). It may reorder them, alter their dominance relations, insert some morpheme adjacent to C or C', or delete C or C' (subject to the recoverability condition: cf. Chomsky, 1965, Chapter III). I insist only on the strictly local nature of this class of rules, and on the restriction that one of the two constituents affected not be a phrase node. Carlos Otero has pointed out to me that this definition of local transformation is NOT the same as that of a "local transformation with respect to a category A" defined in Chomsky (1965, Chapter II, n.18). In Section VI.4 I claim that there is always an A that immediately dominates either C or C' so that a transformation that is local in the sense here defined is always also "local with respect to A" in Chomsky's sense. In order to keep these concepts clear, it might be necessary to refer to the sense of local transformation here defined as "completely local."

I have replaced the use of the term MINOR (MOVEMENT) TRANSFORMATION found in Emonds (1970) with the term LOCAL because the former term seemed to often be confused with the notion "not important" or "not central to the grammatical system" in informal discussions of that work. I in no way mean to sanction that impression; cf. especially Section V.9.

Two well-known rules of English that can be written as local movement transformations are the optional interchange of an object NP and a postverbal particle and the obligatory reordering of a head adjective and the modifying intensifier (degree word) *enough* (cf. *too big, so big, as big, very big,* but *big enough*). According to the preceding definitions, such local transformations can depend on the structural and lexical characteristics of the constituents interchanged, but not on other characteristics of the phrase markers to which the rules apply. Similarly, a rule that inverts a preverbal clitic sequence around the verb depending only on conditions on the verb and on the clitic sequence is a local movement transformation. (Such a rule can account for the position of clitics in Spanish, as the preverbal—postverbal alternation appears to depend on whether the verb is finite or not.)

---

[3] Phrase nodes are, roughly, nodes that dominate phrases rather than lexical items or grammatical formatives. I return later to an explicit characterization. The set of phrase nodes for English includes S, NP, AP, VP, PP, and perhaps one, two, or three others, depending on the exact formal framework used. The choice of a formal framework is of course dependent on empirical adequacy.

On the other hand, a rule like subject—auxiliary inversion in standard English cannot be a local transformation, because it is dependent on the presence in the string of a WH (or NEG) constituent at the beginning of the clause. The same remark holds for the inversion of the clitic pronoun subject around the verb in questions in French. A third case of interchange of adjacent constituents that cannot be a local transformation is the placement of object clitics after the verb in affirmative imperatives in French, for this rule depends on the ABSENCE of any material in the string to the left of the verb (except perhaps material set off by commas).

With these definitions, we can state the structure-preserving constraint in the form in which it will be defended in this study.

(6) **Structure-Preserving Constraint:** *Major grammatical transformational operations are either root or structure-preserving operations.*

It should be clear that the structure-preserving constraint, if correct, largely solves the problem of how transformations should assign derived constituent structure.

Of course the empirical claim embodied by this constraint is heavily dependent on the correct determination of the phrase structure (or base) rules for any given language, and on any general restrictions that can be placed on possible sets of base rules for any language. The third section of this chapter proposes such restrictions.

Before stating these restrictions, however, I will answer an objection to the dependence of the structure-preserving constraint on the base rules that might be made no matter how severely the latter were restricted, and two other plausible general objections to the "sense" of the constraint.

Given that the formal method for stating structure-preserving rules to be used here often requires that such transformations substitute constituents for nodes that dominate only "dummy" or "empty" nodes, one may ask, What is to prevent one from making any non-structure-preserving rule that moves category A into C—D into a structure-preserving one simply by including A as an optional expansion in the base rule(s) generating C—D. This criticism has been made most clearly in Hooper (1973, pp. 41—42); her statement of it bears repetition in full:

> In order for the SP constraint to make any strong claims about the nature of language or transformational rules, the PS rules must be independently motivated. All PS rules postulated must be necessary to generate surface word orders that cannot be shown to be derived by transformation. Emonds' hypothesis is weakened considerably by the postulation of nodes that are always empty in deep structure, because such nodes can have no independent justification, i.e. they cannot be shown to be necessary for generating surface word orders except through the application of SP transformations.

I believe that Hooper's criticism of my previous work is well taken [there is a discussion of this difficulty in Emonds (1970) in the section on WH preposing], and that a condition should and can be placed on the grammar that excludes categories being generated by base rules that are "filled" only by grammatical transformations and never by lexical insertion.

Thus in the present study I exclude the possibility that semantic projection rules defined on deep structure—if they exist—can play a role in "filtering out" whole sets of base structures that exhibit anything but an empty or dummy node in a given base position. That is, for every position of a node C on the right side of a base rule expanding a node B, there is a productive class of semantically and syntactically well-formed deep structures that exhibit "B over C" with C from this position.[4]

I.2 POSSIBLE GENERALIZATIONS OF THE CONSTRAINT

At first glance, when one compares the preceding formulation of the structure-preserving constraint to some rather obvious grammatical processes in languages other than English, it appears that the constraint is seriously inadequate. However, it seems likely to me that the constraint can be generalized in certain ways so that the general idea of the constraint remains intact. I will discuss two types of such inadequacies and suggest ways in which the structure-preserving constraint might be revised in order to account for these cases.

The most general form of the structure-preserving constraint may contain language-specific variables other than the set of phrase structure or base rules, so that the preceding statement of the constraint would be in fact a special case of a more general formal universal.

In particular, in some languages where movement transformations are more freely applicable in certain embedded clauses, a somewhat larger class of nodes may play the role that root S's play in English and French. (This possibility has been suggested by Ken Hale.)

As a case in point, the analysis of Classical Arabic given by Saib (1972) suggests a generalization of the structure-preserving constraint in this direction. Saib argues that the verb is first in deep structure in Classical Arabic, and that the two types of subject—verb—object order that do occur in surface

---

[4]It may be possible to impose the stronger restriction that every CONFIGURATION generable by a base rule must give rise to a productive class of semantically interpretable (well-formed) structures. However, I do not rule out at this point a possibility like a base rule of the form

$$A \rightarrow (B) - \begin{Bmatrix} C \\ D \end{Bmatrix} - (E)$$

all of whose expansions are semantically interpretable except, say, B—C—E.

structure (besides the verb—subject—object order) are transformationally derived.[5] These orders are:

(7)   a. $\begin{bmatrix} NP \\ + NOM \end{bmatrix} - V - \begin{bmatrix} NP \\ + ACC \end{bmatrix}$

           b. $\begin{bmatrix} \begin{Bmatrix} \text{'}inna \\ \text{'}anna \end{Bmatrix} \\ COMP \end{bmatrix} \begin{bmatrix} NP \\ + ACC \end{bmatrix} - V - \begin{bmatrix} NP \\ + ACC \end{bmatrix}$

Order (7a), according to Saib, occurs only in roots S's, in accordance with the structure-preserving constraint. Order (7b) is an optional variant of the verb—subject—object order in main clauses and in certain LIMITED types of subordinate clauses. The deep structure verb-first order is ALWAYS possible, although the clause in question is sometimes introduced by '*an* and sometimes by '*annahu*.

As Saib has pointed out to me, order (7b) is a counterexample to the structure-preserving constraint if the definition of root S given here is to hold for Arabic. The rule that moves an NP to the left of the verb to yield (7b) applies only in subordinate clauses introduced by '*annahu*, and it sometimes moves the object NP, which is not adjacent to the verb, so it cannot be a local movement transformation. Thus it may be that in Classical Arabic certain complements S's—those introduced by '*anna(hu)*—can play the role of root S's, in line with the suggestion of Hale's mentioned earlier.[6]

---

[5]There are relatively few VSO languages. If VSO is a base order, the notion of "deep structure subject NP" would not be realized in just these languages. These facts suggest that VSO languages might be derived from SVO base orders by a local transformation, counter to Saib's proposal. His arguments are therefore of great import for grammatical theory if they stand up under comparison with carefully worked out alternative analyses with an SVO base.

[6]The types of subordinate clauses in which order (b) occurs in Arabic are similar, I believe, to the indirect discourse contexts in which the structure-preserving constraint is sporadically violated in English, giving sentences of doubtful acceptability. Cf. Sections II.6 and II.7. In Arabic, however, the acceptability of the (b) order in the appropriate contexts is not in doubt, as in English.

In Hooper and Thompson (1973) it is argued that certain dependent clauses even in English (those that are "semantically asserted," in their terms) act like root S's, suggesting that the definition of root S as given previously may be too restrictive even for English. At present Hooper and Thompson's notion of assertion can be formalized as a list of different clause types or by a feature +ASSERTION to be associated with main clauses and certain other structurally definable clauses.

I cannot yet definitively evaluate these claims, as I have not yet been able to systematically investigate the data in areas where different claims than mine are made. A comparative critique is to be found in Ogle (1974, Chapter 6), who also argues for a different analysis regarding the applicability of root transformations. My impression is that their alternative analysis faces as many counterexamples as mine (not the same ones, by any means—which gives the proposal interest), and that there is also, unfortunately, much disagreement over the acceptability of the data in crucial areas. In some cases, however, I am not sure that really different claims are made. For example, it may be that nonrestrictive relative clauses, which Hooper and Thompson consider to be semantically asserted, are derived from a coordination of root S's

However, at this point I am not in a position to define what are the possible sets of nodes that may function as root nodes in languages other than those like English. A reasonable working hypothesis would be that only S nodes can play the role of root nodes in any language; a stronger one would be that only left- or right-branching S nodes can play this role. Interesting work in this regard I must leave for future research.[7]

Footnote 6 continued

transformationally—for example, by means of the root transformation of parenthetical formation discussed in Section II.9:

> *John came in late, and he is usually reliable* (by Parenthetical Formation, which here postposes the first VP).
> *John, and he is usually reliable, came in late.*
> *John, who is usually reliable, came in late.*

Such an analysis predicts that the following example is unacceptable, because parenthetical formation normally moves only constituents:

> *?Bill asked John, who is usually responsible, for the rent money Sunday.*

Part of the evidence that should be used in determining whether such a derivation of nonrestrictive relatives is correct is of course whether or not root transformations freely apply in such clauses, as Hooper and Thompson claim. But if they do, it seems that the preceding analysis makes unnecessary a special extension of the notion "root S of English" for nonrestrictive relatives.

    Similarly, Hooper and Thompson claim that "nonrestrictive" subordinate clauses such as (i) freely allow root transformations:

(i)	*John isn't coming, because I just talked to his brother.*
≠ (ii)	*John isn't coming because I just talked to his brother.*

However, Edward Klima (personal communication) has pointed out that preposability is a characteristic of subordinate, but not coordinate, clauses:

$$John\ isn't\ coming,\ \begin{Bmatrix} although \\ but \end{Bmatrix}\ the\ rest\ of\ the\ family\ will\ attend.$$

$$\begin{Bmatrix} Although \\ {*}But \end{Bmatrix}\ the\ rest\ of\ the\ family\ will\ attend,\ John\ isn't\ coming.$$

$$John\ isn't\ coming,\ \begin{Bmatrix} because \\ for \end{Bmatrix}\ the\ car\ isn't\ running.$$

$$\begin{Bmatrix} Because \\ {*}For \end{Bmatrix}\ the\ car\ isn't\ running,\ John\ isn't\ coming.$$

By this test, the nonrestrictive use of *because* in (i) acts like a coordinating rather than a subordinating conjunction:

(iii)	*Because I just talked to his brother, John isn't coming.*

Sentence (iii) means the same as (ii), but not the same as (i). Thus if nonrestrictive *because* clauses freely exhibit root transformations, we can assign nonrestrictive *because* to the class of coordinate conjunctions and thereby account for both (i)—(iii) and the data of Hooper and Thompson.

    The nonpreposability of nonrestrictive *because* does not REQUIRE that we assign it coordinate conjunction status; it only makes it possible. It may be that nonrestrictive subordinate clauses and coordinate clauses simply share a structural similarity that excludes preposing. Also, if nonrestrictive *because* is a coordinate conjunction (meaning that the clause it introduces is a root S), there is no requirement in the structure-preserving constraint that all root transformations be applicable in all root S's.

    [7] If some languages have a larger set of root S's than English, another question that is immediately raised is whether such variation is random or related to other formal properties of the languages in question.

A second kind of violation of the structure-preserving constraint appears to occur when certain phrasal constituents move about within a sentence somewhat freely. For example, Banfield (1973b) notes that certain "stylistic transformations" that account for the "free phrase order" and "gapping" patterns in English poetry of the grand style (Milton, Donne, Pope, etc.) are neither root nor structure-preserving operations. It is to be noted, however, that such stylistic transformations exhibit, according to Banfield, certain other formal characteristics that differentiate them from strictly grammatical transformations: They follow all other syntactic rules, including agreement and case assignment; they cannot be "triggered" by the presence or absence of specific morphemes in the tree (by contrast, say, to English indirect object movement, which is "triggered" by the prepositions *to* and *for*); they cannot introduce morphemes, nor delete morphemes except under identity; they appear to be subject to some version of Chomsky's "up-to-ambiguity" principle (1965, pp. 126–127); they do not seem to be statable (without loss of generalizations) in terms of the left-to-right analyzability conditions that are appropriate for grammatical transformations. Informally, their inputs appear to be systematically as acceptable or MORE acceptable (even in the case of deletion under identity) than their outputs. For discussion of these characteristics see Banfield (1973b, Chapter III).[8]

From this point on, then, I use the term STYLISTIC RULE to refer only to rules with these formal properties, and NOT in any loose sense.

It is clear, however, that stylistic rules that break the structure-preserving constraint are not allowed freely. As Banfield points out, the stylistic movement rules of English poetry in the grand style are not part of spoken Modern English, and the rules of Modern English that seem to formally qualify as stylistic (e.g., topicalization) obey the structure-preserving constraint.[9] A revision of the structure-preserving constraint in the following form therefore suggests itself:

(8)   ***Under certain conditions*** *stylistic (as opposed to grammatical) transformations may break the structure-preserving constraint.*

A revision of this type should account for many of the phenomena traditionally called "free word order." At this time, I can offer only preliminary suggestions for stating these "certain conditions," all of them based on traditional linguistic ideas about free word order in Indo-European languages.

---

[8] In many ways these stylistic transformations resemble the feature-changing performance rule proposed by Otero (1972) for certain acceptable but ungrammatical utterances of Spanish—in particular, the "up-to-ambiguity" limitations on such utterances and the impression that they involve a partly conscious "intervention for effect" by the speaker are similarities.

[9] It has been pointed out to me by Ann Banfield that if one considers topicalization and negated constituent preposing as the same rule, as seems plausible, then this rule must precede auxiliary inversion, an obligatory rule. Thus topicalization in Modern English could not be stylistic in any case.

For one thing, stylistic transformations apply more freely in literary and poetic language than in conversational language. This dimension may be all that is involved in differentiating Milton's use of free word order from the prohibition against it in spoken Modern English.

We also know that phrasal categories (NP, AP, PP, etc.) are more likely to be subject to free word order in inflected languages. To simplify discussion I assume with Banfield that stylistic transformations take surface structures as their INPUT. (This terminological decision can be made because stylistic transformations are optional rules that follow all grammatical transformations; it is also suggested by the fact that the input—not the output—of stylistic rules is judged to be grammatically more acceptable, as pointed out by Banfield.) This means that surface structures are subject to the structure-preserving constraint without reservation, and that the task is to specify when stylistic transformations that break the structure-preserving constraint can be added to the grammar of a language. The formal relation between inflection and non-structure-preserving free word order rules might now be stated along the following lines:

(9)   *Nodes of phrasal category* C *may (not must) be moved within subtrees of category* B *(e.g.,* B = *embedded* S*) by a stylistic rule that breaks the structure-preserving constraint (* = *"a free word order rule") if, in a "sufficiently wide" class of cases, the surface structure grammatical relations of* C *to other elements in* B *are not obscured—e.g., if these relations are indicated by a set of syntactic features that are phonologically realized in* C.[10]

Thus a set of phonologically realized "case features" on head nouns or on determiners that differentiate subject NP's, object NP's, and various indirect object or oblique NP's in the surface structure of a "sufficiently wide" class of S's would permit (not require) a language to have a free word order rule for noun phrases within a sentence. In Latin, which has free word order of NP's, nouns exhibit case features (nominative, genitive, etc.). In Modern English, only pronouns exhibit such features. In Modern French, not even pronouns (within NP's) exhibit case features (cf. the analysis of French clitics in Chapter VI). In spoken Modern English and French, free word order of NP's within the S is prohibited. The free word order in Milton's poetry may be due solely to the poetic dimension, or to the fact that case features on pronouns were more indicative than they are today of surface grammatical relations, or to both factors.

---

[10]Notions such as "phrasal category," "head of a phrase," etc. are defined formally in the next section. "Sufficiently wide" is probably to be construed differently for literary and for conversational language styles.

Similarly, a set of "agreement features" between adjective phrases and the nouns that they modify (such as agreement in grammatical gender, number, and case), and an adverbial feature marker for adjective phrases that do not directly modify nouns, could "sufficiently" indicate the surface relations of adjective phrases to other elements inside an S so as to permit the free word order of some or all adjective phrases.

Thus in Latin there are overt agreements in gender, number, and case between adjectives and nouns, and there is a distinct adverbial form for adjectives. Concurrently, Latin exhibits very free ordering of adjective phrases, to the extent that, in literary language at least, adjectives may be moved out of noun phrases by stylistic rules.

By contrast, Modern French adjectives agree with the noun they modify overtly only in gender and—in rare cases—in number; further, there is one less grammatical gender in French than in Latin. Modern French retains an adverbial marker for adjective phrases (*-ment*). Consequently we may expect to find less free word order. Schlyter (1973) proposes that French adverb phrases are subject to a number of structure-preserving transformations and that they are also subject to Keyser's "transportability convention."[11] This "convention" is in fact a typical stylistic transformation—in Schlyter's analysis it can follow all grammatical transformations; it is optional; it does not depend on or introduce specific morphemes; and it cannot be stated adequately in terms of left-to-right analyzability conditions that are subject to a structural change. However, transportability (i.e., interchange with sister constituents) is a more limited type of free word order than is found in Latin, especially since it applies only to adverbial adjective phrases and not to AP's in general. If Schlyter's analysis of French is correct, it would seem that the surface relations of adjective phrases are "sufficiently marked" in French to permit some free word order of AP's, but less than is found in Latin.

It seems, then, that the following problems present themselves:
(i)   Under what conditions may embedded S's play the role of root S's?
(ii)   Under what conditions (on the rule, or on the grammar in which the rule appears) can a stylistic transformation break the structure-preserving constraint?

I claim that the conditions for either possibility, whatever their nature, do not exist in Modern English, i.e., that all major transformational operations in English ARE root or structure-preserving, with root S as defined earlier. But I am not claiming that careful analyses of other languages, such as those undertaken by Saib and Schlyter, will not lead to different, though ultimately com-

---

[11]According to Keyser (1968), a node is transportable if it can freely appear before or after any of its sister constituents. He claims that English adverbial phrases are in general transportable, but I argue in Section V.2 that this is not true.

patible, conclusions about the grammars of other languages, and to important modifications in the structure-preserving constraint.[12]

I.3   RESTRICTIONS ON BASE RULES

In the model of transformational grammar described in Chomsky (1965), the deep structures are generated by a set of context-free phrase structure rules and the lexicon. As research has developed and refined this model, it has become clear that the notion of "possible set of base rules" (excluding any rules that may be in the lexicon) can be considerably restricted without loss of generality. In particular, the work of Bowers (1969), Chomsky (1970), Dougherty (1970a), Jackendoff (1971), Milner (1973), Ruwet (1969), Selkirk (1970, 1972), Shopen (1972), and others suggests that all phrasal categories of the grammar are best defined in terms of at most four "head-of-phrase category nodes": N, V, A, and P (noun, verb, adjective, and particle).[13] The restrictions on base rules that will be proposed here follow from this basic premise (which is also implicit in the work of Z. Harris).

The adverbs that are formed from adjectives—by adding *ly* in English, for example—will be treated simply as adjectives in a verb-modifying rather than a noun-modifying function. The basic justification for this is that such adverbs, with few exceptions, are formed regularly from adjectives, and that

---

[12]In subsequent chapters I entertain the possibility only once that a stylistic (not a grammatical) transformation of English breaks the structure-preserving constraint. In Section II.10 I give an analysis of the preposing of adverbial prepositional phrases that are "outside the VP" in deep structure that is in accord with the structure-preserving constraint. As noted there, the analysis is questionable and perhaps should be replaced by a (stylistic) adverb-preposing rule that can apply in a variety of dependent clauses. I think the evidence weakly favors the analysis given in Section II.10 (and not the stylistic rule), but the question is far from decided.

Were the stylistic rule finally adopted, I would propose that such a free word order rule is possible in English only because the PP's moved by it (those "outside the VP") enter into a single surface grammatical relation (as a sister to VP), which is not obscured by the existence of one free word order rule in the language.

Carlos Otero has pointed out to me that the postposing of the subject NP in Spanish (much freer than in French; cf. Section III.4.3) may well not be construable as a stylistic rule in the sense here defined—under certain conditions it may be obligatory. If so, this constitutes a situation not compatible with the form of the structure-preserving constraint here defined.

[13]"Preposition" as a name for the fourth lexical category would be unfortunate. On the one hand, the category includes many "intransitive prepositions," which are not "preposed" in any sense, such as *together, away, back* (cf. Emonds, 1972a); on the other, many elements traditionally termed prepositions, such as *à* and *de* in French, may well not be in a head-of-phrase category (cf. Ruwet, 1969). A better term that would also have grammatical tradition behind it might be ADVERB; however, many elements traditionally termed adverbs (e.g., adjective-modifying words like English *very*) are not members of the fourth lexical category. Further, the category in question can modify nouns as well as verbs (*the weather **around** the airport*), and ADVERB cannot be assigned a single mnemonic symbol (because A = adjective). I will continue the usage that has begun in transformational grammar and retain the symbol P for the fourth lexical category. However, as a name for the category PARTICLE is perhaps the least misleading. As I argue in Emonds (1972a), prepositions belong to this category.

they are modified by exactly the same type of grammatical constructions (comparatives, superlatives, etc.) as adjectives. For English and French, at least, similar statements would not hold for any two categories of the N, V, A, P group.

As a basis for the discussion, it is useful to have a formal definition of the term PHRASAL CATEGORY. In order to be as noncommittal as possible on nonessential points, I will not exclude the possibility that phrase nodes directly dominate certain formatives (i.e., the pronoun *I* could conceivably be an NP but not an N), nor the possibility that nonphrase nodes like N may occur on the left side of certain base rules (i.e., a rule of the form N → V−P could conceivably be the source of compound nouns like *lean-to, walk-on, take-off, build-up, talking-to, run-about*, etc., as suggested in Kuiper, 1972). So I will not identify phrase nodes with nodes that do not dominate lexical entries, nor claim that they are the only nodes that occur on the left of (nonlexical) base rules, although it is quite likely that one or both of these are also properties of phrase nodes.

A definition of phrasal category compatible with a model in which neither, one, or both of the preceding properties hold is the following:

(10)   **Phrasal Category:** *A grammatical category that can dominate* NP
        *by virtue of applying the base rules in a given language without
        using lexical rules is a "phrasal category" or a "phrase node" in
        that language. All other categories are "nonphrasal."*

Even though it may be that N dominates NP in $[_N\ [_{NP} American\ history]_{NP}$ *teacher* $_N]$ and that V dominates NP in $[_V\ take\ [_{NP}\ unfair\ advantage]_{NP}\ of\ _V]$, these configurations can arise only if lexical insertions with internal syntactic structures are utilized.

It follows from the definition that no nonphrasal category can dominate a phrasal category; if it could, it could dominate NP and hence would itself be phrasal. The nodes that one might informally call "phrase nodes" in grammatical descriptions of English (S, NP, VP, AP, PP) clearly satisfy this definition. (Note that the definition does not specify immediate dominance.) On the other hand, descriptions of English have been proposed in which DET → NP is a phrase structure rule (for generating possessive noun phrases), which would mean DET was a phrasal node. We will see later that such a phrase structure rule is excluded by the restrictions we will place on base rules, which would dictate, rather, an alternative such as

$$(11) \qquad\qquad NP \rightarrow \begin{Bmatrix} DET \\ NP \end{Bmatrix} \ldots N \ldots$$

for possessive noun phrases; in Section V.9 corroborative empirical evidence is given that, in this case at least, the formal restrictions to be proposed here have the right result.

It seems that base rules are permitted by which any phrasal category can dominate any other. In the case of English the base rules proposed here will yield almost every possible combination of IMMEDIATE dominance among the phrase nodes S, NP, AP, VP, and PP. (A nonoccurring case might be PP → . . . VP . . . ; PP apparently immediately dominates even AP in sentences like *The atmosphere changed from very depressing to quite gay when she arrived.*)

Given this fundamental distinction between phrasal and nonphrasal categories defined by the base rules, we can proceed to formalize a number of restrictions on base rules that have generally been observed in practice by transformationalists, if not explicitly recognized.

(12) **Definition:** *The three categories* N *(noun),* V *(verb), and* A *(adjective) are "lexical categories." The category* P *is the nonlexical head-of-phrase category; the head-of-phrase categories are* P *and the lexical categories.*

(13) **Lexical Restriction:** *Only lexical categories can be "productive"; that is, only lexical categories may have several hundred or even thousand members, and only in these categories can speakers of the language "coin" new members.*[14]

(14) **Base Restriction I:** *A head-of-phrase category of a language* L *appears on the right side of at most one base rule of* L.[15]

One might be tempted to extend Base Restriction I to all nonphrasal categories. However, there are plausible analyses of negation, questions, etc. that propose more than one deep structure source for morphemes like WH and NEG, so any simplistic extension of this type appears premature at best. On the other hand, one might be able to impose the requirement that any nonphrasal category can appear but once in the base rules, except that it may COOCCUR as an optional syntactic feature on some other category without breaking the restriction. Thus a feature like NEG could have a "principal" position in the base—say, in the auxiliary in English—and could also appear as an optional feature on other categories, such as DET and/or COMP. (An analysis of negation compatible with such a restriction would be that of Lasnik, 1972.) But I will not pursue this further here.

---

[14] I deny that lexical categories MUST be productive. A relevant point that supports my position has been made by Vida Samiian, an Iranian linguistics student; she feels that the standard literary dialect of Modern Persian may be best analyzed as having only noun and adjective as productive categories, with verbs being a nonproductive category.

[15] If one feels that base rules must also be used to define the possible categorial combinations in derivational morphology (such as the N → V—P rule for compounds like *lean-to* and *walk-on*), then Base Restriction I applies only to those base rules with phrasal categories on the left side. The set of possible rules of this type is further specified later.

The specification of possible base rules using Base Restriction I that has been developed in the works cited earlier (Bresnan, Chomsky, Dougherty, Jackendoff, Milner, Ruwet, etc.) depends crucially on utilizing the notion "head of a phrase." This signals an attempt at formulating within a generative model a central principle in the work of Harris. Further refinements and modifications in this area will no doubt depend crucially on how exactly the generative model can capture some of the properties of heads of phrases defined and discussed in, for example, Harris (1957, 1968).

In defining further restrictions I will use neither the superscript notation of Harris nor the bar notation of Chomsky (1970) but, rather, the prime notation of Selkirk (1972). This is meant to reflect the fact that no formal properties of either Harris' or Chomsky's notation will be used unless they are explicitly defined here. In particular, I do not require that a single schema of base rules serve for N, V, and A. Also, I will use the symbol H for "lexical category" or "head of a phrase," as I feel that Chomsky's "X" is too easily confused with a variable for an arbitrary string.

The only base rules for expanding phrase nodes that seem to have gained some acceptance,[16] except those for expanding S and those for generating coordinate conjunction (which are taken up later), are as follows, where $H_0 = H$, H', or H'', and the number of primes of H_0 does not exceed that of the phrase node being expanded.

(15) **Base Restriction II:** *All phrase node expansions, except those of S and of coordinate conjunction, are of the following form:*

> i. $H'' \rightarrow X_1 H_0 X_2$
> ii. $H' \rightarrow X_3 H_0 X_4$
> iii. $H'' \rightarrow$ PRO

where H is a head-of-phrase category node and X_i is a variable.

Base Restriction II claims that all phrases are endocentric, with the exception of S. This possibility is proposed in Harris (1951, Chapter 16).

(16) **Definition:** *In (i)–(iii) the category H, H', or H'' (whichever has the fewest primes) on the right side of the rule is called the head of the phrase H'' or H' on the left side of the rule.*

(17) **Uniqueness Condition:** *A well-formed base rule given by Base Restriction II has a unique head.*

---

[16]In part this may just reflect the fact that the languages extensively investigated in generative frameworks have been limited in number. But making precise hypotheses about base rules in general is the only way to see if and exactly how other languages require that we modify these hypotheses.

In more usual terminology, which will for the most part be retained in the text, $N'' = NP$, $V'' = VP$, $A'' = AP$, and $P'' = PP$.

Since the restrictions being discussed are intended to put LIMITS on possible base rules, it is not relevant here to determine precisely what even narrower limits can be set on base rules in an adequate grammatical theory; if more such restrictions can be imposed without loss of explanatory adequacy elsewhere in the theory, so much the better.[17] In particular, it is possible that there do not exist phrase nodes "between" NP and N, VP and V, etc. Thus it may be that H' ($\overline{H}$ in the bar notation of Chomsky, 1970) does not exist separately from H'', so that ONLY the phrase node expansions given in (i) and (iii) are theoretically possible. In this study, I do not utilize H' nodes unless I explicitly note the contrary.

A third restriction on base rules that can be imposed is that all complement and modifier constituents of phrasal category are optional (at the deep structure level), whereas heads of phrases are obligatory. Another way to put this, which will prove useful later, is as follows:

(18) **Base Restriction III:** *In the metatheoretical statements of possible base rules, the phrase nodes contained in the variables are optional; the specified (phrasal and lexical) nodes are obligatory.*

As far as Base Restriction II is concerned, Base Restriction III simply means that the phrase nodes in the variables X_i are optional and that the heads of phrases are obligatory. The observation of this characteristic I would attribute to Harris (1951, Chapter 16), although I believe that it can be accurately formulated only in a framework that admits of deep structure.

There are thus head nouns, verbs, adjectives, and prepositions whose LEXICAL entries require obligatory complements of various sorts, but there are no object, adverb, predicate attribute, relative clause, or comparative complements that must appear within ALL H'' structures given by a particular base rule.

On the other hand, it does appear that heads of phrases are obligatory at the level of deep structure. For example, in English the deep structure head noun is deleted after the determiner (but not after an adjective) in many contexts, yielding surface noun phrases of the form *the good, the just, which, some, all, the shorter, the first,* etc. Thus, *these small lamps are beautiful, but*

---

[17] It will be of interest later that these restrictions exclude NP → S or NP → NP—VP (unless the NP on the right is the head of the construction) as possible base rules. They do not, of course, prevent equivalent configurations in surface structure that might arise as a result of deletion rules. In English the two configurations appear in surface structure as free (= "independent" or "headless") relative clauses and as gerunds, respectively. The two cases are discussed in Chapter IV.

some big ones are ugly and *these lamps are beautiful, but some are ugly.* In
the case of mass nouns, English lacks a lexical "pro-noun" like *one*, so that
the string that results when the head deletion rule does not operate is **that
dark wood is beautiful, but some light is ugly.* The fact that this string is
ungrammatical indicates that the dummy terminal symbol Δ is present in the
surface structure, which, in turn, indicates that it must be obligatorily generated
in deep structure. (It is a condition on derivations that the dummy terminal
symbol Δ must be removed either transformationally or by lexical insertion—
see the discussion of agent postposing in Chomsky (1970). Cf. *that wood is
beautiful, but some is ugly*, where the noun head deletion rule has deleted Δ,
giving a grammatical sentence.) Of course surface nouns as well as verbs can also
be deleted ("gapped") under identity. Cf. Jackendoff (1971) for a comparative
study of the two cases. In these cases also, the most convincing analyses in the
end hypothesize obligatory heads of phrases in deep structure.[18]

We can now approach the question of whether the subject NP node in
English is dominated by V″; if it is not, then V″ cannot be identified with S.
In the literature one finds differing opinions: Chomsky (1970) keeps the two
distinct, while Jackendoff (1971) does equate them.

There are two ways in which the subject NP node in a sentence S differs
from other nonhead phrase nodes in English: (i) It is obligatory in deep
structure, independent of the selection or subcategorization features of the verb
(although it may consist only of a dummy element that is filled in during the
transformational derivation with an expletive subject such as *it*); (ii) it is a
phrase node to the left of the head node (the VP) and also exhibits free right-
branching recursion in surface structure. I return later to the second characteristic of the subject NP, but for the moment let us use the first in order to
determine what the form of initial symbol (S) expansions should be.[19]

If the base expansions for S are to be subject to Base Restriction III,
as are the expansions for other phrase nodes (those given by Base Restriction
II), then the obligatory subject NP and predicate VP nodes must be specified
in the appropriate metatheoretical statement (Base Restriction IV):

---

[18]I do not put forward any hypothesis for predicting when nonphrasal nodes in the expansions of H″ and
H′ are optional. While most such nodes seem optional, the French article (or determiner) and TENSE in
English and French are potential counterexamples to any claim that all such nodes are optional. Similarly,
H. Van Riemsdijk (personal communication) argues that in Dutch each predicate contains an obligatory
assertion or negation marker in deep structures. So I continue to assume that nodes that are neither phrase
nodes nor lexical category nodes must be marked as optional or obligatory in each base rule.

[19]Some recent work by Banfield (1973a), Quang Phuc Dong (1969), and Shopen (1972) indicates that
there is a nonrecursive initial symbol E or U (expression or utterance) in which nonembedded epithets,
expressions, and constructions occur; this symbol, in turn, can dominate the highest S of a sentence. The
arguments for this position seem convincing to me, so that the problem being dealt with in the text is actually
the determination of the expansions of the node that can dominate propositions.

(19) **Base Restriction IV (Tentative):** *The possible base rules for expanding* S *are of the following form:*

    iv. $S \rightarrow Y_1 N'' Y_2 V'' Y_3$, *or* $S \rightarrow Y_4 V'' Y_5$

where Y_i *is a variable and* Y_i *does not contain* N'' *or* V''.

Like the schema in (i)—(iii) for expanding other phrase nodes given in Base Restriction II, (iv) is subject to Base Restriction III. The second disjunct of (iv) is for languages without subjects in deep structure. If these do not exist, it should be eliminated (cf. note 5).

It is plausible that (iv) should be generalized, even for English, to include predicates that are verbless NP's, AP's, and PP's. There are, of course, languages where the copula does not appear in certain surface sentences of the form NP—NP, NP—AP, or NP—PP. But even when finite forms of the copula do appear before predicate attribute NP's, AP's, and PP's, they may be——in some languages at least——realizations of the node TENSE or some node other than the node V.[20] In this view, sentences like *John is a doctor, John is very nice,* or *John was behind the house* might contain no verb at all. In order not to exclude such verbless deep structure sentences (whatever other category name is given to the copula), I extend the schema for the base expansions of S from (iv) to (v):

(20)   v. $S \rightarrow Y_1 N'' Y_2 H'' Y_3$, *or* $S \rightarrow Y_4 H'' Y_5$,

    where Y_i *is a variable,* Y_i *does not contain* N'' *or* H'', *and* H *is a head-of-phrase category node.* H'' *is the head of* S. *The second disjunct is needed only if there are languages without deep structure subjects.*

Let me now return to the observation made earlier that the subject NP in English, UNLIKE phrase nodes to the left of the head within an NP, AP, PP, or VP, exhibits free right-branching recursion in surface structure——e.g., *Your decision about the report that the men who had been elected would take bribes dismayed us.* By contrast, such free surface recursion is not exhibited in English by possessive noun phrases (*the king of England's hat*), prenominal adjective phrases, preadjectival measure phrases (*three tiring miles long*), intensifying adverbial adjective phrases (*so magnificently attired, quite simply boring*), preverbal adverbial adjective phrases (*politely put it away, very quickly finished his work*), or preprepositional measure phrases (*put it three feet*

---

[20]TENSE might better be considered as the node that marks the presence of an assertion, with (in English) +PAST as an optional accompanying syntactic feature. It should be noted that nothing in what has been said so far prevents base rules such as VP → AUX—VP, VP → ... V ... VP, or VP → AUX—... V ... VP. I take up this question in Chapter VI, but the restrictions set up here do not predetermine our choice of analyses.

beyond the table). I have not investigated in detail how this restriction on recursion in surface structure can best be stated, but it certainly seems to exist.
The important point is that this restriction does not apply to subject NP's,
and hence this corroborates the prediction made by Base Restriction III that
subject NP's are not within the VP $= $ V''.

However, for purposes of making this claim somewhat more precise, I
will venture a partial formulation of a "surface recursion restriction":

(21) **Surface Recursion Restriction:** *Given a surface configuration of
the form* $\left[_{H_i^n} \ldots A \ldots H_i \ldots \right]$, *if the base rules permit right
sisters* H_k'' *to* H_i, *then* A $\neq$ XS Y, A $\neq$ X PP Y, *where* PP
dominates a lexical preposition, and A $\neq$ WA Z, *where W and
Z* $\neq \emptyset$. *In such cases we say that* A *does not exhibit free recursion.*

Quite clearly this restriction, if correct, excludes the possibility that V''
dominates the subject NP. It should also be noted that the restriction as
stated does not apply to sentences (S). And in fact not only subject NP's but
also presubject adverbial phrases exhibit free recursion: *The day that John
said that* . . . , *Bill died*. Further, the restriction does permit, say, an NP in
the surface configuration $\left[_{VP} \ldots NP \ldots V \ldots S \right]$ to have surface recursion,
because only H'' (and not S) to the right of the head prevents recur-
sion before the head. It has been pointed out to me by H. Van Riemsdijk
that this possibility should be allowed for the analysis of Dutch and German. For further discussion of this restriction on recursion, see Zwarts
(1974).

A consequence of the surface recursion restriction is that either all freely
recursive phrase nodes (except a subject NP and perhaps S) appear to the left
of a given head of a phrase in surface structure, or else all appear to the right of
the head. Thus it makes sense to speak of the "recursive side of (the head of)
a phrase" as that side of the head which exhibits *all* the freely recursive nodes
other than S.

Finally, we must specify the possible base rules for coordinate conjunction
of phrase nodes. In this, I use the rules proposed by Dougherty (1970a). He has
demonstrated, in my opinion, that all coordinate conjunction in English, except
what may be called "conjunction across constituent boundaries,"[21] should be
generated by the base; he proposes the following base rules:

(22) $$ X \rightarrow (Q) \; X^n \; (ADV) $$

---

[21] An analysis of coordination across constituent boundaries in terms of a stylistic deletion transformation
is given in Banfield (1973b). In a similar vein, I understand that Blom (1972) argues against conjunction
reduction, and for a late deletion rule, in deriving such constructions.

where X = S, NP, or VP; Q (the "distributive quantifier") = each
all, both, either, neither. ADV *(the "distributive adverb")* = at
once, simultaneously, concurrently, en masse, in different directions,
respectively, correspondingly, at one time, together, *etc.*

I will replace Dougherty's X by H'' and S to be consistent with what has gone
before, and slightly generalize his formula for base conjunction in writing a
schema for possible base rules for conjunction. Conceivably X should be extended to H and/or H' as well.

(23) **Base Restriction V:** *The possible base rules for coordinate*
conjunction of phrase nodes are of the following form:

$$\text{vi.} \quad H'' \rightarrow U_1 \, H''^n \, U_2; \; S \rightarrow U_3 \, S^n \, U_4$$

U_i *is a variable and* H *is a head-of-phrase category node.*

These expansions are subject to the same restrictions as those of (i)−(v):
H'' and S are the specified nodes and hence are obligatory; any phrasal categories in U_i are optional. By Base Restriction I, $U_1 U_2$ and $U_3 U_4$ cannot contain any
lexical category nodes.

Conceivably more than two primes are needed in the phrasal category
notation developed here. See, in particular, the suggestive work of Williams
(1972) and Ronat (1973). I do not mean to imply that extension of the bar notation or the prime notation in this direction is formally undesirable.

II

Root Transformations

In this chapter, I will discuss transformations of English that are neither structure-preserving nor local, and can be analyzed as movements of nodes into positions where such nodes are immediately dominated by a root S. The burden of showing that transformations that cannot be so formulated (indirect object movement, WH fronting, clitic placements in French, affix movement, etc.) are in fact either local or structure-preserving falls on subsequent chapters.

The definitions of root sentence and root transformation are given in Chapter I.

II.1   SUBJECT–AUXILIARY INVERSION

In standard American speech the subject NP and the auxiliary verb invert in direct questions, except when the subject itself is questioned. By AUXILIARY, in this study, I will always mean just those verbal elements that undergo this rule: modals, *have* (in certain uses), *be*, and *do*. The full justification for this category (AUX) is given in Chapter VI. This inversion is also used in certain exclamations, wishes, and sentences with preposed negative constituents:

(1)   *Is Mary coming?*
                     Will they support us?
                     How would we escape?
                     Why weren't they cooperative?
                     Did you burn the papers?
                     Who has John helped?

> *Wasn't that brave of him!*
> *Isn't it cold out!*
> *May you always be as thoughtful as she was!*
> *Never in my life have I spoken to him.*

The mechanics of this transformation are well known; if the subject of the highest S is preceded by a questioned (WH) or negated constituent, the order of the subject and the following auxiliary, which includes a TENSE affix and a possible *n't*, is reversed. According to Katz and Postal (1964), there is an underlying preposed questioned constituent *whether* within *yes—no* questions that causes auxiliary inversion like other WH constituents. This *whether* appears explicitly in embedded questions:

(2)   *John wonders whether Mary is coming.*
      The question of whether they will support us is still undecided.

The rule has the form given in (3), where COMP is the sentence-initial "complementizer" node justified in Bresnan (1972a), under which we can assume that WH constituents are transformationally placed:

(3)   **Subject—Auxiliary Inversion**:
      $$\text{COMP}-\text{NP}-\text{AUX}-X \Rightarrow 1-3-2-4$$
      where 1 *dominates* WH *or* NEG *or* so.

The important characteristic of this inversion rule for our purposes is that it applies only in the HIGHEST S; it does not apply in relative clauses and indirect questions:

(4)   *We talked about how we would escape.*
                      She doesn't know why they weren't cooperative.
                      The papers that you burned were important.

"Root S," as defined here, describes the contexts for subject—auxiliary inversion more exactly than "highest S," since this rule also applies in conjoined sentences immediately dominated by the highest S:

(5)   *She didn't do the dishes, and why should she?*
      I know it was expensive, but never in my life have I been so thrilled.
      When is he coming, and where is he from?
      Come in right now, or do I have to use force?

(The conditions under which such mixed sentence types can be conjoined are not known with precision, but this is of no consequence here.)

Sometimes the conjoined sentence exhibiting inversion is only an abbreviated (tag) form of a full sentence. Thus *neither—auxiliary—NP* is derived from NP—auxiliary—*not either* by preposing the negated constituent *not either*, which, in turn, causes the inversion. Like full sentences containing inversion, such tags cannot be embedded:

(6)   **Bill didn't come to the party because neither did Mary.*
      *John thought that Bill hadn't come, and that neither had Mary.
      *Mary doesn't know why Susan is leaving, and we don't know
          why is she either.

The affirmative tag NP—auxiliary—*too* can be paraphrased by preposing *too*
and changing it to *so*, yielding, after inversion, "*so*—auxiliary—NP." Again,
the inverted form cannot be embedded:[1]

(7)   **I am in great danger, and the knowledge that so are you isn't very*
          comforting.
      *I'm worried, and I'm sure (that) so are you.

Another class of root S's in which subject—auxiliary inversion applies are
the "reported sentences" or "quotes" of direct discourse. As stated in Chapter
I, I adopt the "two-sentence" analysis of direct quotes of Partee (1973) and
Banfield (1973a):

(8)   *John said, "What should she eat?"*
          The man asked, "Can my son have a key?"
          She exclaimed, "Isn't it cold out!"

A typical surface structure in (8) is as follows:

(9)

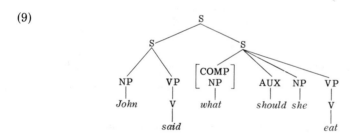

In the cases covered so far, A ROOT S (IMMEDIATELY) DOMINATED BY ANOTHER
S is set off by commas. We will be able to extend this to many other cases as
we proceed.[2]

It is reported in Labov, Cohen, Robbins, and Lewis (1968, Section 3.7)

---

[1]Inversion in negative imperatives also takes place only in a root S:

> *Don't you be so impolite!*
> *Don't you talk like that, or I'll send you home!*
> *Don't anybody move!*

[2]There are a few other contexts in which subject—auxiliary inversion occurs, especially in very
"literate" speech, but in which rule (3) does not apply freely. For example, there are such inversions
after the complementizers *than* and *as*. The auxiliary inversion that occurs in "sentence relatives"
introduced by *as* is quite free, but may be attributed to the fact that these S's can be assigned a

that Black English exhibits subject—auxiliary inversion (and the absence of *whether*) in dependent clauses:

(10)   *I don't know how did I do it.*
                Where did she get the coat from I don't know.

The absence of a complementizer in a dependent clause suggests that this construction is like the "mixed" indirect discourse of German,[3] in which the tenses

---

Footnote 2 continued

root status (that is, we can analyze sentence relatives as S sisters to the main clause; note the comma intonation):

> *John must do his own laundry, as must every student here.*
> *I was looking for faults in his presentation, as was my friend.*

Comparative clauses introduced by *than* and *as* are not root S's, unless they are to be assigned that status in sentence-final position by a special raising transformation, a possibility suggested to me by Thomas Huckin. They therefore should not exhibit inversion according to the rules of Modern English proposed in this study. If the following sentences were all completely regular and to be accounted for by the subject—auxiliary inversion rule, my analysis would be deficient:

> *We saw the same man as did John.*
> *She hasn't bought as many souvenirs as has her husband.*
> *She spoke more convincingly than did Harry.*
> *?Bill seems smarter in math than does Harry in science.*
> *?The Chinese are as ready to fight as are the Japanese to talk.*
> **I hope you found the play more interesting than did we.*
> **Our friends can't afford to buy records as often as can you.*
> **John likes Beethoven more than do I.*
> **He'll cut more cake than will Mary be able to eat.*

However, the fact that pronouns cannot invert in these sentences indicates that subject—auxiliary inversion does not operate the same way in *as* and *than* clauses as it does in questions, exclamations, etc. Furthermore, even the acceptable sentences with inversion are somewhat less acceptable than their counterparts without inversion:

> *We saw the same man as John did.*
> *She hasn't bought as many souvenirs as her husband has.*
> *She spoke more convincingly than Harry did.*
> *Bill seems smarter in math than Harry does in science.*
> *The Chinese are as ready to fight as the Japanese are to talk.*

Another difference between inversion in *as* and *than* clauses and normal subject—auxiliary inversion is that the former is optional and the latter obligatory.

For these reasons, I am willing to regard the *as* and *than* clauses (other than sentence relative *as* clauses) that exhibit inversion as (i) not fully grammatical in English [they would be derived by application of a prestige-oriented performance rule of the type proposed in Otero (1972) for an ungrammatical class of acceptable utterances in Spanish] or (ii) derived by a secondary inversion rule in the class of local transformations. In this case, the class of local rules would have to be extended slightly to permit structural descriptions with sequences of at most one phrase node specified without a variable and TWO adjacent non-phrase nodes (COMP and AUX, in this case).

[3]German has two indirect discourse constructions. In one of these, the reported sentence is like other nonroot S's in that it is introduced by *dass*, its verb is in final position, certain fronting transformations cannot occur in it, etc.:

> *Er sagte dass er krank sei.*

and pronouns of indirect speech appear in clauses that otherwise have all the characteristics of main clauses (i.e., of direct quotation). In fact such a construction appears in Standard English after a verb like *wonder*:

(11)   *John wondered (mused), (why) should he be early.*

Such "complement" sentences have main clause status throughout the transformational derivation; i.e., they are derived from two-sentence sources as in (12) and transformed into $\left[{}_s S - S \right]$ structures:

(12)   *John wondered thus: Why should he be early.*
            John asked me this: Why was he supposed to be early.

In this view, the characterization of dialects, languages, or literary styles (cf. the discussion in Banfield, 1973a) depends on what classes of verbs appear as first clause main verbs in those sequences like (12) that can be transformed into single S's. (This transformation is discussed in Section II.9.2.)

It therefore seems plausible that Black English differs from Standard American in allowing question clauses to appear in "mixed indirect discourse," and that it does NOT allow auxiliary inversion in true dependent clauses. Alternatively, Black English (and Irish English—cf. Baker, 1969) may exhibit auxiliary inversion more freely because of a larger class of root S's. (Hale's suggestion in Section I.2 is relevant.)

II.2   VERB PLACEMENT IN GERMAN

German is in interesting contrast to English with regard to the placement of the verb. In German the finite verb, i.e., the verb that carries the tense ending, is generally in second position in a root S:

(13)   *Gestern **ist** er nach Hause gekommen.*
            *Welches Buch **können** die Studenten nehmen?*
            *Mit einem Messer **wird** er den Kuchen schneiden.*
            *Hans **stahl** ein Buch.*
            *Mich **hat** er geschlagen.*

Footnote 3 continued

        *Er sagte dass gestern er nach Hause gekommen sei.
        *Er sagte dass mich sie geschlagen habe.

In the other type of indirect discourse, the reported sentence, like the reported sentence in direct discourse, is a root S. The verb is second, certain fronting transformations can apply, *dass* does not introduce the clause, and the clause is sometimes set off by a comma:

        Er sagte, er sei krank.
        Er sagte, gestern sei er nach Hause gekommen.
        Er sagte, mich habe sie geschlagen.

In embedded (nonroot) sentences the finite verb is last in the verb phrase. (In this section, LAST means "last except for sentence complements.")

(14) *Ihm tat es leid, dass er gestern nach Hause gekommen **war**.*
      *Er weiss nicht, welche Bücher die Studenten genohmen **haben**.*
      *Er wird mehr Kuchen mit dem Messer schneiden, als ich essen **kann**.*
      *Weil Hans einen Bleistift gestohlen **hat**, wird er bestraft.*
      *Dass er ein Auto stehlen **würde**, erstaunte seine Eltern und seinen*
          Lehrer.

If the German verb is last in its clause in deep structure, as argued in Bierwisch (1963), the rule that moves it to second position in root S's can be formulated as a root transformation. That is, the V moved can be attached to the highest S. The alternative position would be to assume that the German verb is generated in second position by the phrase structure rules and is moved, in nonroot S's only, to final position in the VP. Cf. Ross (1967b), and a refutation in Maling (1972).

The structure-preserving constraint is in fact inconsistent with this assumption, since in principle it excludes such a movement rule. At the same time, it predicts that a rule moving the verb from final position to second position can apply ONLY in root S's. Thus if the constraint on transformations proposed in this study is correct, the German verb must be last in its clause in deep structure.[4] For a discussion of the relation of this hypothesis to the acquisition of German by children, see Roeper (1972).

II.3 TAG QUESTIONS

A TAG QUESTION is a declarative sentence followed by a repetition of the first auxiliary (*do* if the preceding declarative has no auxiliary) and a pronominalized form of the subject. Some typical tags are *shouldn't he? hasn't he? did they? were you?* Two rules might be involved in forming tag questions: A tag formation rule might copy an entire declarative sentence, probably with the addition of *whether* (deleted, as usual, in root S's in surface structure),[5] and the subsequent deletion of what follows the first auxiliary would then be due to an independently motivated "VP deletion" rule:

---

[4]See n. 3.

[5]I am ignoring the problems associated with positioning NEG correctly in these constructions. If pronouns are in the base, as seems correct to me, then the tag question rule must introduce pronouns rather than a copy of the subject.

(15)   *Mary had come, hadn't she?*
                         Mary won't buy this dress, will she?
                         Bill dates someone, doesn't he?
                         You were dissatisfied, were you?

I assume that the surface structure that results from the tag formation
rules is as in (16). The fact that the right-hand S in (16) is a root means
that subject—auxiliary inversion may apply. Also, the comma that sets off the
tag from the preceding declarative follows from the principle relating commas
and root S's proposed in Section II.1.

(16)

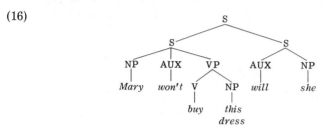

The tag formation rule itself is a root transformation, since tag questions
are never nonroot S's; the highest S immediately dominates the tag S:

(17)   **Bill wanted to know whether Mary had come, hadn't she?*
       *Bill asked if he could date someone, could he?
       *The question of who Mary dates, doesn't she, doesn't bother him.
       **The idea that Bill knew whether Mary had come, hadn't she, is
           preposterous.*

Sometimes the tag S is a copy of the complement to *I imagine, I suppose,
I guess*, etc., as in (18). (This can occur only with a first-person singular present
tense form.) Cf. the discussion in R. Lakoff (1969).

(18)   *I imagine he is dating my wife, isn't he?*
                         I guess he likes foreign beers, doesn't he?

However, the definition of a root transformation demands only that the constituents copied by tag formation be immediately dominated by a root S in
DERIVED structure. There is no reason to believe that the tags in (18) are not so
attached, given the examples in (19):

(19) *The idea that I imagine he is dating my wife (*isn't he) bothers
         him.*
     The foreign beers that I guess he likes (*doesn't he) are expensive.

II.4   ADVERB PREPOSING

Several kinds of adverbs may be preposed in a sentence. A basic division can be made between those that, in preposed position, are followed by an optional (sometimes obligatory) comma or breath pause, and those that are not. This division is further justified by noting that the former class never causes inversion in the main clause, while the latter does in almost every instance.

Possible deep structure sources for the former class of adverbs, and the question of whether they can freely appear in embedded sentences, are discussed in Section II.10; I will say no more about them here. The latter class, which we can call INVERSION adverbs, result from root transformations and can appropriately be treated here.

II.4.1   Negated Constituent Preposing

Preposed negated constituents, which are sometimes NP's but usually adverbs, cause subject—auxiliary inversion and are not separated from the main clause by a comma:

(20)   *Under no conditions may they leave the area.*
            Never have I had to borrow money.
            At none of the beaches are the lifeguards alert.
            Only on weekends did I see those students.
            It was expensive, but seldom has John been so pleased.
            Few movies have we enjoyed so thoroughly.
            Nothing did I see that I liked.
            In not many years will Christmas fall on Sunday.
            (Cf. *In not many years, Christmas will fall on Sunday.*)

The examples in (21) generally indicate that this preposing is limited to S's that are roots.[6] Nagahara (1974, Section 3.3) cites some acceptable embedded preposed negative constituents followed by inverted auxiliaries, and some marginal ones (according to judgments he reports). Besides the remarks of note

---

[6] Some of the examples in (21) do not sound totally unacceptable. However, the fact that auxiliary inversion occurs after WH constituents only in roots indicates that such examples may not be strictly grammatical. Moreover, the general heuristic subscribed to here for classes of sentences of doubtful grammaticality (acceptability judgments in such classes being erratic) is that they are ungrammatical, provided that they are not semantically difficult or of undue length or embedding. The reason for this is that it would be hard to explain even slight unacceptability for sentences that are relatively short and simple, semantically clear, and perfectly grammatical. But it is to be expected that intelligent language users would possess strategies of interpretation to render certain types of sentences that are relatively simple, semantically clear, and slightly ungrammatical perfectly understandable and acceptable. According to this heuristic, then, I take the sentences in (21) to be ungrammatical. See Otero (1972, 1973) for discussion of such matters.

6, I simply extend the observations of Section II.7 (taken without change from Emonds, 1970) to negated constituent preposing and subject—auxiliary inversion.

(21)   *If under no conditions may they leave the area, how can they pay*
  their debt?
  ?I have worked hard so that never have I had to borrow money.
  *The proof that at none of the beaches are the lifeguards alert is that
  there have been many fatalities.
  *The students that only on weekends did I see are living in the
  country now.
  ?We wouldn't do it again, even though seldom has John been so
  pleased.
  *The employees are happy that in not many years will Christmas
  fall on Sunday.

II.4.2   Directional Adverb Preposing

If the verb of a sentence is in the simple past or present tense (no auxiliaries being allowed), a prepositional phrase indicating spatial direction may be preposed. This includes adverbs of direction that, like other adverbs of time and space, are in the preposition category (cf. Emonds, 1972a). This construction seems limited to exclamatory statements. Also, the simple present seems to paraphrase the present progressive of sentences with normal word order:

(22)   *In came John!*
  Down the street rolled the baby carriage!
  Up trotted the dog!
  Round and round spins the fateful wheel!
  Here he comes! (Cf. the synonymous *He is coming here.*)
  Away they ran!

Substituting verb forms containing auxiliaries into (22) generally produces ungrammatical examples.

The sentences in (22) are not obtained by simply exchanging the first and last constituents of the corresponding declaratives, since pronoun subjects are not inverted. Rather, two processes seem involved. The first is the preposing of the adverbial PP, which is perhaps part of some other rule, and the second is the movement of the simple verb into second position. This is similar to the movement of the auxiliary into second position after the preposing of WH and negated constituents (cf. Section II.1). I will call this SUBJECT–SIMPLE VERB INVERSION (because ordinarily no auxiliaries can be involved).[7]

Both of these rules, directional adverb preposing and subject—simple verb inversion, take place in the highest S; i.e., they are root transformations:

(23)   *I noticed that in came John.
            *It seems that away then ran.
            *The fact that down the street it rolled amazed her.
            *I was surprised when up trotted the dog.

Simple verb inversion cannot be combined with auxiliary inversion because (i) in this case, if an auxiliary is present, the rule does not apply, whereas in the other case, the rule applies ONLY to auxiliaries, and (ii) pronominal subjects do not count as taking up the second position in simple verb inversion, but in auxiliary inversion they do.

Actually it is hard to combine the preposing of the directional adverb with any other rule, because it depends on the sentence's verb form's not containing any auxiliaries, and no other adverb-preposing rule has this proviso:

(24)   *In John was coming!
            *Down the street the baby carriage was rolled!
            *Here he **does** come!
            *Round and round the wheel has spun!
            *Away they didn't run!

It appears therefore that directional adverb preposing and subject—simple verb inversion are distinct rules, and that moreover they are, respectively, separate from other adverb-preposing rules and subject—auxiliary inversion. If this is true, two adverb-preposing rules are root transformations——negated-constituent preposing and directional adverb preposing——and two subject inversion rules are root transformations——subject—auxiliary inversion and subject—simple verb inversion. Although directional adverb preposing occurs only with (noun) subject—simple verb inversion, the latter has another use in direct quotation, described in Section II.9.

II.5 SOME OTHER PREPOSING RULES

II.5.1 Topicalization

Consider the following sentences:

---

[7]At the point of this inversion in a derivation, the pronoun subject may already be attached to the verb form as a prefix, so that the verb is already in second position after the preposing of the directional adverb.

(25)   *These steps I used to sweep with a broom.*
              Each part John examined carefully.
              Our daughters we are proud of.
              Poetry we try not to memorize.

These examples result from a transformation, called TOPICALIZATION, that moves noun phrases to the front of the sentence; that is, it attaches them to the highest S. This transformation is a root transformation, since examples like (25) cannot be embedded (however, see note 9):

(26)   **Have I shown you the broom (that) these steps I used to sweep with?*
       *I fear (that) each part John examined carefully.
       **We are going to the school play because our daughters we are proud
          of.*
       *Are you aware (of the fact) that poetry we try not to memorize?
       *Do you think socialist theory many Czechs would deny?
       *That this house he left to a friend was generous of him.

II.5.2   VP Preposing

Consider the following sentences:

(27)   *Mary once predicted that John would pass an exam eventually, and
          pass one he now has.*
       John hoped that Mary would find his hat, but find it she could not.
       John intends to make a table, and make one he will.
       *We thought someone would fail the exam, and fail it plenty of people
          have.*

These sentences are derived from the structures underlying those in (28) by preposing a VP to the front of an S:[8]

(28)   *Mary once predicted that John would pass an exam eventually, and
          he now has passed one.*
       John hoped that Mary would find his hat, but she could not find it.
       John intends to make a table, and he will make one.
       *We thought someone would fail the exam, and plenty of people have
          failed it.*

(I show in Chapter VI that the first auxiliary *have*, *be*, or *do* is outside the VP in AUX position when rules like this apply to VP; hence, the rule is not overly complicated.)

---

[8]Actually the rule may be misnamed here, since it applies to any phrase node following the first auxiliary: *Mary said he was a bad risk, and a bad risk he was; We thought she would be in the running, and in the running she is.* Paul Postal first brought this rule to my attention.

The rule in question, VP PREPOSING, cannot apply in nonroot S's:

(29)   *Mary once predicted that John, who now has passed an exam,
        would pass one eventually.*
        **Mary once predicted that John, who pass(ed) an exam now has,
        would pass one eventually.*

        *John hoped that Mary would find his hat, but I wonder how she
        ever could find it.*
        **John hoped that Mary would find his hat, but I wonder how find
        it she ever could.*

        **John intends to make a table, and his wife thinks that make one he
        could.*
        **John intends to make a table, and we're afraid that make one he
        will.*
        **John intends to make a table, and I'll get the materials so that
        make one he can.*

        **We are looking for someone who failed the exam, and now we've
        found someone who fail(ed) it (he) has.*

Thus VP preposing is also a root transformation.

II.6   RIGHT AND LEFT DISLOCATION

In this section, we consider rules that remove NP's from their ordinary
position in sentences, set them off by commas, and replace them with pronouns.
One such rule, LEFT DISLOCATION, moves an NP to the beginning of the sentence:

(30)   *This room, it really depresses me.*
             John's sister, she won't do anything rash.
             These clams, I buy them right at the shore.
             This movie, I told you you wouldn't like it much.
             Jane, she visits this park every weekend.

This rule apparently attaches NP's to the highest S;[9] if this condition is not
fulfilled, the impression is that of broken speech:

---

[9]This observation is due to Ross (1967a, pp. 233–234). He states that left dislocation "only places
constituents at the head of main clauses," and observes that the same restriction holds for the topicalization
rule discussed in the preceding section. He also notes that sentences in which these two rules apply "in
certain object clauses seem to be acceptable." To exemplify this exceptional behavior, Ross provides the
following:

                ?*I acknowledged that my father, he was tight as a hoot-owl.*
                I said that my father, he was tight as a hoot-owl.

(31)   **I told you that this movie, you wouldn't like it much.*
       *Bill hopes that John's sister, she won't do anything rash.
       *They put so much furniture in here that this room, it really
           depresses me.
       *The fact that these clams, I buy them right at the shore means that
           they are sure to be fresh.
       *He doesn't like the park that Jane, she visits it every weekend.

I conclude that left dislocation is a root transformation, if not a base construction. (If the latter, it would be generated under the nonrecursive initial symbol E discussed in Section II.9.2. This was suggested to me by N. Chomsky and by H. van Riemsdijk.)

   Corresponding to left dislocation there is a rule of RIGHT DISLOCATION, as exemplified in (32):

(32)   *It really bothers me, John's big cigar.*
               She won't do anything rash, John's sister.
               I buy them right at the shore, these clams.
               I told you you wouldn't like it much, this movie.
               Jane visits it every weekend, this park.

   The crucial examples for determining whether or not right dislocation is a root transformation are trees containing an embedded sentence that is not rightmost in a constituent (NP or VP) immediately dominated by a root. An S that is rightmost in a subject NP or in a VP immediately dominated by a root does not qualify because the right- "dislocated" NP could be attached

---

Footnote 9 continued

       *That informers they never use is claimed by the Revenooers.
       ?The Revenooers claim that informers they never use.

   The remarks in Section II.7 (which I have left unchanged from Emonds, 1970) about exactly this possibility of root transformations applying in certain object clauses so as to produce sentences of marginal grammaticality (note, for instance, the last example in the preceding set) clearly extend to left dislocation and topicalization. Invariably object clauses of the same type exhibit the phenomenon in question (those of indirect discourse; cf. the following section).

   A different explanation of why topicalization leads to well-formedness only when the preposed constituent is in the root S is given in Chomsky (1973). This alternative, if correct, would throw doubt on the necessity of the "sentence boundary condition" (Chapter III), and hence merits comparison on more than one count.

   I do not agree with Ross's judgment that RIGHT dislocation can attach constituents to dependent clause S's (the depth of embedding of the NP in the input of the rule is not relevant here). The discussion in the text, moreover, shows that Ross's judgments on the following two sentences (that they are acceptable, which I do not think they are) do not, even if correct, provide evidence against the claim that right dislocation attaches NP's to S's:

       That they spoke to the janitor about that robbery yesterday, the cops, is terrible.
       That the cops spoke to the janitor about it yesterday, that robbery, is terrible.

to the root, as in (33). [On the other hand, if (33) is unacceptable, it may mean
that right-dislocated NP's appear only on the right of the highest VP; thus we
can conclude nothing from a judgment on (33).]

(33)

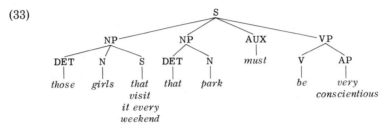

Crucial examples are therefore those in (34):

(34)   *John has sold the garage that you store it in, that old car, to Mary.*
        *I predicted that her attempt to do something daring, John's sister,
            would end in disaster.*
        *The fact that the girl Bill bought it for, the camera, is visiting him
            doesn't seem to improve his disposition.*
        *He doesn't realize that the girl he bought it for, the camera, doesn't
            like him.*
        *I didn't say that it bothered me, riding in the back seat, on the trip
            out.*
        *John gave the boy she used to go out with, his girl friend, a
            dollar.*

Since these crucial examples are unacceptable, I conclude that right dislocation is a root transformation. But I leave undecided the question of whether it
can attach NP's between the subject NP and the VP, as in (33). For arguments
that left-dislocated NP's are base constructions in French and Dutch, see
Hirschbühler (1974) and van Riemsdijk and Zwarts (1974).

II.7   PREPOSING AROUND BE

In this section, I discuss some constructions that are not so clearly root
transformations as those previously discussed. Rather, these constructions
throw into relief the possibility of falsification of the structure-preserving hypothesis, and ways in which other syntactic or semantic processes may interrelate
with the constraint on transformations I propose. The rules that produce these
constructions are not structure-preserving; nonetheless, they SOMETIMES and
FOR SOME SPEAKERS ONLY can apply in nonroot S's in normal English speech. In

order to retain the hypothesis that non-structure-preserving, nonlocal movement rules must be root transformations (the structure-preserving constraint), I assert that the use of these rules in embedded sentences is ungrammatical in the strict sense, and that the structure-preserving constraint is being broken for purposes of emphasis, clear communication, etc. Since I am not in a position to be able to characterize the conditions under which ungrammatical sentences can be used, my theory, in the only sense that I can make it precise, does not always coincide with judgments of acceptability. However, it is likely that the way to correct it is to study the conditions under which the structure-preserving constraint can be broken, and not to abandon the constraint itself.

Consider first the rule by which predicate adjective phrases whose heads are compared by means of *more, less, most, least,* or *as* are permuted with the subject NP. (Whether or not the rule operates in sentences that have linking verbs other than *be* is of no interest here.) Call this rule COMPARATIVE SUBSTITU-TION:

(35)   *More important has been the establishment of legal services.*
        Just as surprising was his love for clothes.
        Most embarrassing of all was losing my keys.
        No less corrupt was the ward boss.
        Equally difficult would be a solution to Russell's paradox.

The substitution of an AP for an NP is not a structure-preserving rule according to the definition given in Chapter I.

Therefore, comparative substitution should be a root transformation, and constructions like those in (35) should not occur in embedded sentences. And in some embedded sentences they are indeed unacceptable:

(36)   **Bill wonders why more important has been the establishment of legal services.*
        *A love for clothes that just as surprising was also got him into debt.
        ?That equally difficult would be a solution to Russell's paradox is not at all clear.
        *The deputies could extort with impunity, as long as no less corrupt was the ward boss.

In other instances, however, the sentences in (35) sound acceptable when embedded, at least to some speakers:

(37)   *? We convinced the authorities that more important would be the establishment of legal services.*
        ?Your admission that just as surprising was his love for clothes indicates a lack of understanding.
        ?I am sure that most embarrassing of all was losing your keys.

John Bowers (personal communication) has pointed out that the embedded sentences that violate the structure-preserving constraint in (37) all seem to be complements to verbs, nouns, or adjectives that report attitudes or statements of their subjects; i.e., these verbs, nouns, and adjectives are functioning to introduce indirect discourse. If those parts of the meaning of a sentence that involve connected discourse (presupposition, new information, etc.) are to be found in the surface structure and surface order of elements (for a discussion of this, see Chomsky, 1971, and Jackendoff, 1972), then the simplest way to report this sort of meaning in indirect discourse would be to break the structure-preserving constraint and reproduce the surface order directly.

By mentioning the possibility of an explanation along these lines, I do not mean to deny that the structure-preserving constraint, as it now stands, makes some doubtful predictions about the sentences in (37). But as I said earlier, the proper path for further study would seem to be investigation of the conditions under which the constraint can be broken. In the great majority of cases, as we will continue to see, the constraint makes just the right predictions; for example, if the constraint were abandoned, what would explain the unacceptability of sets of examples like (36)?

Another rule that preposes constituents around *be* we might term PARTICIPLE PREPOSING. In Chapter VI I give evidence that what follows the progressive or passive uses of *be* is a single sister constituent to *be* (a VP). The sentences in (38), which have limited use in English, seem to corroborate this contention:

(38)   *Speaking at today's lunch will be our local congressman.*
       Taking tickets at the door was a person I had previously
           roomed with.
       Examined today and found in good health was our nation's chief
           executive.
       Taking turns, as usual, were his two sisters.

Inasmuch as participle preposing is used as a rule of English, it exhibits root transformation behavior quite clearly:

(39)   **Bill wonders why speaking at today's lunch will be our local*
           congressman.
       *The person who taking tickets at the door was had roomed with
           me at Yale.
       *Since examined today and found in good health was our nation's
           chief executive, we can all breathe more easily.
       *The fact that taking tickets at the door was my old Yale roommate
           made it easy to get in.
       *Bill said that taking turns, as usual, were his two sisters.
       ?Bill announced that speaking at today's lunch would be our local
           congressman.

A third transformation that permutes constituents with subject NP's over *be* (and a few other verbs, in this case) is a rule we can call PP SUBSTITU-TION:

(40) *In each hallway is (hangs, has long stood) a large poster of Lincoln.*
      Among the guests were (sat) John and his family.
      On the porch is a large wicker couch.
      Upstairs is (stands, lies) all the wine we bought in Europe.
      Here will be (will stand) the memorial to the war dead.

Since PP substitution is not a structure-preserving nor a local rule, it should be, according to the structure-preserving constraint, a root transformation. And as in the case of comparative substitution, there are embedded S's in which it may not apply:

(41) **I have no idea how often among the guests were (sat) John and his family.*
      *The posters that in each hallway are (have long stood) subtly influence the children.
      *That here will stand a memorial to the war dead upsets the pacifists.
      *I won't be satisfied until upstairs is all the wine we bought in Europe.
      *Now that on the porch is a large wicker couch, we can all relax.

However, there are also cases of acceptable embedded sentences that exhibit PP substitution (at least for some speakers):

(42) *?The belief that in each hallway is (hangs, has long stood) a large poster of Lincoln is erroneous.*
      ?She convinced Bill that among the guests were (sat) John and his family.
      ?Bill is happy that on the porch is a large wicker couch.
      ?I've noticed that upstairs is (lies) all the wine you bought in Europe.
      ?Bill was just explaining that here will be (will stand) a war memorial.

I believe that what was said earlier about comparative substitution is also appropriate here. It should be remarked that the contexts in (36) and (41) are similar, as are those in (37) and (42). I propose that the structure-preserving constraint be retained in its present form in the face of such data, and that efforts be made to isolate properties (especially potential discourse properties) of the rules and lexical items involved in (37) and (42) to see what allows the constraint to be (for some speakers) neutralized.

A germane discussion is to be found in Hooper and Thompson (1973), who propose to modify the class of root S's so as to permit non-structure-preserving rules to apply in a wider class of sentences. A few comments on their proposal are given in note 6 of Chapter I, but lack of time has prevented me from giving a fuller treatment.

In Aissen and Hankamer (1972) there is a discussion of some sentences closely related in structure to those given by PP substitution:

(43)   *They are planning to destroy the old church under which are buried*
        six martyrs.
    They destroyed the church in whose basement is buried the town's
        founder.
    These are the causes to which are attributed most of the financial
        catastrophes of the decade.
    I met the social director to whom fell that terrible task.

In these cases, WH fronting (discussed in Chapter V) rather than PP substitution fronts a prepositional phrase.

Aissen and Hankamer are concerned with what rule effects the interchange of the verbal complex and the subject NP in the sentences in (43). They suggest extending the rule of subject—simple verb inversion discussed in Section II.4.2 to cover the cases in (43), and conclude that this rule, if so extended, would not be a root transformation. They also note that this extension, contrary to what was proposed in Emonds (1970), must allow inversion of compound tenses of the verb (*are buried, are attributed,* etc.).

However, my original discussion of this rule states—as does the discussion in Section II.4.2—that compound verbs produce ungrammatical sentences in the two uses for which I proposed the rule—directional adverb preposing and direct quote preposing:

(44)   *In has come John!*
      Down the street was rolling the baby carriage!
      Up has trotted the dog!
      Into the street was kicked John!
      Across the park will be thrown the ball!
      (Cf. *Across the park will be erected a war memorial.*)

      "Bill is crazy," was repeating Mary.
      "I am late," has exclaimed Bill.

This would seem to indicate that the original proposal to limit the rule to simple verbs is correct.

The rule needed to effect the subject shift in both (40) (the PP-substitution cases) and (43) (the WH-fronting cases of Aissen and Hankamer) is a restricted version of the rule of "stylistic inversion" that Kayne (1970) has proposed for French.[10] In Chapter III (and in Emonds, 1970) I argue that this rule of French is structure-preserving precisely BECAUSE it cannot apply when the verb phrase contains a direct object NP. That is, I claim that stylistic inversion in French is a structure-preserving substitution of the subject NP for an empty object NP node.

The same analysis can be made for English. The inversions in (43) can be effected by a structure-preserving substitution of the subject NP for an empty object NP node:

(45)

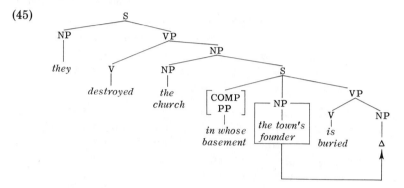

This analysis is also that justified in Nagahara (1974, Section 3.2). He adds the following interesting example:

(46)   "All these attest how varied and how far-flung have been the influ-
       ences which have moulded the modern English vocabulary [From
       C. L. Wrenn, *The English Language*. Tokyo, Kenkyusha, p. 70]."

[Nagahara points out that (46) suggests the correctness of an analysis utilizing the concept of a doubly filled predicate attribute node in deep structure; for further discussion of this concept, see Chapter III, n.26.]

An "object replacement" analysis for (40) and (43), as exemplified in (45), predicts that, as in French, the movement of the subject NP will be blocked if a direct object NP is present in the surface structure.

Aissen and Hankamer note that this (for them accidental) restriction on moving the subject in fact holds for what they take to be instances of subject—verb inversion in (47) (i.e., for the inversion of the subject in sentences where WH fronting or PP substitution has fronted a PP); this means that the English

---

[10]The French version is not generally limited by the type of main verb appearing in the clause, but only by what kinds of constituents appear within the VP when the rule applies. Incidentally, stylistic inversion (Kayne's term) is not a stylistic rule in the sense of Chapter I. For discussion see Section III.4.3.

as well as the French version of stylistic inversion should be formulated as a structure-preserving rule:

(47)   **Under the old church buried the former inhabitants of the town six martyrs.*
       *They are planning to destroy the old church, under which buried the former inhabitants of the town six martyrs.

       *Under the old church buried six martyrs the former inhabitants of the town.
       *They are planning to destroy the old church, under which buried six martyrs the former inhabitants of the town.

       *To these causes attributed the senator most of the financial catastrophes of the decade.
       *These are the causes to which attributed the senator most of the financial catastrophes of the decade.

I therefore agree with Aissen and Hankamer that the rule inverting the subject and the verbal complex (stylistic inversion) in (43) is not a root transformation; it is, rather, structure-preserving. But I do NOT agree that the rule I call subject—simple verb inversion (as opposed to what they call by this name) is not a root transformation.

II.8   A CONDITION ON TRANSFORMATIONS THAT MOVE CONSTITUENTS OVER VARIABLES

There is evidence that all the root transformations that front phrasal constituents without inducing comma intonation are substitutions for the sentence-initial COMP node. The evidence is the fact that only one of these transformations can occur in a given clause. To show this, I first list the preposing root transformations of this type so far studied, together with sentences in which the boldface constituents have been fronted by each of the rules in question:

(48)   a.   **Negated Constituent Preposing:**
                Never *will she buy a car.*
                Only a few students *did he meet in the East.*

           b.   **Directional Adverb Preposing:**
                Away *ran John.*
                Into that house *ran the boys.*

           c.   **Topicalization:**
                These steps *I never swept with a broom.*
                Her *John likes.*

d. **VP *Preposing:***
    *She never has bought a car, and **buy one** she never will.*
    *He said I would like her, and **like her** I do.*

e. ***Comparative Substitution:***
    Easier for us to solve *would be a problem from number
        theory.*
    Equally as welcome *would be a theorem from geometry.*

f. ***Participle Preposing:***
    Speaking to the President now *is our top reporter.*

g. ***PP Substitution:***
    Among the guests *was standing John.*

In (49) we see that combinations of the rules in (48) (within the same
clause) produce ungrammaticality. The notation (x,y) after the examples in (49)
means that first rule 48x and then rule 48y must apply to yield the example
in question:

(49) **That house into ran the boys.*   (b,c)
      *Into the house the chairs the boys shoved.   (c,b)
      (Cf. *The boys shoved the chairs into the house.*)

      *She never has bought a car, and buy one never will she. (a,d)
      *She never has bought a car, and never $\begin{cases} \textit{will buy one she.} \\ \textit{buy one she will.} \end{cases}$ (d,a)

      *These steps never did I sweep with a broom.   (a,c)
      *Never $\begin{cases} \textit{did these steps} \\ \textit{these steps did} \end{cases}$ *I sweep with a broom.*   (c,a)

      *He said I would like her, and her like I do.   (d,c)
      **John said she would help him willingly, and help willingly him
          she does.* (c,d)

      *The President speaking to now is our top reporter.   (f,c)
      *Speaking to now the President is our top reporter.   (c,f)

      In the crowd could be found not a single woman.   (g)
      *Not a single woman could in the crowd be found.   (g,a)

      *She said they would run into the house, and into the house they
          ran.* (b)
      *She said they would run into the house, and run into the house
          they did.* (d)
      **She said they would run into the house, and into the house run
          they did.* (d,b)

      A test question from geometry would be equally scary.

> *A test question from geometry equally scary would be.*   (e,c)
> *Equally scary from geometry a test question would be.*   (c,e)

If, following a suggestion of Higgins' (1973, n.5), we formulate all the transformations in (48) as COMP substitutions, then we can explain the ungrammatical examples in (49). [Even if the node COMP is retained in sentence-initial position as a feature of the fronted constituents in derived structure, Chomsky's recoverability condition (1965, pp. 144—145) guarantees that no COMP substitution can take place later in the transformational derivation.] In Section II.9.3 another root transformation that fronts phrase nodes without inducing comma intonation is seen to have this same property.

Further confirmation of the nature of the root transformations under discussion is the fact that they cannot cooccur with WH fronting. In the sections of Chapters IV and V in which this rule is discussed, we will see that it too must be formulated as a COMP substitution rule. Thus it should be the case that it and any of the rules in (48) cannot apply in the same clause, and this is borne out:

(50)

Which plays of his $\begin{Bmatrix} never\ have \\ have\ never \end{Bmatrix}$ we read?   (a,WH)

Never which plays of his have we read?   (WH,a)
Never have which plays of his we read?   (WH,a)

Who into the house dashed?   (b,WH)
Into the house who dashed?   (WH,b)

What $\begin{Bmatrix} these\ steps\ did \\ did\ these\ steps \end{Bmatrix}$ you use to sweep with?   (c,WH)

These steps what did you use to sweep with?   (WH,c)
Was among the guests standing John?   (g,WH)
Among the guests was John standing?   (WH,g)

What would easier to solve be?   (e,WH)
Easier to solve what would be?   (WH,e)

The root transformations are now divisible into three categories:

1. Those that induce comma intonation—the tag question rule, left and right dislocation, certain transformations that produce parentheticals of various sorts (discussed in the following sections).
2. The COMP substitution rules, which do not induce comma intonation.
3. The two "inversion" rules—subject—auxiliary inversion and subject—simple verb inversion. Like local rules, these rules interchange two adjacent constituents, one of which is not a phrase node. (Unlike local rules, they depend on conditions external to the two interchanged nodes.)

Consider now the other two classes of transformations permitted by the structure-preserving constraint (the structure-preserving and local rules): All structure-preserving rules are substitution rules, and no local transformations move constituents over variables. All these observations lead to the following conclusion:

(51)   *In English at least, all transformations that move constituents without inducing comma intonation are substitutions for categories generated in the base, unless they interchange adjacent constituents.*[11]

That is, a local transformation or an inversion root transformation (item 3 in the preceding list) does not move a constituent over a string specified by a variable in the structural description of the rule.

The only rule that seems to me to be a possible 'free word order" rule in English—i.e., a stylistic rule that breaks the structure-preserving constraint (cf. Section I.2)—is the adverb-preposing rule discussed in Section II.10. Such a rule would of course not be a substitution and would move a constituent over a variable. As predicted by (51), it induces comma intonation.

It may be appropriate to recall the other principle of comma intonation given in Section II.1 (and in Emonds, 1970); for further discussion and a somewhat different formulation, see Downing (1973).

(52)
   A root S (immediately) dominated by another S is set off by commas.

II.9   PARENTHETICAL CLAUSES[12]

II.9.1   The Parenthetical Formation Transformation

In an early study of parentheticals in a framework of transformational grammar, Rardin (1968) proposes that sentence-final parentheticals such as those in (53) should have the structure in (54):

(53)   *John came later than Sue, I think.*
       The books have already arrived, you realize.
       The volunteers must realize the dangers involved, it seems to me.

---

[11]I do not claim that movements of constituents that induce comma intonation are never substitutions, although in most cases it seems that they definitely are not.

[12]This entire section has appeared in Rohrer and Ruwet (1974) and in Corum, Smith-Stark, and Weiser (1973), and is reprinted with permission.

(54)

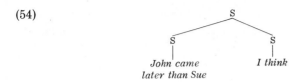

If this structure is correct, all the S's in (54) are root S's. Accordingly, it should be the case that root transformations can apply in both clauses, and they do:

(55)   *Was John here at that time, do you think?*
             "That radio I don't want," exclaimed Mary

Without discussing for the moment how structure (54) is to be generated, let us consider sentences in which the parenthetical is "inserted" into the first clause, as in (56):

(56) *John came, I think, later than Sue.*
     The books, you realize, have already arrived.
     The volunteers must realize, it seems to me, the dangers involved.
     Was John here, do you think, at that time?
     "That radio," exclaimed Mary, "I don't want!"

The sentences in (56) are more closely related to those in (53) and (55) than to those in (57):

(57) *I think John came later than Sue.*
     You realize (that) the books have already arrived.
     It seems to me the volunteers must realize the dangers involved.
     Do you think John was here at that time?
     Mary exclaimed, "That radio I don't want!"

In the first place, the parentheticals in (53), (55), and (56) share the comma intonation and exclude the complementizer *that*, but sentences like (57), except where quotation is involved, lack the comma intonation and permit *that*. The inverted auxiliary in *Was John here at that time?* indicates a WH complementizer in this clause as well as in the *do you think* parenthetical in (55) and (56), but the main verb *think* in constructions like (57) cannot take a complement introduced by *whether*:

(58)   **Do you think whether John was here at that time?*

Further, some parentheticals, such as *as far as I can tell*, *you know*, and *as they say*, either do not occur in main clauses like those in (57) or else do not, in such a use, have their parenthetical meaning:

(59) *You know that the books have already arrived, but Bill doesn't (know).*
     ≠The books, you know, have already arrived, but Bill doesn't know.
     *The books have already arrived, you know, but Bill doesn't.

I therefore propose to transformationally relate sentences with "internal parentheticals" like (56) to those with sentence-final parentheticals, like (53) and (55). In this, I believe I am in agreement with Rardin (1968) and Ross (1973). This decision will further allow us to relate in a similar fashion sentence pairs like those in (60):

(60)   *Will he come tomorrow, in your opinion?*
          Will he, in your opinion, come tomorrow?
          The books have not yet arrived, to my knowledge.
          The books, to my knowledge, have not yet arrived.

The rule involved must be something like the following:

(61) **Parenthetical Formation:**

$$_{s}\left[X-\begin{Bmatrix} NP \\ AP \\ S \\ VP \\ PP \end{Bmatrix}\right]_{s} - \begin{Bmatrix} S \\ PP \end{Bmatrix} \Rightarrow 1\text{--}3\text{--}2$$

[N. Chomsky has pointed out that (61) can be stated without brackets if the place of comma intonation in a string can be referred to in the structural description of a rule.]

There are syntactic restrictions to be imposed on the S that is to become the parenthetical; usually coordinate clauses and sentential relatives (relative clauses modifying the entire main clause) cannot become parentheticals:

(62)   *The books have not yet arrived, but they are due.*
          *The books, but they are due, have not yet arrived.
          The books have not yet arrived, which bothers me.
          *The books, which bothers me, have not yet arrived.
          John put the car in the garage, for the weather was bad.
          *John put the car, for the weather was bad, in the garage.

As a first approximation we might say that the S that becomes a parenthetical by (61) must begin with a COMP that does not dominate a phrase node (such as NP). This will exclude all the ungrammatical examples in (62). The only such complementizers that appear in a nonembedded structure as exemplified in (54) are WH, *as*, the neutral complementizer (phonologically unrealized or deleted in root sentences), and the fronted proform *so*. Examples:

(63)   *Those books are, wouldn't you say, rather late.*
          Those books are, as he said, rather late.
          Those books are, I have no doubt, rather late.
          Those books are, so it appears, rather late.

Exact statement of this and other conditions on the parenthetical S are not important for the first point I wish to make here, which deals, rather, with what kind of derived structure (61) produces.

It is more important that, in a very large class of cases, limiting the second term of parenthetical movement to phrasal constituents makes the correct predictions:

(64) *John should put, I think, down that book.
       John should run, I think, down that street.

       *A donation, it seems to me, to their campaign fund would be preferred.
       They would prefer a donation, it seems to me, to their campaign fund.

       *He likes every, I believe, friend of John.
       He likes, I believe, every friend of John.
       He likes everyone, I believe, on that block.

       *Will, in your opinion, John come tomorrow?
       Will John, in your opinion, come tomorrow?

       Linguists in France, you know, take Chomsky very seriously.
       *Linguists in France take, you know, Chomsky very seriously.
       Linguists in France take Chomsky, you know, very seriously.
       Linguists in France take, you know, very few courses.

       *John pushed, they claimed, a child into the street.
       John pushed a child, they claimed, into the street.
       John, they claimed, pushed a child into the street.

       *These claims will make, I have no doubt, many people quite angry.
       These claims, I have no doubt, will make many people quite angry.
       These claims will make many people, I have no doubt, quite angry.

       *John will buy any dress, as you said, that he likes for the girl next door.
       John will buy any dress, as you said, that he thinks the girl next door likes.

       "I took a hitchhiker from Chicago to Miami," John said.
       (ambiguous)
       "I took a hitchhiker," John said, "from Chicago to Miami."
       (unambiguous——the postparenthetical phrase is interpreted as a constituent, as in *It was from Chicago to Miami that he took the hitchhiker.*)

       *He deprived, I fear, her children of wealth.
       He dispelled, I fear, her illusions of wealth.

*He will urge, I suppose, John to leave.
He would prefer, I suppose, for John to leave.*

*He'll talk about, you realize, his book to your friends.
He'll talk about, you realize, his book on your friends.*

It thus appears that the second and third terms of (61) are normally constituents and not variables. This enables us to pose the question as to the derived structure produced by (61). Does (61) move the second term around the parenthetical clause to the right, attaching it as a right sister to one of the root S's in the input structure in (54), or does it move the third term (the parenthetical clause itself) to the left INTO the left-hand S? The constraint argued for in Schwartz (1972)—that only constituents may be moved by transformations—is satisfied by either of the alternatives, given that we have established that the second as well as the third term of rule (61) is a constituent.[13]

Intuitively the first alternative gives a surface structure—(65a) or (65b)—that seems more accurate than one that might be given by the second alternative—(66a) or (66b):

---

[13]Jorge Hankamer has pointed out that some examples like the starred ones in (64) appear to be acceptable if contrastive intonation appears in the constituent following the parenthetical:

?*John gave, I believe, **Four Roses** to his father.*

I do not think this is systematically possible, however:

*John would consider **Beaujolais**, I believe, very appropriate.
*John would consider, I believe, **Beaujolais** very appropriate.
He'll even talk about **Capital**, I think, to his students.
*He'll even talk about, I think, **Capital** to his students.*

For this reason, I leave the analysis in the text unchanged, lacking any explicit alternative that explains these variations.

It is well known, of course, that contrastive intonation interferes with other tests for constituency (cf. the discussion of coordination across constituent boundaries in Chomsky, 1957). For an interesting initial study of a possible systematic relationship between contrastive intonation and certain root transformations, see Ogle (1974, Chapter VI).

Parenthetical formation must also be restricted so that certain phrasal constituents that are "too deeply embedded" do not serve as the second term of the rule:

*He dislikes the man that Mary works for, I think.
He dislikes the man that Mary, I think, works for.

In this case, Ross's (1967a) "complex NP constraint" or its equivalent will exclude the starred example. However, nothing in the literature, to my knowledge, would properly account for the following contrast:

*She persuaded Bill that you worked for her company, it seems.
She persuaded Bill that you, it seems, worked for her company.

I leave this problem unresolved, as it appears independent of the claim in the text that what follows the parenthetical is normally a constituent and that this constituent, rather than the parenthetical, is moved by parenthetical formation.

(65)

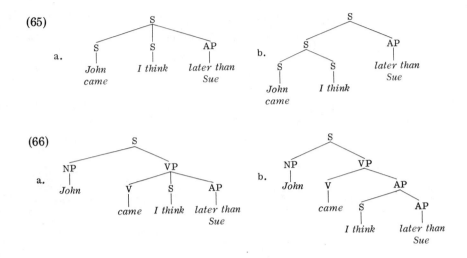

(66)

By virtue of the intonation rule in (52) we are led to prefer the derived structures of (65), since this permits an explanation of the obligatory comma intonation that sets off parentheticals. We can also support this choice with the following two arguments based on syntactic theory.

John Ross has pointed out to me that the second alternative is a counter-example to the constraint proposed in Chomsky (1965), which prohibits transformations from moving morphological material into a clause from a higher sentence. On the other hand, the first alternative [moving the second term of (61) to the right] does not violate Chomsky's proposed restriction on operations performed by transformations. Thus the constraint, motivated on other grounds (cf. Chomsky, 1973), indicates that the first alternative is the correct one. (Actually the restriction against lowering constituents in trees is no doubt more general; see Schwartz, 1972).

The structure-preserving constraint on transformations also decides in favor of the first alternative, i.e., in favor of derived structures like (65) rather than (66). Parenthetical formation as in (61) interchanges two phrase nodes, so it violates one of the restrictions defining a local transformation (the only type of non-structure-preserving rule permitted by this constraint that does not attach constituents to a root sentence). The second alternative (moving the parenthetical itself) does not attach a constituent to a root sentence [cf. (66)], so it is not a root transformation; it does not move the parenthetical S to positions where S can be generated by the base rules, so it is not a structure-preserving transformation either. One must conclude that the second alternative is ruled out by the structure-preserving constraint; only the first alternative is consistent with the constraint. In particular, this parenthetical formation is a typical case of a root transformation.

Thus the structure-preserving constraint, like Chomsky's "lower-S" constraint, leads to the conclusion that parenthetical formation moves a constituent over the parenthetical clause to the right.

The structural change of parenthetical formation written as in (67) reflects the fact that the second, and not the third, term moves.[14]

(67)

$$_s\left[X-\begin{Bmatrix} NP \\ AP \\ S \\ VP \\ PP \end{Bmatrix}\right]_s - \begin{Bmatrix} S \\ PP \end{Bmatrix} \Rightarrow 1-\emptyset-3-2$$

It may be instructive to consider parenthetical formation as in (67) as a rule that in many cases takes the "focus" constituent to the right of the parenthetical clause. (For discussion of the notion of focus, see Chomsky, 1971). Certain kinds of constituents that cannot receive contrastive stress cannot appear as focus constituents in other constructions:

(68)   *?It's down that you should put the cat.*
          *It's down that you should write the address.
          It's themselves that they will sooner or later injure.
          *It's themselves that they will sooner or later perjure.
          It's postmen that Mary perfers to converse with.
          ?It's people that Mary prefers to converse with.

These kinds of constituents do not appear to move by parenthetical formation either:

(69)   *?John should put the cat, I would say, down.*
          *John should write the address, I would say, down.
          They will sooner or later injure, I predict, themselves.
          *They will sooner or later perjure, I predict, themselves
          Mary prefers to converse with, to all appearances, postmen.
          ?Mary prefers to converse with, to all appearances, people.

There are certain parentheticals that are appropriate only with focus constituents that particularize the category mentioned in the parenthetical:

---

[14]It should be noted that both alternative· versions of parenthetical formation provide counterexamples to the coordinate structure constraint on movement proposed in Ross (1967a), meaning that some revision of this (or, alternatively, of Chomsky's A-over-A principle) is needed that will permit (67) to violate such a constraint and yield the following sentence:

John would like fewer courses and, it is likely, more pay.

(70)   * *John wrote a book on semantics, of all places.*
                        John wrote a book in Paris, of all places.

The notion that parenthetical formation very often moves the focus constituent
is confirmed by the requirement that parentheticals as in (70) can appear
sentence-internally only adjacent to the (focus) constituent that particularizes
the category involved:

(71)   * *In Paris John wrote, of all places, a book.*
                        John wrote a book in, of all places, Paris.

Similar examples:

(72)   * *Mary was talking about birth defects to John, of all subjects.*
        Mary was talking to John about birth defects, of all subjects.
        * *Mary was talking about birth defects to, of all subjects, John.*
        Mary was talking to John about, of all subjects, birth defects.

There appears to be at least one case in which parenthetical formation
does not move the focus constituent but, rather, a constituent to the right of the
focus constituent, so as to allow the parenthetical to appear just after (instead
of just before) the focus constituent:

(73)   * *The board of directors gave Nixon the peace award, of all people.*
          (normal, noncontrastive stress)
        The board of directors gave the peace award to Nixon, of all people.
        The board of directors gave the peace award to, of all people.
        Nixon. [movement of the focus constituent, as in (71)–(72)]
        The board of directors gave Nixon, of all people, the peace award.
          (movement of a constituent to the right of the focus constituent
          over the parenthetical, allowing the latter to appear ADJACENT
          to the focus constituent)

These remarks, which informally relate the focus constituent to parenthetical formation, are not to be taken as an adequate formal account of the
phenomenon discussed. Rather, they are meant to show that parentheticals are
related principally to the constituents that follow them and not to the material
on their left. In most cases they serve to put into relief the constituent that
follows them, and, as pointed out, in (68)–(69), constituents that are not
susceptible to being put into relief in other contrastive environments do not
appear to the right of parentheticals either.

With these properties of parentheticals in mind, the parenthetical formation transformation in (67) gives prominence to the constituent following
the parenthetical by attaching it to a root S. Other root transformations, such
as topicalization, right and left dislocation, and directional adverb preposing,
achieve roughly the same "semantic," "rhetorical," or "stylistic" effect on a

"prominent" constituent by essentially the same syntactic process—attachment to a root S.

II.9.2   The Deep Structure Source of Parentheticals

In the first part of this section, I concluded that sentences with "internal" parentheticals, as in (56), are transformationally derived from those with "final" parentheticals, as in (53) and (55), and that the transformation involved is a root transformation, as in (67), that moves a final phrasal constituent of the nonparenthetical clause to the right over the sentence-final parenthetical.

However, I have not yet addressed the question of the source of sentence-final parentheticals, i.e., the structure in (54). There are two initially plausible analyses that I would like to compare. The first claims that the sentence-final parenthetical is a main clause in deep structure, as in (74), and that (54) is derived from (74) by a transformation that fronts the complement S, called SLIFTING in Ross (1973):

(74)

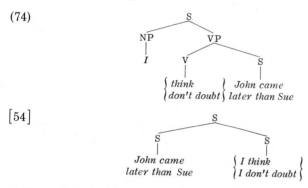

[54]

If this analysis is correct, the complement-fronting rule is a root transformation, since the pairs in (75) should clearly not be transformationally related:

(75)   *They didn't take into account the fact that I thought John came later than Sue.*
      ≠They didn't take into account the fact that John came later than Sue, I thought.

   Bill fears that it appears to us that he doesn't deserve the job.
   ≠Bill fears that he doesn't deserve the job, it appears to us.

   Mary assumes that we don't doubt she'll get the job.
   ≠Mary assumes that she'll get the job, we don't doubt.

   The troops that you admit are in the South are southerners.
   ≠The troops that are in the South, you admit, are southerners.

   She says that you can swim faster than I think you can.
   ≠She says that you can swim faster than you can, I think.

The second analysis of the source of sentence-final parentheticals claims that (54) is relatively close to its deep structure; in particular, its deep structure as shown in (76) would consist of two successive independent clause S's concatenated without a coordinating conjunction, the second of which contains a proform referring back to the first. The same type of deep structure is assigned to (54), in this view, as to clauses connected by semicolons in (77):[15]

(76)

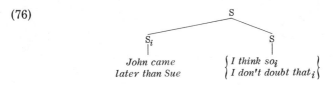

(77) *John came later than Sue; this bothers me.*
      John came later than Sue; I think so anyway.
      John came later than Sue; he warned us ahead that he would do so
          to avoid meeting her uncle.
      John came later than Sue; an event of such magnitude can't be
          overlooked.

This analysis of parentheticals is similar to that proposed in Jackendoff (1972). Instead of a "complement-fronting" rule, the second analysis postulates a "proform deletion" rule. Both analyses, of course, face similar problems in specifying exactly which predicates in the clause that becomes a parenthetical permit, respectively, complement fronting or proform deletion; I will not be concerned further with this problem here.

Before comparing the two analyses of the source for (54), I would like to further elaborate on the second analysis. I do this to avoid an implausible assignment of the same structure to clauses connected by comma intonation and to those connected with semicolon intonation.

In presenting an analysis of direct and indirect speech, Banfield (1973a) proposes that a wide variety of structures that cannot be embedded, including many previously studied in the literature (in particular, see Culicover, 1972; Quang Phuc Dong, 1969; Shopen, 1972), are in fact to be generated under a nonrecursive initial symbol E ("expression"), which is only optionally expanded as S. Thus the boldface elements in (78) are generated under E, but outside of any S:

---

[15]One could claim that (76) underlies (54) and that the proforms in (76) are, in turn, transformationally derived from fully specified S's; I am not arguing here against this position, though it faces some of the same problems as the alternative I am arguing against.

(78)   ***By God**, I know that he is guilty.*
         ***Yes, yes**, that would appeal to John.*
         John, downstairs with those monstrosities!
         ***One more can of beer** and you'll be in trouble.*
         Three cheers for those brave volunteers!
         O, damn that old man!

Banfield further notes that E's, as identified by the presence of such non-embeddable elements, can be coordinately conjoined—the only "recursion" permitted. (*Yes, I want that, but by God, I can't get money for it easily*). We can consider the examples in (77) as exhibiting the same structure as co-ordinately conjoined E's but lacking the conjunction; this corresponds to the notion of school grammar that semicolons "substitute" for coordinate conjunctions between independent clauses. Thus the deep structure in (76) would be revised to that in (79):

(79)

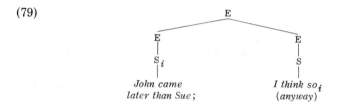

The proform deletion rule that creates a (sentence-final) parenthetical can then be written as a rule that both deletes a proform from the second S in structures like (79) and also attaches this S as a right sister to the first S, yielding (80). This allows us to associate semicolon intonation only with surface sequences of E's that lack the coordinate conjunction:[16]

---

[16]The structure in (80) can also be taken as the structure of sentences modified by the "sentential relative clauses" introduced by *as* and *which*; as noted earlier, such *as* clauses can become sentence-internal parentheticals by the parenthetical formation transformation in (67). In this way, nonrestrictive relative clauses modifying noun phrases and sentences have parallel structures; i.e., the modified constituent and the modifying nonrestrictive relative clause (containing a proform referring back to the first clause) are sister constituents.

I also take $[_S S - PP_S]$ to be the deep structure source of certain sentence-modifying adverbial phrases and clauses—*to my knowledge, in your opinion*, those concessive (*although*) and causal (*because*) clauses that are separated from the main clause by comma intonation and are generally said to modify the sentence rather than the predicate, etc. This structure was first suggested to me by Edward Klima.

In Chapter V I propose a similar deep structure, namely $[_{VP} VP - PP_{VP}]$, for certain adverbial phrases and clauses that modify the entire VP rather than complementing the main verb. In such cases comma intonation is at least not obligatory.

(80)

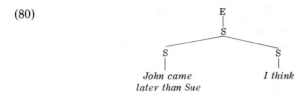

[Alternatively, the S sisters might be immediately dominated by the single E in (80).]

It should be noted that (79) is entirely analogous to the deep structures for direct quotation proposed by Partee (1973) and Banfield (1973a) (although the E node is not used by Partee):

(81)

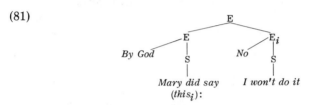

We are justified in formulating proform deletion as moving the S and not the E in (79) because parentheticals that result from this rule, including those in sentence-final position, cannot contain elements generated outside the S by the E expansion rules:

(82) *He said John came later than Sue; by God, I believe that.*
       *He said John came later than Sue, by God, I believe.

      Beer compares favorably with water; yes, we think so anyway.
      *Beer compares favorably with water, yes, we think.

      Mary has been fairly dishonest; John, I don't doubt it.
      *Mary has been fairly dishonest, John, I don't doubt.

      He is not really from this area; oh, you realize that.
      *He is not really from this area, oh, you realize.

However, the examples in (82) can also be accounted for in the earlier analysis involving complement fronting—if one stipulates that this root transformation attaches the complement S to the RIGHT of the exclamatory elements that are generated as left sisters to the root S node by the E expansion rule. In this view, the following pairs of sentences are transformationally related:

(83)   *By God, I believe he said John came later than Sue.*
        By God, he said John came later than Sue, I believe.

        Yes, we think beer compares favorably with wine.
        Yes, beer compares favorably with wine, we think.

John, I don't doubt that Mary has been fairly dishonest.
John, Mary has been fairly dishonest, I don't doubt.

Oh, you realize he is not really from this area.
Oh, he is not really from this area, you realize.

In order to compare the two hypotheses, consider again the following example:

(84)   *Oh, he is not from this area, you realize.*

According to the complement-fronting hypothesis, (84) is to be transformationally related to (85); but according to the proform deletion hypothesis, (84) is to be related to (86):

(85)   *Oh, you realize he is not from this area.*

(86)   *Oh, he is not from this area; you realize this.*

Perhaps no clear judgment is possible, but inasmuch as the parenthetical clause has any semantic content at all, it seems to me that expressive elements like *oh* in a sentence like (84) are related to the rest of the sentence the way *oh* is in (86), and not as it is in (85).

This argument becomes clearer when we examine sentences of direct discourse. If one assumes that sentence-final and sentence-internal direct discourse parentheticals are to be accounted for like other parentheticals, we can ask what the rules of each analysis predict of the following underlying sequences:

(87)   *By God, she said in class, "I hate this damned course!"*

(88)   *"I hate this damned course!"; by God, she said that in class.*

In the complement-fronting analysis, nothing will happen to (88), but (87) [unless direct quote parentheticals are not formed by the same rule as the parentheticals in (83)] will be transformed into the incorrect (89) —recall that the fronted complement, as in (83), must be placed AFTER the exclamatory elements:

(89)   **By God, "I hate this damned course," she said in class.*

In the proform deletion analysis, however, nothing will happen to (87) and nothing will happen to (88) either, as the rule creating parentheticals is blocked by elements under E but not under S [recall the examples in (82)]. Thus the proform deletion hypothesis but not the complement-fronting hypothesis can exclude (89) and still treat direct discourse and other parentheticals uniformly.

A second argument against the complement-fronting hypothesis is provided by examples of the following types, pointed out to me by Edward
Klima:

(90)   a.   *John hasn't completed his book, I don't think.*
          b.   *Will John complete his book on time, do you believe?*

In the complement-fronting hypothesis, these examples are derived from those
in (91); in the proform deletion hypothesis, they are derived from those in
(92):

(91)   *I (do) think that John hasn't completed his book.*
          (or, I don't think that John has completed his book.)
          Do you believe that John will complete his book on time?

(92)   *John hasn't completed his book; I don't think so (anyway).*
          Will John complete his book on time? Do you believe so?

While there is no systematic prohibition against sequences of independent
sentences as in (92), where both are negations or both are questions, there is a
lack of systematic correspondence between (90) and (91). Complement fronting
would have to copy a WH complementizer from the main clause onto the subordinate clause in order to ensure the double inversion in (90b), and it would
have to copy a negative from one clause into another in order to ensure the double
negative in (90a).

   Thus although we cannot say that there are really conclusive arguments
against a root transformation of complement fronting as a source for sentence-
final parentheticals, it seems more likely that such parentheticals are derived
from the deletion of a proform in the second of two independent clauses,
which refers back to the first clause. This derivation of sentence-final parentheticals, as noted earlier, is similar to the derivation of direct speech from
sequences of independent clauses (or E nodes), as in Partee (1973) and
Banfield (1973a). I have not had time to compare the analysis here with the
complement-fronting ("slifting") analysis in Ross (1973). On a first reading
it appears that some but not all of his arguments would carry over against this
analysis.

   Independently of this conclusion in favor of the proform deletion hypothesis
for sentence-final parentheticals, I argued in the first part of this section
that sentence-internal parentheticals are to be derived from the former by
a root transformation of parenthetical formation. The correctness of the
predictions made by this analysis of sentence-internal parentheticals
supports both Chomsky's lower-S constraint and the structure-preserving
constraint.

II.9.3   Concessive Parenthetical Clauses

Consider the following pair of presumably transformationally related sentences:

(93) a.   *Mr. Jones insists on buying stock, though he usually is sensible.*
  b.   *Mr. Jones, though he usually is sensible, insists on buying stock.*

If we assign (93a) the deep structure in (94), as proposed in note 17, parenthetical formation as in (67) will transform (94) into (95), the surface structure for (93b):

(94)

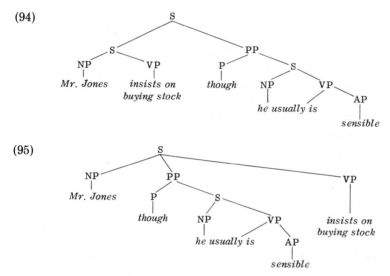

(95)

A further rule of English permits an adjective to prepose around *though* in this construction, yielding (96):

(96) *Mr. Jones, sensible though he usually is, insists on buying stock.*

Clearly the rule could be formulated as a root transformation by making the fronted adjective a sister to the *though* clause in derived structure. (I show later that if the *though* clause is embedded, predictable ungrammaticality results.)

However, certain facts indicate that this is not quite the correct derived structure. First, the condition in (51) on moving constituents around variables requires that this preposing, which does not induce comma intonation (on the adjective's right), must be a substitution transformation. This, in turn, suggests that the adjective is preposed into the COMP position of its clause, and that *though* is inverted with this COMP by a local transformational operation (doubtless the two operations are part of the same rule). As a result of the latter opera-

tion, the subordinate S becomes a root S.[17] (The PP dominating this S dominates no material outside this S, so this S is a root S by definition.) The following surface structure then results:

(97)

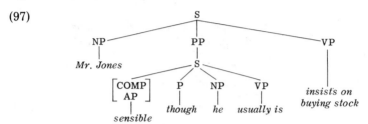

The S to which the preposed AP is attached in the derived structure in
(97) is a root S; it is set off by commas because of the principle in (52) (i.e.,
because it is dominated by another root S).

The claim that the preposed adjective in (97) is in the COMP position is
confirmed by the fact that other COMP substitution (root) transformations cannot apply in this clause:

(98)   ?*Mary, happy though she may seem to you, is on the verge of a
          breakdown.*
       **Mary, happy though to you she may seem, is on the verge of a
          breakdown.*
       **Mary, to you happy though she may seem, is on the verge of a
          breakdown.*
       *Handsome though I believe (that) Dick is, I'm still going to marry
          Herman.*
       (from Ross, 1967a)
       **Handsome though Dick I believe is, I'm still going to marry
          Herman.*
       **Dick handsome though I believe is, I'm still going to marry Herman.*
       Cf. *Dick I believe is handsome.* (from topicalization)

---

[17]The removal of a subordinating conjunction from the P position automatically gives the S under
this PP the status of a root S; this is confirmed by the fact that another such removal, *if* deletion, also
induces main clause behavior; cf. note 2, Chapter I.

> *If he were more circumspect, John would not buy stock.*
> *Were he more circumspect, John would not buy stock.*

Of course *if* deletion and the (limited) auxiliary inversion that accompanies it (**Did he leave, he would
have been happy, etc.*) are probably part of the same rule. My claim is that such a rule (and the rule
being discussed in this section of the text) cannot occur if the nonlocal, non-structure-preserving movements it performs do not attach constituents to root S's.

?Rich though we'll never be, we want to be happy.
*Rich though never will we be, we want to be happy.
*Never rich though we'll be, we want to be happy.

Since I claim that the "sentence-internal" position of concessive parentheticals [as in BOTH (95) and (97)] is due to the parenthetical formation rule of Section II.9.1, the same grammatical contrasts should exist for concessive parentheticals as for the sentential parentheticals treated in that section. As predicted, this parallelism is borne out. The following examples should be compared with those of sentential parentheticals in (64):[18]

(99)

$*$*John shouldn't put,* $\left\{ \begin{array}{l} \textit{though he is tired,} \\ \textit{tired though he is,} \end{array} \right\}$ *down that book.*

?John shouldn't run, $\left\{ \begin{array}{l} \textit{though he is worried,} \\ \textit{worried though he is,} \end{array} \right\}$ *down those stairs.*

?A donation, $\left\{ \begin{array}{l} \textit{though it might be small,} \\ \textit{small though it might be,} \end{array} \right\}$ *to their campaign fund would be preferred.*

They would prefer a donation, $\left\{ \begin{array}{l} \textit{though it might be small,} \\ \textit{small though it might be,} \end{array} \right\}$ *to their campaign fund.*

*He likes every, $\left\{ \begin{array}{l} \textit{though they are poor,} \\ \textit{poor though they are,} \end{array} \right\}$ *friend of John.*

?He likes, $\left\{ \begin{array}{l} \textit{though they are poor.} \\ \textit{poor though they are,} \end{array} \right\}$ *every friend of John.*

He likes everyone, $\left\{ \begin{array}{l} \textit{though they are poor,} \\ \textit{poor though they are,} \end{array} \right\}$ *on that block.*

*Will, $\left\{ \begin{array}{l} \textit{though he is overworked,} \\ \textit{overworked though he is,} \end{array} \right\}$ *John come tomorrow?*

Will John, $\left\{ \begin{array}{l} \textit{though he is overworked,} \\ \textit{overworked though he is,} \end{array} \right\}$ *come tomorrow?*

*Linguists in France take, $\left\{ \begin{array}{l} \textit{though he is American,} \\ \textit{American though he is,} \end{array} \right\}$ *Chomsky very seriously.*

?Linguists in France, $\left\{ \begin{array}{l} \textit{though he is American,} \\ \textit{American though he is,} \end{array} \right\}$ *take Chomsky very seriously*

Linguists in France take Chomsky, $\left\{ \begin{array}{l} \textit{though he is American,} \\ \textit{American though he is,} \end{array} \right\}$ *very seriously.*

---

[18]The preferred position for concessive clauses as in (97) is, however, adjacent to the NP that is described by the preposed adjective. Some of the judgments in (99) are affected by this factor.

*John pushed, $\left\{ \begin{array}{l} \textit{though she was helpless,} \\ \textit{helpless though she was,} \end{array} \right\}$ the child into the street.

John pushed the child, $\left\{ \begin{array}{l} \textit{though she was helpless,} \\ \textit{helpless though she was,} \end{array} \right\}$ into the street.

*These claims will make, $\left\{ \begin{array}{l} \textit{though they are modest,} \\ \textit{modest though they are,} \end{array} \right\}$ many people quite angry.

These claims, $\left\{ \begin{array}{l} \textit{though they are modest,} \\ \textit{modest though they are,} \end{array} \right\}$ will make many people quite angry.

*John will buy any dress, $\left\{ \begin{array}{l} \textit{though it may seem expensive,} \\ \textit{expensive though it may seem,} \end{array} \right\}$ that he likes for the girl next door.

John will buy any dress, $\left\{ \begin{array}{l} \textit{though it may seem expensive,} \\ \textit{expensive though it may seem,} \end{array} \right\}$ that he thinks the girl next door likes.

I conclude that a root transformation of "adjective preposing, *though* inversion" optionally operates on concessive clauses, including concessive clauses that have previously been "inserted" into main clauses by means of parenthetical formation. This root transformation, like others that move constituents over variables without inducing comma intonation, is basically a COMP substitution rule.

II.10   *PREPOSED ADVERBIAL* PP's

In this section, we return to the preposed adverbials first mentioned in Section II.4. These adverbials can be, and usually are, set off by comma intonation and never cause inversion, either of the main verb or of the auxiliary. Nor do they trigger stylistic inversion of the subject NP (cf. Section II.7).[19] The following examples are typical:

(100) *I pledge that, during this examination, I have neither given nor received assistance.*
Mary asked me if, at that time, John saw any chance of a speedy trial.
You can count on trouble when, without thinking, you call the police.
In many cities, the crime rates grow with the number of police employed.

---

[19]In Chapter V I justify treating subordinating conjunctions (as opposed to complementizers) as prepositions with sentence complements; here I assume such an analysis.

Although he is poor, John is extremely conservative.
John claims that, as he reads linguistic work more critically, his
  taste for science fiction becomes more refined.

The data I present in this section, although they concern uncertain judgments of grammaticality, are very much like the data on parenthetical clauses in
Section II.9.1. That is, I find that preposed adverbial PP's as in (100) generally
sound acceptable if what follows them can be construed as a single constituent,
and slightly unacceptable if, other things being equal, what follows them cannot
be so construed. My analyses of the parenthetical clauses in the previous section
and of parenthetical (comma-separated) adverbial PP's in this section both
depend crucially on such data.[20]

If it should be the case that all or some transformationally displaced
parentheticals in English are grammatical in a greater variety of dependent
clause positions than the structure-preserving constraint allows (i.e., if my data
and analyses in this and/or the preceding section are incorrect), then it would
appear that such parentheticals are subject to certain limited stylistic (not
grammatical) transformations of the type discussed in Section I.2. Since the
data in this section are less certain than those in the preceding section, it is also
possible that my analysis there is correct but that here a stylistic adverb-
preposing rule should front the PP's in examples like (100).

With this caveat, we can return to the construction under discussion. The
fronted PP's in (100) can be distributed as parentheticals throughout the clause
they originate in, but they cannot go into a higher clause. For example, the
second example in (100) has the variants in (101) but not the (nonsynonymous)
variants in (102). The phrase *at that time* may appear with comma intonation
in any of the blanks in (101) without change in meaning.

(101) *Mary   asked   me   if_____John_____saw_____any   chance*
  _____of (?)_____a speedy trial.

---

[20]Since we are dealing in this section with dependent as well as independent clauses [e.g., (100)],
the generalization that what follows parentheticals is a constituent depends on and supports Bresnan's
(1972a) hypothesis that the complementizer (COMP) of a sentence is a sister constituent to the rest of
the sentence. That is, she proposes that COMP is generated by the following base rule, and that $\bar{S}$ and
not S is what generally appears on the right side of other base rules:

$$\bar{S} \rightarrow COMP–S$$

Nagahara (1974, Section 2.3) gives many examples like those in (100), including some interesting
complex cases—cf. especially his examples (12)−(14). He also gives cases where adverbial PP's, set
off by commas, intervene before M−VP sequences and *not*−V−... sequences. Independent evidence
that the former sequence must be a constituent is given in Dougherty (1970b), although this constituent
is generally not notated in the present volume. Similarly, I think the noncontracted *not* must be independently analyzed as part of the VP in sentences like *John couldn't not try* and *John may simply not attend*
(cf. the discussion of adverbials like *simply* in Section V.2). Thus the claim in the text that preposed
adverbial PP's are followed by single constituents is consistent with Nagahara's sets of examples.

(102) *Mary asked me, at that time, if John saw any chance of a speedy trial.*

Mary, at that time, asked me if John saw any chance of a speedy trial.

In the first example in (100), *neither given nor received* is a constituent; hence, the ungrammaticality of the starred examples in (103) is because the materials following the parentheticals are not constituents:

(103) *I pledge that I, during this examination, have neither given nor received assistance.*

I pledge that I have, during this examination, neither given nor received assistance.

*I pledge that I have neither, during this examination, given nor received assistance.

*I pledge that I have neither given, during this examination, nor received assistance.

Another similarity between the adverbial parentheticals in (100) and those formed by the parenthetical transformation in (67) is that neither can precede a constituent that may not be given "prominence" (i.e., many idioms, stressless postverbal particles, etc.) [cf. (69)]:

(104) *I pledge that I have neither given nor received, during this examination, assistance.

*It's assistance that you shouldn't have given or received.

*The better students give the poorer ones, he claims, assistance.

*I don't think you should walk, during this exam, about.

*It's about that they were walking.

*The students were walking, he claims, about.

I have not been able to formulate a satisfactory set of restrictions on the variables and terms of an adverbial parenthetical formation rule, so I restrict myself to claiming only that the material following an adverbial parenthetical is a constituent, and that such constituents are attached to root S's. Such a claim, if true, means that it should be possible in principle to formulate a root transformation of adverbial parenthetical formation that moves a constituent to the right over an adverbial PP and attaches this constituent to a root S.

The first part of the claim was discussed and exemplified above. In order to find evidence about the second part—whether the material to the right of "preposed" parenthetical adverbials can be attached to root S's—we must examine the acceptability of sentences where the material to the right of such an adverbial could not be attached to a root S.

As with right dislocation, discussed in Section II.6, the behavior of embedded clauses that terminate the subject NP of the main clause is NOT crucial, for in such cases the boldface constituents in (105), for example, could possibly be attached to the root S:

(105) *?The realization that after the dinner **I would be sick** didn't stop me from ordering.*

*?Any child who by writing to Washington **can improve his fortune** is exceptional.*

The crucial cases are those like the following, where the constituents in boldface cannot possibly be attached to a root S. In these cases, the evidence weakly indicates that adverbial parenthetical formation is in fact blocked:

(106) *The decision that the parks that millions visit in the summer are to be barred to cars is a great victory for naturalists.*

*?The decision that the parks that in the summer **millions visit** are to be barred to cars is a great victory for naturalists.*

Any suspicion that John was red-headed in his youth that you might be harboring is certainly false.

*?Any suspicion that in his youth **John was red-headed** that you might be harboring is certainly false.*

Mary foolishly revealed the fact that Bill was friends with communists in the thirties to his long-time employer.

*?Mary foolishly revealed the fact that Bill, in the thirties, **was friends with communists** to his long-time employer.*

I'll gladly keep the men who wear hats in the presence of ladies company.

I'll gladly keep the men who in the presence of ladies **wear hats company.*

John stayed angry over the fact that we had called the police without thinking for weeks after it happened.

*?John stayed angry over the fact that without thinking **we had called the police** for weeks after it happened.*

They wanted to discuss the idea that we should leave even if it was dangerous in a general meeting.

*?They wanted to discuss the idea that even if it was dangerous **we should leave** in a general meeting.*

As noted earlier, the judgments are not clear in cases like (106) (for example, the corresponding judgments with right dislocation are clearer); this may mean that the analysis proposed here is incorrect and should be replaced by one of the alternatives mentioned at the beginning of this section (a stylistic transformation). However, since the judgments in (106) have some validity for me, and since they support the strongest claim about the structure-preserving constraint, I retain the claim that a root transformation of adverbial paren- thetical formation is the source for the preposed adverbial parenthetical PP's in (100) and similar cases.[21]

---

[21] Of course the analysis here claims that these adverbial parentheticals are not "preposed" but that the constituent following them has been "postposed."

III

Structure-Preserving NP *Movement* *Transformations*

In Chapter II I enumerated and discussed most of the root transformations of English.

The bulk of this chapter is devoted to showing that the (nonroot) transformations of English that move NP's have been or should be formulated as structure-preserving. For many transformations this means only a small formal modification in a widely accepted formulation of the rule, while for others it involves showing inadequacies in accepted formulations that can be removed by assuming that they have the structure-preserving property.

In later chapters I discuss transformations that move other nodes besides NP's, and show that they too have the structure-preserving property, provided that they are not local or root transformations. Again, in some cases accepted formulations need major revisions. But in each case of a major revision, evidence that this revision is necessary is presented. As might be expected, some currently accepted notions of grammatical structure must be modified in order to make my claim hold in general. Although one of these modifications will slightly weaken the initial statement of the structure-preserving constraint in Chapter I, the narrowing of the notion "possible transformational rule" that emerges from this study is considerable.

III.1 THE PASSIVE CONSTRUCTION

III.1.1 The Active—Passive Relation in English

Transformational grammarians generally agree that English contains a "passive" rule (or rules) relating pairs of sentences like the following:

(1)   a.   *Russia defeated Germany.*
             b.   *Germany was defeated by Russia.*

Furthermore, the trees corresponding to (1a) and (1b) after the application of the passive rule can be represented as (2) and (3), respectively. [There is disagreement over the status of the passive auxiliary *be*, which I return to in Chapter VI; in (3) it is simply represented in ad hoc fashion.]

(2)

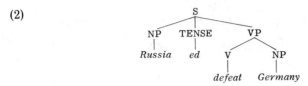

(3)

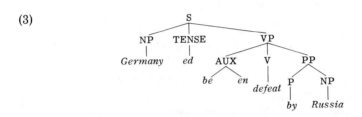

There is ample justification for assigning the structure $[_{PP} [_{P} by] [_{NP} X]]$ to an "agent phrase" like *by Russia* in (3). For example, it behaves like a PP in relative clauses and questions:

(4)   *By whom has this book been read?*
             Who has this book been read by?
             The people this book has been read by are not typical.

Also, this *by*, like other prepositions, cannot have a *for–to* (infinitive) object:

(5)   *The tension would be lessened by for Europe to disarm.*
             The bankers would be angered by to suggest devaluation.

The relation in (1), the ACTIVE–PASSIVE relation, is sometimes thought to hold also between pairs of noun phrases such as (6) and (7):

(6)   *Russia's defeat of Germany*

(7)   *Germany's defeat by Russia*

There are, however, differences between "passive noun phrases" like (7) and passive sentences. If and exactly how passive noun phrases and passive sentences are grammatically related is not of direct interest here, since I will be demonstrating only that the rule or rules that derive passive sentences from active ones have a certain property. I return to the derivation of passive noun phrases in Section III.5.

There is some disagreement over what the common deep structures of actives and passives should look like. In particular, it is not certain whether the agent phrase (*Russia* in the preceding examples) should originate in subject position or in the *by* phrase. The force of what follows does not depend on the resolution of this question. For purposes of exposition I assume that agent phrases are subjects in deep structure, in line with most transformational work. Under this assumption, (3) is a transform of (2) (for a complete discussion see Section III.5.3.).

A second question concerning the proper formulation of the passive rule(s) is whether one rule that moves two NP's or two rules that move one NP apiece are involved. Again, the results of this section are neutral with respect to this question, and for purposes of exposition I assume that one rule moves the deep structure subject NP into the *by* phrase, and that a separate rule moves a deep structure object into the subject position. Following the terminology of Chomsky (1970), I call these rules AGENT POSTPOSING and NP PREPOSING, respectively.

III.1.2   The Structure-Preserving Property

Agent postposing and NP preposing are both good examples of the structure-preserving transformations defined in Chapter I and studied extensively in this chapter. Both move NP constituents into positions where NP's are permitted by independently motivated phrase structure rules. Agent postposing moves the subject NP into the NP position provided for in the rule PP → P−NP. NP preposing moves an object NP into the position provided for by the rule S → NP−TENSE−(M)−VP. This notion of moving a constituent labeled X into a position where a node X is already provided for by the phrase structure rules is the central idea in the definition of a structure-preserving transformation.

To formalize this notion, I drop the requirement in the theory outlined in Chomsky (1968, Chapter V) that all nodes dominate nonexpandable (terminal) elements, and permit the designated terminal element Δ to be inserted by convention under any node at any point in the (phrase structure) derivation. This insertion then terminates any further expansion at that point in the tree (phrase marker). I call any node that dominates only Δ an EMPTY NODE.

Thus we allow Δ to be inserted not only under lexical category nodes but immediately under phrase nodes and grammatical formative nodes (WH, NEG, M, DET, etc.) as well. Following Chomsky (1972, n. 12), WE REQUIRE THAT Δ NOT APPEAR IN A WELL-FORMED SURFACE STRUCTURE. In particular, this means that either Δ must be replaced by the insertion of a lexical item (or a grammatical formative, inasmuch as these are to be distinguished) at the deep structure level, or else some grammatical transformation must delete it or substitute another constituent for it. There is NO rule-independent convention for removing unwanted Δ's in surface structure.

Informally we can say that no node is permitted to remain empty throughout the transformational derivation of a well-formed surface structure. Moreover, semantic interpretation rules and any selectional or strict subcategorization features of the type discussed in Chomsky (1965) ignore empty nodes completely in the framework to be developed here. That is, an empty NP cannot fulfill or violate the required presence or absence, respectively, of an NP in some rule of this type.[1]

We can now give a definition of a structure-preserving rule that is somewhat more abbreviated than the general definition given in Chapter I:

(8)   ***Structure-Preserving Transformation:*** *A transformational operation* T *that substitutes a node* B *and all the material dominated by it for some node* C *that is a constituent of the same category is structure-preserving.*

If T specifies the location of B in the tree it is applying to, T is a movement or a copying rule, depending on whether T deletes B from its original position or leaves the constituent B there (besides substituting B for C). If T explicitly specifies B in its structural change, then T is an insertion rule. Of course I do not require that any given transformation be purely an insertion or a movement or a copying rule; different operations may be combined, up to certain limits that are not our concern here. Further, there is no implication that ANY structure-preserving rule is a possible rule; these rules are subject to many constraints, such as those discussed in Ross (1967a) and Chomsky (1973).

The deletion of the node C entailed by the preceding definition is subject to a recoverability condition, as in Chomsky (1965). That is, either C is empty or it dominates some "designated element" (designated in linguistic theory rather than in particular grammars) that may be freely deleted, or the rule in question specifies what C dominates, or—conceivably—C dominates material that is identical to that dominated by B.

I further assume that a structure-preserving rule, unless it is specified otherwise, OPTIONALLY leaves an empty node B (of the form $[_B \, \Delta \, _B]$ in the position of B in the input tree. This means that the original position of B may, but need not, serve as the "C position" (the empty node) for a subsequent

---

[1] I do not rule out the possibility that Δ may sometimes be accompanied by a phonetically nonrealized feature at some level of structure (say, +ANIMATE) that itself contributes to semantic interpretation. But in this case, the node dominating Δ is not empty at the level of structure in question, on the one hand, and on the other, this instance of Δ (as well as any other) must be removed by rule during the course of deriving any well-formed surface structure.

structure-preserving movement or insertion.[2] A structure-preserving rule may also specify a morpheme to be inserted into the original position of B. If we ever need to require that a rule NOT leave an empty node in the original position of B, we may use the symbol $-\Delta$ in the structural change of the rule in this position.

Under these conventions, a structure-preserving rule moving a constituent to the right typically transforms (9a) into (9b):

(9)   a. $W-[_{\text{B}}\,X\,]-Y-[_{\text{B}}\,\Delta\,]-Z$
             b. $W-([_{\text{B}}\,\Delta\,])-Y-[_{\text{B}}\,X\,]-Z$

An obligatory node may be empty in deep structure, just as an optional node may be. However, an obligatory node differs from an optional one by definition in that it must be chosen. Since I require (in the third paragraph of this section) that EVERY node is nonempty at some point in a transformational derivation, it follows that obligatory nodes are just those that must be present and nonempty at some point in a transformational derivation. (Optional nodes need not be, since they need not be chosen in deep structures.) Lasnik and Fiengo (1974) argue for an interesting revision of this principle: that at least the subject NP of an S must be filled AT THE END OF THE CYCLE ON THAT S.

III.1.3   The Passive Rules in the Structure-Preserving Framework

The agent-postposing rule (or the part of the passive rule that moves the subject) moves an NP into the *by* phrase object position, as shown by the arrow in (10). By formulating this rule as structure-preserving (i.e., we either assume that *by* and its empty object NP are present in the deep structure of the passive, or assume that there is an empty PP and insert *by*), we can account for the derived PP structure that results from this rule without postulating any ad hoc symbols such as PASSIVE in deep structure:

(10)

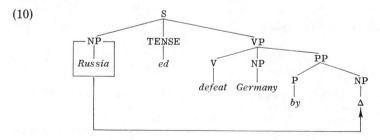

---

[2]When Δ is left behind but no later grammatical transformation removes it, an ill-formed surface structure of course results.

The optional phrase structure choice of a PP with the preposition *by*[3] or an empty P provides an empty node for receiving a postposed agent NP. This formal mechanism [essentially that utilized in Chomsky (1965) to account for the PP structure of the *by* phrase] explains why the output of agent postposing results in a prepositional phrase similar to other prepositional phrases in its position under VP, in its internal structure, and in its transformational behavior.

When agent postposing applies in a sentence, it must be followed by NP preposing. I am not concerned here with the fact that this rule MUST apply; an explanation for this is proposed in Section III.5.2. The important fact about NP preposing here is that it is structure-preserving: It moves object NP's into the empty NP position of the subject NP, as in (11). Of course it is well known that subjects of passive sentences behave in a wide variety of syntactic processes (case, number agreement, etc.) like other subject NP's. (The passive auxiliary is represented ad hoc here; the auxiliary is discussed in more detail in Chapter VI.)

(11)

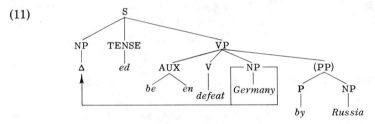

Thus we see that both the NP movements involved in the formation of the passive construction in English (i.e., in defining the active—passive relation) are paradigm cases of structure-preserving rules.[4]

It may be well to dwell here on the importance of showing that transformations have the structure-preserving property, even if no other problems could be resolved by this observation. The reason we want to limit transformations to certain types (root or local or structure-preserving) is that the expressive power of the theory of transformations is too great. Many hypothetical rules that are

---

[3] See Emonds (1972a) for a demonstration that many other prepositions are subcategorized as intransitive in deep structure.

[4] It may be superfluous to remark that I do not claim that absolutely compelling evidence will present itself for every structure-preserving rule considered in isolation to the effect that the rule must be formulated in this way. Rather, I claim that every major transformational operation (in the precise sense of nonlocal, given in Chapter I) that can apply freely in embedded sentences MAY be written as structure-preserving, subject to the constraints on base rules given in Chapter I.

In the majority of cases (e.g., with agent postposing), independent arguments can be given that the rule must be so written if explanatory adequacy on the question of how transformations assign derived structure is to be achieved. If there were no structure-preserving constraint, agent postposing could as well assign AP as PP structure to the *by* phrase, and NP preposing could assign PP structure to the subject NP and/or insert a preposition marker, etc.

non-structure-preserving are just as easily expressed in the generally accepted algebra of transformations as those that are.

For example, let A be a hypothetical language identical to English except that the agent phrases in passive constructions are placed immediately before the passive verb or noun rather than among the other complement PP's. Thus the grammar of A yields the following grammaticality judgments, where # signifies ungrammatical in A and * represents ungrammatical in English:

(12)   *Some countries couldn't defeat Germany with conventional arms.*

       #*Some countries couldn't with conventional arms defeat Germany.*

       #*Some countries couldn't Germany defeat with conventional arms.*

(*$\neq$#) #*Germany couldn't be defeated with conventional arms by some countries.*

(*$\neq$#)   *Germany couldn't be by some countries defeated with conventional arms.*

       this country's second defeat of Germany in this century

       # *this country's second Germany defeat in this century*

       # *this country's second in this century defeat of Germany*

(*$\neq$#)# *Germany's second defeat by this country in this century*

(*$\neq$#)   *Germany's second by this country defeat in this century*

(*$\neq$#)# *the second defeat of Germany in this century by this country*

(*$\neq$#)   *the second by this country defeat of Germany in this century*

In previous transformational theory the grammars of A and of English differ in an accidental way—in the formulation of the agent-postposing rule—and each language is equally highly valued. Yet English seems a more regular language in a significant way: The postposed agent PP in English appears in a typical PP position. (Recall that language A has the SAME phrase structure rules as English.) Thus it would seem that the theory should be revised to favor English over langage A. Adoption of the structure-preserving hypothesis achieves this, since A could not be described without an ad hoc addition of a PP to the phrase structure rules for VP and NP expansion.[5] More generally, adoption of the structure-preserving hypothesis excludes on principle any language whose transformations, like those of language A, do not "obey" its phrase structure rules in embedded sentences.

---

[5]Such an addition is in fact completely excluded by the condition on base structures proposed in Chapter I, as no base construction in A would utilize this PP.

Any number of hypothetical alternatives to English can be devised whose passive rules, like those of language A, do not have the structure-preserving property. In all cases there are fairly clear intuitions that these languages are irregular in a sense that English is not. It is this sense that the claim that nonroot transformations are structure-preserving makes precise.

III.1.4   The Optionality of the *By* Phrase in the Passive

The agent *by* phrase is optional in English passive constructions:

(13)   *Germany was defeated (by Russia).*
               Germany's defeat (by Russia)

Some transformationalists have accounted for this by postulating an optional rule that deletes *by*—NP. In the framework of this study, an alternative to this ad hoc device is to attribute the optional presence of the *by* phrase in passive constructions to the optionality of PP under the nodes VP or NP. In this view, the deep structure of a passive lacking an agent phrase in surface structure has an empty NP in the subject position. Agent postposing cannot apply to such deep structures, since there is no empty node to move the subject NP onto. Thus the deep structures of (14) would be (15a) or (15b):

(14)   *Germany was defeated.*

(15)

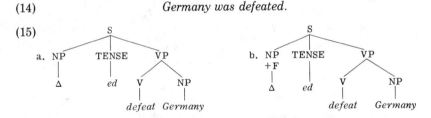

In this way, *by* phrase deletion can be eliminated from the grammar.[6]

Eliminating *by* phrase deletion also eliminates the syntactic problem of determining what element is actually deleted in this rule. That is, in (16) the understood agents are, respectively, *everyone, someone,* and *his father*:

---

[6] One might ask what the difference is in such a framework between the differently interpreted *the corn grew* and *the corn was grown*. One possible answer is simply that the deep structure grammatical relation of *the corn* to *grow* is the subject relation in the first case and the object relation in the second. Another possible answer is that the deep structure of the second example (as well as that of *one grew corn*) contains the deep structure of the first and, also, an abstract "causative" verb that is replaced by *grow* in surface structure. Thus the deep structure of *the corn was grown* would be as in (i), while that of *the corn grew* would be as in (ii). I see no reason to choose between these alternatives at this point.

(16)   *John wants to be left alone in his room.*
       A hitchhiker here will probably be picked up.
       He was never physically harmed by his father, but he was often
          threatened.

This analysis of agentless passives will also account for a verb like *be born*
(in the sense of *be given birth to,* not that of *be carried*), which cannot appear in
the active and never occurs with an agent *by* phrase:

(17)   **This child was born by my sister on Memorial Day.*
           *My sister bore this child on Memorial Day.

Footnote 6 continued

(i)

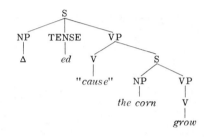

(ii)

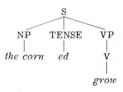

   A third alternative is that the passive rule includes the deletion of an optional deep structure
feature F on the otherwise empty subject (as in 15b), where F either is mentioned explicitly in the
passive rule or is "recoverable" in the sense of Chomsky (1965). Not all verbs that can occur in
the passive would necessarily have to cooccur with such an element; for example, if F = ANIMATE,
then the deep structure subject of *The book has been read* could be [$_{NP}$ + ANIM], while that of *The
door has been scratched* could be simply [$_{NP}$ △].
   Culicover (1973) points out the important observation of Kurylowicz that any language with
a passive permits deletion of the agent phrase. According to the conditions on base rules in Chapter
I, any phrase node complement to a verb must be optional; hence, any agent phrase in a passive
construction (by definition such a phrase is within the complement system rather than the subject
of the verb) cannot be obligatory by virtue of the base rules. Thus in the analysis of the passive
in this section, in which the agent phrase arises from the replacement of an empty deep structure PP,
there cannot in principle be anything but an optional agent; this explains Kurylowicz's observation.
Previous transformational accounts of the passive could not insightfully do this.
   In a later section the possibility of the agent phrase's being nonempty in the base is discussed.
Again, in this case, the normal situation must be that the agent phrase is optional. However, this
view would permit certain verbs to be lexically subcategorized for an OBLIGATORY agent phrase. If
some verbs in some languages do not permit "agent deletion" in the passive, even though Kurylowicz's
observation holds for normal verbs, then the latter view is supported over that presented in this
section.

The use of the progressive with *be born* shows that it is a verb rather than an adjective, since the progressive is not used with adjectives formed from past participles:

(18)   *Unwanted children are being born every minute.*
              **Unwanted children are very often being stillborn.*

We need only stipulate that *bear* (in the sense of *give birth to*) is sub-categorized to not take a deep structure subject; it is immaterial that an (empty) subject NP appears before this verb in deep structure, in which lexical material is never inserted, once we admit the notion of an empty node. We will see other instances of verbs that may not take a deep structure subject throughout this study. Thus the deep structure of (19) is (20):

(19)   *This child was born on Memorial Day.*

(20)

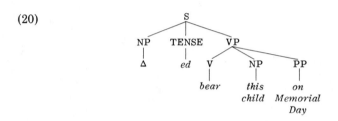

In connection with *bear* (*give birth to*), which cannot have a deep structure subject, a few verbs that MUST can be mentioned, such as *precede, follow, own*:

(21)   **The dinner was preceded.*
              **The speech was followed.*
              **Some of the chairs are owned.*

The normal case is that a verb may or may not take a deep structure subject.

This concludes the introduction of the concept of a structure-preserving transformation. The main purpose of this section has been to illustrate how the two NP movement transformations, NP preposing and agent postposing, which together account for the passive construction in English, satisfy what I have defined as the structure-preserving property. In the remainder of this chapter, other nonroot transformations that move NP's are shown to have this property. In Chapters IV and V, a number of structure-preserving transformations that move other phrase nodes (AP, S, and PP) are studied, and in Chapter VI, rules that move nonphrase nodes are discussed in some detail. In all, almost every movement transformation that has found acceptance in transformational literature as relevant to the description of English is discussed somewhere in this study.

III.2   MOVEMENTS OF NOUN PHRASES INTO HIGHER SENTENCES

Agent postposing and NP preposing, the two NP movement rules involved in describing the English passive, move NP's within single S's in structure-preserving fashion. In later sections we return to more rules of this type. But here we consider some NP movement rules that transfer constituents from lower to higher clauses. As these are almost universally construed as structure-preserving, there is little reason for us to dwell on the details of their behavior.

Rosenbaum (1967) argues that a rule of SUBJECT RAISING transforms structures like (22) into structures like (23).[7] While this is almost universally accepted in transformational grammar, it can further be argued (Baker & Brame, 1972) that the same rule directly transforms (24) into (25). I agree that this is so, but different views on this question are not of relevance here. As with NP preposing, the "raised" subject displays all the characteristics of subject NP's (TENSE is omitted in this section):

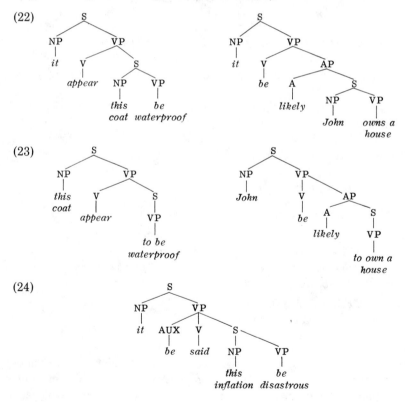

(22)

(23)

(24)

---

[7]Rosenbaum's term is *it* REPLACEMENT.

(25)

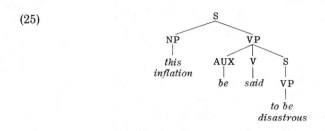

Subject raising is clearly a structure-preserving rule.

A rule somewhat similar in its formal effects, but whose existence is less agreed upon, is the RAISING-TO-OBJECT rule that transformationally relates pairs of sentences like the following:

(26)   *John believes that he has won the contest.*
       John believes himself to have won the contest.

       We can depend on it that their paper will expose crooked politicians.
       We can depend on their paper to expose crooked politicians.

It is sometimes claimed that subject raising and raising to object are the same rule, but I do not believe this can be maintained; cf. Berman (1974) and Akmajian (1973). In any case this debate is also peripheral to our present concerns.

It is possible that raising to object could exist as a transformational rule, but that its effect would simply be to postpose the VP of the sentences in (26) to the end of the nonembedded VP. In this case, it would suffice to formulate a local transformation to effect this change in constituent structure (i.e., to eliminate the deep structure embedded S node), since the subject NP and the VP of this sentence cannot be separated by raising to object:

(27)   *She believes with all her heart that she has won.*
            ?She believes that she has won with all her heart.

            *She believes herself with all her heart to have won.
            *She believes with all her heart herself to have won.
            ?She believes herself to have won with all her heart.

            *She assumed for a while John to be guilty.
            *She assumed John for a while to be guilty.
            ?She assumed John to be guilty for a while.

However, for reasons that will become clear in the next chapter, it seems more likely that the (nonfactive) clauses that can undergo raising to object originate in the VP-final S complement position and not under the object NP. In this case, a (structure-preserving) NP movement would be involved; the pairs in (26) would be related by movements as in (28):

(28)

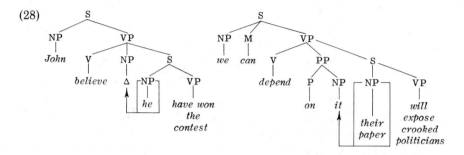

Whether these rules that move the subject NP of embedded sentences replace NP's that dominate *it* (deleting *it* in the process) or empty NP's[8] is not of direct interest here. As far as the structure-preserving hypothesis is concerned, the important fact is that the subject-raising and raising-to-object rules (or appropriate modifications) move NP's into positions where the phrase structure rules generate NP's—subject position, direct object position, and prepositional object position.

Another much discussed subject replacement rule relates the pairs of sentences in (29). This rule differs from the previous subject replacement rule (subject raising) in that it removes NP's from the VP of embedded sentences rather than from subject position. We can call it OBJECT RAISING:

(29)   *It is easy to lift John onto the horse.*
              John is easy to lift onto the horse.

              It is hard to lift John onto the horse.
              The horse is hard to lift John onto.

              It would be a lot of fun to talk to a movie star.
              A movie star would be a lot of fun to talk to.

Object raising is also structure-preserving, as is shown in (30):[9]

---

[8]It may be that some or all of the *it*s in (22)—(28) are transformationally inserted, and that the NP's dominating them are still empty when they are replaced by the subject NP of the embedded S.

[9]By citing any movement rules that have been discussed in the literature of generative grammar, I do not mean to imply that I am arguing that they should not or could not be replaced with another analysis that might use, say, a deletion rule. I simply mean to point out that if a movement rule is involved, the rule is (i) structure-preserving, (ii) a local movement rule, or (iii) a root transformation, as the case may be. Lasnik and Fiengo (1974) argue in the present case that no movement rule is involved.

(30)

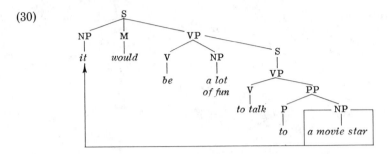

We have seen three rules that raise NP's into higher clauses, of the type permitted by the structure-preserving constraint. The value of the constraint is that it explains why such rules exist and why English does not have rules that move NP's out of embedded S's into a non-NP position, such as, say, the beginning of a VP that is a sister to M, as in (31):

(31)   *It may this coat appear to be waterproof.*
         The fact that it will John be likely to be away disturbs me.
         The man who it is Bill believed to dislike is here.
         It has this task been easy to finish.

III.3   *INDIRECT OBJECT MOVEMENTS*

INDIRECT OBJECT MOVEMENT rules in English relate pairs of sentences such as the following:

(32)   *The paper that I wrote John a letter on was old.*
         The paper that I wrote a letter to John on was old.

         To refuse visitors permission to enter is bad enough.
         To refuse permission to enter to visitors is bad enough.

         John's parents are happy because he carved them a statue.
         John's parents are happy because he carved a statue for them.

         They were talking about building the residents a park.
         They were talking about building a park for the residents.

Thus indirect object (or "dative") movement has two functions: (i) It deletes a preposition (*to* or *for*), and (ii) it reverses the order of two postverbal NP's.[10]

---

[10]Fillmore (1965) proposes that English has two dative movement rules because the indirect objects derived from deep structure *to* phrases can undergo the NP-preposing (passive) rule, while those derived from deep structure *for* phrases cannot. That is, most speakers of American English find the sentences of the first group in (i) completely acceptable and those of the second group somewhat unacceptable:

The deletion of a preposition is not unparalleled in English grammar. Another example of a preposition deletion rule in English is the optional deletion of *for* and *on* in certain adverbial expressions of time:

(33)   *John has been working on this table (for) three hours.*
    I'm going to step outside (for) just a moment.
    The guests registered here (on) October first.
    You should pay your bill (on) the last day of the month.

The deletion of a preposition before adverbs of time is obligatory in certain cases:

(34)   *He paid the rent (*on) last Saturday.*
    They deliver the paper at noon (*on) every weekday.
    I'll finish my dessert later (*in) this afternoon.
   (Cf. *I'll finish my dessert later in the afternoon.*)

Postulating a P deletion rule for time adverbial NP's means that the phrase structure rule expanding NP need only allow PP's and S's (and not NP's) after the head noun. That is, the boldface NP's in (35) can be derived from deep structure PP's:

(35)   *The discussion **last Saturday** disturbed him.*
    *They predict a big storm **this afternoon**.*
    *The traffic jam **every weekday** makes city life less desirable.*

The deletion of *to* and *for* in indirect object movement(s) is formally similar to the deletion of *on, for,* or *in* in time adverbials, and is a part of any formulation of these rules. On the other hand, the reversing of order of the two postverbal NP's that results from this P deletion could logically be formulated in various ways: The second NP could move over the first, the first could move over the second, or the two could exchange positions. The first two possibilities are not structure-preserving, as illustrated in (36):

Footnote 10 continued

(i)   *The visitors must have been refused permission.*
          The children were told a bedtime story.
          A few natives are being taught Spanish by the volunteer.
          John has just been promised a large refund.

          *The visitors must have been found some food.
          *His parents were carved a statue.
          *Mary is being built a table by John.
          *The guests have just been roasted a duck.

This discrepancy can be explained by assuming that the objects of *to* phrases but not those of *for* phrases are moved in front of the direct object (optionally) before the NP-preposing rule applies, and are hence subject to being preposed. That is, ordering *to* dative movement before NP preposing and *for* dative movement after it accounts for the difference between the two groups of sentences.

(36)

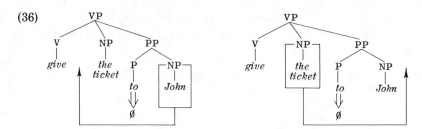

On the other hand, a rule interchanging the positions of two constituents OF THE SAME CATEGORY is always structure-preserving in the sense that both constituents are moved into positions where the phrase structure rules allow such constituents.

More precisely, recall that in Section III.1.2 the general form of structure-preserving rules is as in (37):

(37) $X-B-Y-B-Z \Rightarrow 1-4-3-(\Delta)-5$ (movement to left)

         $X-B-Y-B-Z \Rightarrow 1-(\Delta)-3-2-5$ (movement to right)

We can formulate the permutation of indirect object movement as structure-preserving by writing the right-hand side of (37) as $1-4-3-2-5$ (permutation). Such a formulation of indirect object movement makes crucial use of the fact that this rule reverses the order of two constituents of the same category (given deletion of the preposition as a separate part of the rule). In this view, *to* indirect object movement has the following form:

(38) $X + V-NP-to-NP-Z \Rightarrow 1-4-\emptyset-2-5$

(There are other restrictions on (38); the head of VP must be in a certain class, the second NP in most cases must be $+$ ANIMATE, etc.)

According to (38), the derived structure of sentences like (39) is (40):[11]

(39)
$$John \begin{Bmatrix} gave \\ taught \\ paid \\ read \\ promised \end{Bmatrix} Bill \begin{Bmatrix} a\ letter. \\ French. \\ the\ rent. \\ the\ verdict. \\ a\ book. \end{Bmatrix}$$

[11]For some verbs, like *give, bring, deny, sell,* etc., *to* dative movement does not apply if there is no (nonempty) direct object NP: **John gave Bill, *We read Bill,* etc. For others, like *pay, teach, tell,* etc., *to* dative movement MUST apply if a direct object NP is missing: *We paid (*to) the landlord, John told (*to) his brother, He teaches (*to) children,* etc. Cf. also *He is writing (to) the President.*

(40)

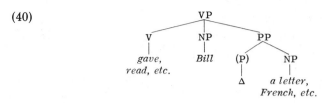

There is evidence to confirm the claim that the derived structure of sentences like (39) may have an empty P, as in (40). This evidence is the existence in English of a class of verbs that, like *give, deny, sell, pay, teach*, etc., have complements in which *to* dative movement applies and, furthermore, require that a preposition be inserted into the empty P provided for by the dative movement rule. Such verbs are *supply, furnish, provide*, and *credit*, which appear in examples like (41):

(41)   *They credited Smith (with this discovery).*
         They credited this discovery to Smith.

         The company furnishes us with a car.
         The company furnishes a car (to us).

         France used to supply Israel (with jets).
         France used to supply jets (to Israel).

Verbs like *supply* can be analyzed like other verbs with indirect objects, with the added stipulation that the preposition *with* be inserted into the empty P of (40). This use of the empty P accounts in simple fashion for a paradigm like (41), which differs from the ordinary indirect object paradigm, and hence justifies in some measure the derived structure that a structure-preserving formulation of indirect object movement assigns to sentences with indirect objects.

We have now seen that indirect object movement MAY be written in structure-preserving fashion. Furthermore, a strong argument can be made that it MUST be written as an interchange of two NP's just to achieve descriptive adequacy, independent of any consideration of the structure-preserving constraint. This argument concerns the interaction between the "postverbal particles" of English and indirect objects.

Many verbs that take indirect objects also appear with particles. In sentences where the indirect object is not moved in front of the direct object (assuming these to be the deep structure configurations given by the rule VP → V—(NP)—(PP)—...), particles can precede or follow the direct object:

(42)   *The secretary sent a schedule out to the stockholders.*
         The secretary sent out a schedule to the stockholders.

         Some student paid his loan back to the bank.
         Some student paid back his loan to the bank.

John read the figures off to Mary.
John read off the figures to Mary.

A clerk will type a permit out for John.
A clerk will type out a permit for John.

Bill fixed a drink up for John.
Bill fixed up a drink for John.

He has brought some cigars down for Dad.
He has brought down some cigars for Dad.

The teacher put the trucks together for the children.
The teacher put together the trucks for the children.

In Emonds (1972a) many arguments are given to show that these "postverbal particles" are in fact intransitive prepositions (i.e., instances of PP). It follows that they follow the direct object NP in deep structure, and that a particle movement transformation—(43), a local transformation—optionally moves them next to the verb:

(43) ***Particle Movement***: $X + V - \begin{bmatrix} NP \\ -PRO \end{bmatrix} - \begin{bmatrix} P \\ _{PP} \end{bmatrix} - Y \Rightarrow 1-3-2-4$

According to these conclusions, the first sentences of the pairs in (42) represent the deep structure order of constituents.[12]

Let us now consider the possible positions for particles in sentences where the *to* or *for* indirect object movement rules have applied:

(44)   *The secretary sent the stockholders out a schedule.*
              Some student paid the bank back his loan.
              John read Mary off the figures.
              A clerk will type John out a permit.
              Bill fixed John up a drink.
              He has brought Dad down some cigars.
              **The teacher put the children together the trucks.*

(45)   **The secretary sent the stockholders a schedule out.*
              **Some student paid the bank his loan back.*
              **John read Mary the figures off.*
              **A clerk will type John a permit out.*
              **Bill fixed John a drink up.*
              **He has brought Dad some cigars down.*
              **The teacher put the children the trucks together.*

[12]For the next several pages (82—86) in this section, I am following the text in Gross, Halle, and Schützenberger (1973) and in Emonds (1972a), except for renumbering and slight rewordings, with permission.

(46)   *?The secretary sent out the stockholders a schedule.*
              ?Some student paid back the bank his loan.
              ?John read off Mary the figures.
              ?A clerk will type out John a permit.
              ?Bill fixed up John a drink.
              ?He has brought down Dad some cigars.
              *The teacher put together the children the trucks.

In all the idiolects I have investigated, the most favored and natural
position for particles in sentences with verb—indirect object—object order is
BETWEEN the two object NP's, as in (44). Furthermore, in all idiolects the
position of the particle after the direct object, as in (45), is rejected. [There
are differences in acceptability among the particles; *together* resists acceptance
in sentences with two NP objects, while *back* sometimes is acceptable in
sentences like (45). I am ignoring those differences that seem unsystematic and
are quite limited in number.]

Idiolects seem to differ with regard to sentences like those in (46). In one
dialect (dialect A), the sentences in (46) are acceptable. In another (dialect B),
they are not, although they are not rejected as firmly as those in (45). (This may
be due to the presence of other speakers in the speech community with dialect
A). In a third dialect (dialect C), which I believe is my own, the sentences in
(46) that derive from sentences with an underlying *to* indirect object are
acceptable, while those that derive from sentences with an underlying *for*
indirect object are not. Since in my own dialect underlying *to* indirect objects
can be subjects of passives whereas underlying *for* indirect objects cannot, it is
not surprising to see this difference reflected elsewhere in the transformational
component, although it remains to be seen how these differences are to be
formally related. I return to this point later.

I will now consider the interrelation of particle movement as in (43) and
indirect object movement in all three dialects, A, B, and C. In dialects A and B,
we can assume that there is only one indirect object movement rule for the
purposes of this study. The structural description of this rule would be of the
form shown in (47) (here I ignore conditions on the verb and on the animateness
of the indirect object, which are irrelevant to the discussion):

(47) $X + V - \begin{bmatrix} NP_1 \\ -PRO \end{bmatrix} - (P) - \begin{bmatrix} _{PP} & \begin{Bmatrix} to \\ for \end{Bmatrix} & -NP_2 \end{bmatrix} - Y \Rightarrow ?$

[The subscripts in (47) are merely for reference in exposition.]

Before filling in the structural change of (47) for any of the three dialects,
we can ask whether this indirect object movement rule moves NP_1 to the
right over NP_2, whether it moves NP_2 to the left over NP_1, whether NP_1 and
NP_2 exchange positions (both moving), or whether perhaps such a question has

no possible empirical consequences so that the theory should be designed to make the question ill-formed.

If we move NP_2 to the left over NP_1, an optional position for particles will be after two object NP's, as in (45), no matter what order is used for particle movement and indirect object movement. To avoid this, an ad hoc condition must be added to particle movement as in (43) that states that the rule is obligatory in a second context, V—NP—NP—PRT. [It is also required that particle movement follow indirect object movement so that this condition and context can be stated. I use the symbol PRT (particle) for expository purposes only.] But if particle movement is obligatory in sentences with two object NP's, a second undesirable consequence is that particle movement cannot be used to account for the two positions of particles in dialects A and C. This leads to complication in the indirect object movement rule. Thus in all three dialects assuming that NP_2 moves to the left over a stationary NP_1 introduces ad hoc complications in the contexts and conditions of the particle and indirect object movement rules.

If we move NP_1 to the right over NP_2, and if particle movement as in (43) follows indirect object movement, there is no principled way to obtain the favored order, V—NP_2—PRT—NP_1, since PRT precedes NP_2 in deep structure. If we move NP_1 to the right over NP_2 but order particle movement before indirect object movement, we can get the particles in the favored position between the two NP objects only by moving them to the right with NP_1, and thus complicating the context for the indirect object movement rule: Its structural description would then be

$$V-(PRT) + NP-(PRT) - \begin{Bmatrix} to \\ for \end{Bmatrix} -NP$$

and the structural change would be $1-3-\emptyset-5-2$. What is worse is that this is a solution only for dialect A; in dialects B and C no solution is possible under this set of assumptions. These complications lead me to reject moving NP_1 over a stationary NP_2.

In contrast to the two types of indirect object movement just rejected, the third alternative, an interchange of NP_1 and NP_2 [terms 2 and 5 in (47)] leads to a perfect description of dialect A if we order this rule before particle movement:

(48) $\quad X + V - \begin{bmatrix} NP \\ -PRO \end{bmatrix} - (P) - \begin{bmatrix} \\ PP \end{bmatrix} \begin{Bmatrix} to \\ for \end{Bmatrix} - NP \end{bmatrix} - Y \Rightarrow 1-5-3-\emptyset-2-6$

According to this analysis, the sentences in (45) are ungrammatical because the corresponding source sentences in which particles follow indirect objects in prepositional phrases are also ungrammatical:

(49)   *The secretary sent a schedule to the stockholders out.*
       Some student paid his loan to the bank back.
       John read the figures to Mary off.
       A clerk will type a permit for John out.
       Bill fixed a drink for John up.
       He has brought some cigars for Dad down.
       The teacher put the trucks for the children together. (where *the
          trucks for the children* is not an NP)

Whether or not (48) applies, (43), which follows (48) in dialect A, can then optionally apply to place the particles next to the verb. If it does not apply, the particles appear in surface structure after the first NP after the verb.

We can account for dialect B by ordering particle movement BEFORE indirect object movement. If particle movement does not apply and indirect object movement does, the particle ends up between the indirect and direct object NP's. If particle movement does apply, the structural description for (48) is not met (since a particle intervenes between the verb and the direct object), so the rule cannot apply and the sequence V—PRT—NP—NP is correctly (for this dialect) excluded.

In dialect C, my own, the *to* and *for* indirect object movement rules are distinct, according to Fillmore's (1965) analysis. Furthermore, Fillmore postulates that *to* indirect object movement precedes *for* indirect object movement, thus allowing *to* indirect objects to become subjects of passives, but not *for* indirect objects.

By ordering particle movement as in (43) after *to* indirect object movement and before *for* indirect object movement, we can account for dialect C. That is, with regard to *to* indirect objects, dialect C is like dialect A, and the indirect object rule containing *to* precedes particle movement to account for this; but with regard to *for* indirect objects, dialect C is like dialect B, and the indirect object rule containing *for* follows particle movement to account for this.

We have been able to account for the three different ways that postverbal particles interact with indirect objects by formulating indirect object movement(s) as rules that interchange the positions of two NP's, making crucial use also of the fact that postverbal particles are generated after direct object NP's in deep structure, as shown in Emonds (1972a).

There is another formally different way to express the rule order of dialects B and C—(i) particle movement and (ii) indirect object movement, which is worth mentioning as an alternative although it does not affect any of our conclusions. If rules (43) and (48) are simply collapsed as in (50), we also obtain the sentences of dialect B [$\emptyset$ stands for the identity element under concatenation in (50)]. Note that (50) is a collapse of a local transformation and a structure-preserving transformation; I leave open the question of whether our algebra of transformations should be allowed to do this:

$$(50) \quad X+V-\begin{bmatrix} NP \\ -PRO \end{bmatrix}-(P)-\begin{bmatrix} \left\{ \begin{matrix} \emptyset & -P \\ \left\{ \begin{matrix} to \\ for \end{matrix} \right\} & -NP \end{matrix} \right\} \end{bmatrix}_{PP}-Y \Rightarrow 1\text{-}\text{-}5-3-\emptyset-2-6$$

Similarly, dialect C can be obtained by postulating a *to* indirect object movement rule and a following collapse of particle movement and *for* indirect object movement identical to (50) except for the absence of *to*.[13]

We see that there are two possible formal analyses for dialects B and C, provided that braces are permissible in transformational notation. Which of these is correct is an open question; but in either case it remains true that straightforward analyses of dialects A, B, and C that are free of ad hoc stipulations can be made only in terms of indirect object rules [(48) or (50)] that interchange two NP's rather than moving one NP over another stationary NP.

The formulation of the indirect object movement rule as an interchange of two NP's, as in (48) or (50), has been justified here because it correctly and simply accounts for the positions of particles in sentences containing indirect objects. That is, an accurate description of these constructions requires that indirect object movement be formulated as structure-preserving. The fact that such formulations are the ONLY ones permitted by the structure-preserving constraint testifies to its explanatory power; i.e., the constraint can lead to the selection of a descriptively adequate grammar (for one of three possible dialects) on the basis of data that concern ONLY indirect object constructions without particles and particle constructions without indirect objects.[14]

---

[13] Rule (50) appears to permit the second of two consecutive postverbal particles to interchange with a direct object. That this is not possible is easily seen from the following examples:

> *John brought the radio back down.*
> **John brought down back the radio.*
>
> *He pushed the shovel down in.*
> **He pushed in down the shovel.*

However, the starred examples are excluded by the fact that constituents interchanged by a local transformation are required to be adjacent.

[14] One might claim that in order to formulate (48) the speaker would have to know that particles (term 3 of the transformation) can in fact cooccur with predirect indirect objects. In line with this, some English speakers have recently informed me that they do not permit indirect object movement at all with particles; in this case, the rule of indirect object movement lacks term 3 of (48).

III.4   FURTHER STRUCTURE-PRESERVING NP MOVEMENTS WITHIN SENTENCES

III.4.1   Obligatorily Reflexive Noun Phrases

Certain verbs in English cannot appear with a direct object other than a reflexive pronoun:

(51)   *The witness perjured herself.*
            *The witness perjured the lawyer.

            Mary absented herself yesterday.
            *Mary absented Martha yesterday.

            The guests should avail themselves of the hotel's services.
            *The guests should avail each other of the hotel's services.

            The children were behaving (themselves) wonderfully.
            *The children were behaving each other wonderfully.

            They braced (themselves) for a shock.
            *They braced their parents for a shock.

            The panelists repeat (themselves) too much.
            *The panelists repeat the moderator too much.

Some of these verbs (*perjure, absent, avail*) have an obligatory reflexive object NP, while others (*brace, behave, repeat*) have an optional reflexive object NP.

Especially since certain of these verbs do not require a reflexive object, it would seem that in deep structure they are all intransitive verbs in the sense that their meanings have only a subject position that may be interpreted. If this is the case, we can assume that the source of the reflexive object pronouns is a structure-preserving transformation that inserts a pronoun copy of the subject NP into the object position. (The subject NP is, of course, not removed, but there is nothing in the definition of a structure-preserving movement rule that DEMANDS that an empty node be left behind; cf. Section III.1.2.) This rule, the IDENTICAL OBJECT rule, is illustrated in (52) (TENSE is omitted):

(52)

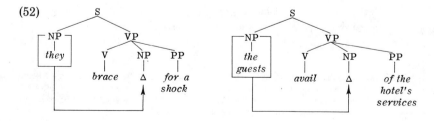

I assume that the appearance of a reflexive pronoun in (52) is due to the fact that reflexivization applies after the identical object rule.[15]

A structure-preserving formulation of the identical object rule implies that it is not an accident that the redundant reflexive pronouns in sentences like (51) appear in object position rather than, say, before the verb, immediately after the subject, at the end of the VP, etc. Since the latter are not NP positions, a copying of an NP is not allowed in them, according to the structure-preserving constraint. That is, the structure-preserving constraint rules out a language A in which reflexives that alternate with other object NP's appear in object position but in which redundant reflexives, as in (51), appear in a position not typical of NP's. In (53) # signifies "ungrammatical in A":

(53)   *The witness killed herself.*
          # *The witness herself killed.*

          # *The witness perjured herself.*
          The witness herself perjured.

          The children were bathing themselves.
          # *The children were themselves bathing.*

          # *The children were behaving themselves.*
          The children were themselves behaving.

In Helke (1973) it is argued that ALL reflexives, including those we have been examining here, are derived by making a pronoun copy of the subject NP in the possessive NP position of an NP whose head in deep structure is *self*. That is, reflexivization consists of an operation graphically representable as (54):

(54)

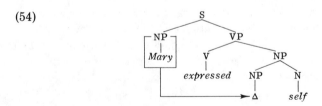

Since the grammar must independently generate NP's in possessive position, this operation is structure-preserving. The structure-preserving constraint does not strictly require that the empty NP be a base NP, although the posses-

---

[15]An alternative analysis of the verbs in question could simply insert the reflexive pronoun NP into object position. This would be necessary if the usual source of reflexives (those that alternate with other NP's) is the base rather than the transformational component. But this insertion would be structure-preserving, in the sense that the remarks in the text à propos the examples in (53) apply equally well to an identical object insertion rule as to a pronoun-copying rule.

sive NP appears to have this status; cf. Chomsky (1970) and Section III.5.[16]

One of Helke's strongest arguments in favor of generating reflexives by a structure-preserving copying rule is that the rule plays a role in many other constructions; for example, it would also account for the obligatory subject NP—possessive pronoun agreement in (55), as represented in (56):

(55)   *John lost his temper.*
             **John lost her temper.*

             We nodded our heads.
             **We nodded my head.*
             **We nodded their heads.*

             They held their own in the race.
             **They held his own in the race.*

(56)

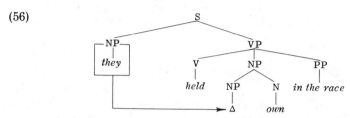

If Helke is right, the structure-preserving rule creating obligatory possessives is part of a very general process in English that inserts an NP (in pronoun form) into the independently generable possessive NP position. On the other hand, were he wrong (which does not seem to me to be the case), there would be two structure-preserving rules necessary to account for the data in this section—one for obligatorily reflexive NP's, as in (52), and one for obligatorily agreeing possessive NP's, as in (56). In either case we have further evidence that the transformations that move NP's within clauses that are needed for English are structure-preserving.

III.4.2   Another Replacement of the Subject

In Chomsky (1962) a transformation he terms simply INVERSION derives sentences of the following sort from deep structures in which the surface subject is the direct object (an alternative nontransformational solution is given in Chomsky, 1972):

(57)   *The book reads easily.*
             Cotton garments iron well.
             Those children frighten quickly.

[16]An alternative is mentioned in note 31 with regard to extending a formalism to be introduced in Section III.7. However, such an extension does not seem to me to be warranted at present.

Again, since these surface subjects exhibit all the characteristics of subject NP's (case, number agreement, etc.), Chomsky's inversion rule simply places a deep structure object into subject position in the following structure-preserving manner:

(58)

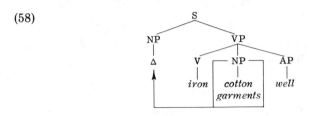

Ruwet (1972, Chapter 3) argues for a similar transformation ("*se—moyen*"), which plays a somewhat more central role in the grammar of French.

III.4.3   Certain Object Replacements in French

The "inversion" rule just discussed moves a deep structure object to the subject NP position. In French, which seems to resemble English at least in that it also is subject to the structure-preserving constraint,[17] there are two rules that move subject NP's into object position. The two rules in question are Kayne's (1970, 1972) STYLISTIC INVERSION rule, which relates the pairs of sentences in (59) by means of the operation displayed in (60), and EXTRAPOSITION OF INDEFINITES, which relates the pairs in (61) by means of the operation displayed in (62):

(59)   *Le pays que Pierre a visité est très passionant.*
                Le pays qu'a visité Pierre est très passionant.
                'The country that Pierre visited is very exciting.'

                Je voudrais savoir où Pierre est allé.
                Je voudrais savoir où est allé Pierre.
                'I would like to know where Pierre went.'

---

[17] Preverbal clitic placement, which might seem at first to be a counterexample to the constraint, is in fact confirmation of it. This is because there are two preverbal clitic nodes, one for reflexive clitics and one for the clitic *en*, which must be present in certain base constructions (*s'en aller, s'en prendre à quelq'un*, etc.). In turn, these are the only nodes necessary for the clitic placement rules that involve variables (i.e., that must be structure-preserving, according to the constraint). A third clitic placement rule can be formulated as a local movement transformation. The analysis is presented in detail in Chapter VI.

(60)

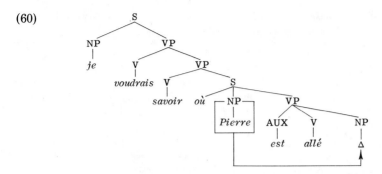

(It should be noted that "stylistic inversion" is not a stylistic rule in the sense of Chapter I, because in Kayne's formulation it depends on the presence of the formative WH in the input string.)

(61)   *Quelqu'un est venu hier.*
          Il est venu quelqu'un hier.
          'Someone came yesterday.'

          Beaucoup de monde a été contenté.
          Il a été contenté beaucoup de monde.
          'Lots of people were made happy.'

(62)

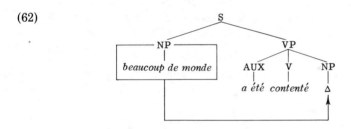

Ruwet (1972, p. 21) shows that these rules, which may apply in embedded sentences in French, are structure-preserving; I translate:

Thus, it might be expected that (15a) or (15b) could be generated by stylistic inversion from (15c) [cf. (59)—(60)]; but (15a)—(15b) include a sequence V—NP—NP which is not generated by the phrase structure rules for French. As the constraints of Emonds predict, (15a)—(15b) are ungrammatical:

(15a)   **La ville où rencontrera Pierre cet homme est très provinciale.*
(15b)   **La ville où rencontrera cet homme Pierre est très provinciale.*
(15c)   *La ville où Pierre rencontrera cet homme est très provinciale.*
           'The city where Pierre will meet that man is very provincial.'

Another example of a "structure-preserving" transformation in French is the rule of extraposition of indefinites (cf. Kayne, 1969; Picabia, 1970), which derives (16a) from (16b) but which cannot derive (17a) from (17b) [see n. 18]:

(16a)	*Il est venu quelqu'un hier.*
(16b)	*Quelqu'un est venu hier.*

(17a)	**Il a rencontré Paul quelqu'un.*
	*Il a rencontré quelqu'un Paul.
(17b)	*Quelqu'un a rencontré Paul.*
	'Someone met Paul.'

Here again, the constraints of Emonds permit one to explain why, even though (18a) is possible (extraposition of indefinites being applied after the passive rule) (19a), which one could expect to derive from (19b), superficially very similar to (18b), is ungrammatical:

(18a)	*Il a été contenté beaucoup de monde.*
(18b)	*Beaucoup de monde a été contenté.*
(19a)	**Il a été content beaucoup de monde.*
(19b)	*Beaucoup de monde a été content.*
	'Lots of people were happy.'

The reason is that *contenté* in (18) is the past participle of a verb, and that the sequence V–NP can be generated by the base rules, whereas *content* in (19) is an adjective, and there is no independent reason for having a base rule such as VP → *être*–AP–NP (where AP = adjective phrase).

Ruwet, quoting Kayne (1972), goes on to point out that the structure-preserving constraint does not, as currently formulated, suffice to account for ALL the restrictions on a rule like stylistic inversion. For example, the rule is blocked in most dialects if some PP follows the verb, as in (63):

(63) a. *La ville où Pierre parlera aux boulangers est très provinciale.*
     b. **La ville où parlera Pierre aux boulangers est très provinciale.*
         'The city where Pierre will speak to the bakers is very provincial.'

The structure-preserving constraint does not predict this restriction, but of course I make no claim that the structure-preserving constraint eliminates the necessity for stating contexts in transformational rules. Rather, I claim that the contexts that achieve descriptive adequacy for particular transformations will be in accord with the structure-preserving constraint (i.e., the constraint explains why certain contexts can appear and others cannot).

In fact, as I understand the situation in French, the unacceptability of (63b) is not as strong as that of Ruwet's (15a) or (15b), nor is it as strong as that of (64):

(64) **La ville où parlera aux boulangers Pierre est très provinciale.*

---

[18]Again, the reason is that this would require the base rule VP → V–NP–NP– ..., which is not a rule of French required for deep structures.

It would appear that (64), which is forbidden by the structure-preserving constraint, shares a higher degree of unacceptability with those other examples (15a–b in Ruwet, 1972) that are forbidden by the structure-preserving constraint, and that an example that is excluded only on the basis of how a particular rule of French is stated, such as (63b), is less unacceptable.[19]

In any case, whatever the reasons for these differences in acceptability, the two NP movements of French under discussion obey the structure-preserving constraint: They apply in dependent clauses but do not create phrase structure configurations that the base rules do not generate (i.e., they can be formulated as substitutions for empty nodes).[20]

III.4.4 Conjunct Movement

Lakoff and Peters (1966) have proposed that the second sentences in the pairs in (65) be derived from the first sentences by a rule called CONJUNCT MOVEMENT. There are arguments against this rule in Dougherty (1968) and Newmeyer (1969). I do not mean to counter these arguments; I wish only to discuss the rule in light of the structure-preserving constraint in case that, given some revision in the theory of grammar, these criticisms can be answered and the rule retained.

(65) *Bill and Mary walked downtown.* ("together," not "both")
      Bill walked downtown with Mary.

      My brother and his friends are reading Marx.
      My brother is reading Marx with his friends.

      Sam and Mary and Sue and Fred are cooperating.
      Sam and Mary are cooperating with Sue and Fred.

      Beer and chocolate don't mix well.
      Beer doesn't mix well with chocolate.

---

[19]I am not claiming that violations of the structure-preserving constraint lead always to strong unacceptability; we saw in Chapter II that under certain conditions the opposite is true. But in the present case Ruwet's examples (15a–b) and example (64) may be strongly unacceptable because the structure-preserving constraint AND a rule of French exclude them independently. In (63), only a rule of French is broken; in the examples of topicalization in certain dependent clauses discussed in Chapter II, only the structure-preserving constraint is broken.

[20]Stylistic inversion cannot be a local movement transformation because it depends on the presence of a preceding element in the COMP position such as WH.

Stylistic inversion shows clearly that it is erroneous to allow empty nodes to satisfy obligatory subcategorization features, as suggested in Emonds (1970). The requirement that a verb like *compléter* be transitive is never satisfied by its being followed by an NP in surface structure: **Le jour où a complété Pierre était très heureux.* In Emonds (1970) I utilized this notion crucially only in the treatment of "*there* insertion"; this mistake is corrected in Section III.6.1.

This formal effect of conjunct movement described by Lakoff and Peters can be trivially modified in the structure-preserving framework, so that this rule fills an empty deep structure PP as in (66):

(66)

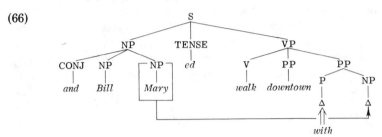

III.5   MOVEMENTS OF NP's WITHIN NP's

III.5.1   The Possessive Transformation; Comparison with NP Preposing

In this section, I utilize a base rule that provides for the possibility of a "possessive" NP before the head noun:[21]

(67) $NP \rightarrow \left\{ \begin{matrix} DET \\ NP \end{matrix} \right\} - \cdots -N-(PP)^*-(S)$

An alternative to (67) is (68). I am not concerned with any differences between these here; I choose (67) for expository purposes only.

(68) $NP \rightarrow \left[\begin{matrix} DET \\ (NP) \end{matrix} \right] - \cdots -N-(PP)^*-(S)$

Chomsky (1970) has given two arguments that the phrase structure rules should generate NP's in the DET position. First, he argues that noun phrases such as those in boldface in (69) cannot be derived from the corresponding sentences in (70) without reducing the notion of "grammatical transformation" to vacuity:[22]

(69)   *The enemy' destruction of the city was complete.*
         The destruction of the city by the enemy was complete.
         The city's destruction by the enemy was complete.

---

[21]It is not always the case that a possessive NP renders the larger NP definite: *There was a farmer's daughter in the field.* Cf. Jackendoff (1968).

[22]Although Chomsky's arguments for this are convincing, they can be strengthened by considerations given in Section III.5.2.

The corn's growth was amazing.
The growth of the corn was amazing.

John's stupidity exceeded only his desire for books.
The stupidity of John exceeded only his desire for books.

He didn't measure *the table's length.*
He didn't measure *the length of the table.*

(70)   *The enemy destroyed the city.*
          The corn grew.
          John was stupid.
          The table was long.

Given this, if we want to have the same order of elements and grammatical relations in the deep structures of the noun phrases in (69) as in the corresponding sentences in (70), we must generate "subject" NP's of noun phrases inside NP's by a rule like (67). [That is, the deep structure order of elements in (69) must be *the enemy's destruction, the corn's growth, John's stupidity, the table's length,* etc.]

Second, Chomsky points out that certain uses of possessive NP's (those followed by *'s*), such as those in bold face in (71a), cannot be plausibly derived from deep structures in which these NP's are not in the DET position. For example, the (normally stressed) sentences in (71b) are not paraphrases of those in (71a):

(71)   a.   ***John's*** *bad eyes are his greatest handicap.*
                Have you seen ***John's*** *measles?*
                Bill doesn't like ***Mary's*** *father.*
          b.   **The bad eyes of John are his greatest handicap.*
                **Have you seen the measles of John?*
                **Bill doesn't like the father of Mary.*

In view of these arguments, I incorporate (67) into the grammar of English.[23]

It will be necessary to speak of the NP on the right-hand side of (67) as the "subject NP" of the NP on the left, whatever the correct definition for this is in grammatical theory.

---

[23]The asterisk after (PP) in (67) implies that the limitations on the number and order of post-nominal PP's are determined by the lexical properties of the head noun, and not by a general constraint on internal NP structure. (Of course one could alternatively define this asterisk as, say, "three at most," rather than "indefinitely many," if a principled reason to do so were found.) The (S) in the source for full sentence and infinitive complements to nouns. It cannot be used as a source for relative clauses, however, since the latter cooccur with clause complements to nouns. I leave open the question of a deep structure source for relative clauses. Perhaps, since more than one such clause can modify a single noun, a recursive rule such as NP → NP—S is appropriate.

Consider now the "passive noun phrases" in (72). These noun phrases are paraphrases of the "active noun phrases" in (73) and the "mixed noun phrases" in (74):

(72)   *the city's destruction by the enemy*
              the offer's acceptance by John
              John's arrest by the police

(73)   *the enemy's destruction of the city*
              John's acceptance of the offer
              the police's arrest of John

(74)   *the destruction of the city by the enemy*
              the acceptance of the offer by John
              the arrest of John by the police

If we assume that the sentences in (72)–(74) are transformationally related, and if we assume that the deep structure order of the head and its object should be the same as that in the corresponding active sentences in (75), it would appear that the noun phrases in (72) are derived from the structures underlying the mixed noun phrases in (74) by some transformation that preposes (inside the NP) a deep structure object NP.

(75)   *The enemy destroyed the city.*
              John accepted the offer.
              The police arrested John.

I assume that the *ofs* following the head nouns in (73) and (74) are not present in deep structure; this allows us to enter noun–verb pairs such as *destroy–destruction* in the lexicon as both transitive (i.e., it is not necessary to specify one as appearing before *of*). If a rule of *of* insertion follows the rule that derives (72) from (74), then the latter rule need not mention *of*.

Given the rule in (67) for expanding NP's, the derivation of (72) from the structures underlying (74) can be expressed by a structure-preserving rule having the effect shown in (76) (as just mentioned, *of* is not yet inserted when this rule applies):

(76)

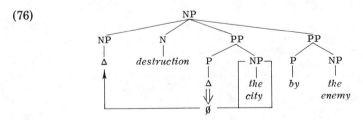

I now give several arguments that the structure-preserving rule operating in (76) is not the previously discussed NP-preposing rule, which yields passive sentences, but a separate structure-preserving rule we can call the POSSESSIVE TRANSFORMATION.

First, NP preposing moves an NP over a verb (or adjective) followed by a LEXICAL preposition in many cases, but the rule operating in (76) never does. [No *of* follows the head noun in (76); in any case NP preposing moves NP's over other prepositions besides *of*, and these prepositions are retained in surface structure]:

(77)   *The strike was referred to briefly in the communiqué.*
         **I saw the strike's brief reference to in the communiqué.*

         Correct procedure was insisted on by Mary.
         **Correct procedure's insistence on by Mary was admirable.*

         A recession is now hoped for.
         **A recession's hope for has receded.*

         The delay was compensated for by an increase in cost.
         **The delay's compensation for was more than adequate.*

         This problem was worked on by the Germans.
         **This problem's work on by the Germans was extensive.*

         John approved of my behavior.
         **My behavior's approval (of) by John was gratifying.*

Cf. *John approved the contract.*
         The contract's approval by John was gratifying.

         Such a tactic was unheard of fifty years ago.
         This was an unprepared for surprise.
         Jonn is very well cared for.

Second, NP preposing in sentences with passive verbs or adjectives is associated with the insertion of the morphemes *be—en*, whereas these morphemes never appear in passive noun phrases.

Third, NP preposing is obligatory in sentences, once agent postposing has applied, whereas the possessive transformation is not. Thus the "mixed" sentences corresponding to the "mixed" noun phrases of (74) are ungrammatical:

(78)   **Destroyed the city by the enemy.*
                 **Accepted the offer by John.*
                 **Arrested John by the police.*

Fourth, the possessive transformation apparently can apply to other NP's besides the one immediately following the head noun, whereas NP preposing applies only to NP's that are not separated from V by an intervening NP. The condition on the possessive transformation appears to be that the NP moved is the object of an empty P when the rule applies (i.e., is of the form $[_{PP} NP]$) [compare the examples in (77)]. This condition allows certain time adverbial NP's whose preposition is deleted (cf. Section III.3 for discussion) to be preposed by the possessive transformation, and this in fact happens:

(79)   *I liked the discussion of novels by the librarian last week.*
        I liked last week's discussion of novels by the librarian.

        The speech this morning by the president was optimistic.
        This morning's speech by the president was optimistic.

But such time adverbial NP's are not movable by NP preposing:

(80)   **I like it that last week was discussed novels by the librarian.*
        *This morning was spoken by the president.

[One could claim that the rule operating in (79) is different from the one operating in (76); but all I am arguing for here is a preposing rule inside NP's distinct from the NP preposing that produces passive sentences, and (79) is evidence for this in any case.]

These arguments all indicate that the possessive transformation is a separate (structure-preserving) rule in the grammar of English.

While we are speaking of movement rules inside NP's, it is appropriate to mention that the rule relating the pairs of sentences in (81) is also structure-preserving:

(81)   *The corn's growth was rapid.*
        The growth of the corn was rapid.

        The king's sleep should not be disturbed.
        The sleep of the king should not be disturbed.

        Mary commented on John's stupidity.
        Mary commented on the stupidity of John.

        The table's length exceeds its width.
        The length of the table exceeds its width.

        They disregarded John's strange belief that the world was cubic.
        They disregarded the strange belief of John that the world was cubic.

In view of the deep structure order of elements in sentences like those in (82), it appears that the first sentences in the pairs in (81) are more basic, whether or not one accepts the arguments in Chomsky (1970) that the sentences in (81) are not derived directly from structures underlying those in (82):

(82)   *The corn grew.*
              The king slept.
              John was stupid.
              The table was long.
              ? John strangely believed that the world was cubic.

This means that the rule relating the pairs in (81) is not the possessive transformation, but some different structure-preserving rule, say, "NP postposing."
Again, we can assume that this rule precedes *of* insertion and the insertion
of *'s*, so that it applies as in (83).

(83)

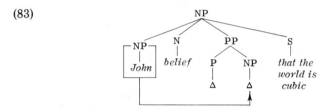

Thus in this section we have seen two structure-preserving NP movements
that operate within larger NP's.

III.5.2   The Questionable Nature of Agent Postposing

In Section III.1, I simply assume that the *by* phrase in English passive
constructions is derived by a transformation that moves a deep structure subject
to this position; cf. (10). In this section, I compare this view with an alternative
view and put forward three considerations that favor the alternative view over
the more usual one. Both views, however, are EQUALLY compatible with the
structure-preserving hypothesis, since both utilize the same number of
structure-preserving transformations in accounting for English passive constructions. In this sense, the whole section is a digression from the main theme.

In note 22 I allude to the possibility of strengthening Chomsky's (1970)
arguments in favor of generating "derived nominals" (e.g., *the enemy's fre-
quent allegations of atrocities*) as noun phrases in deep structure rather than
at transforms of sentences. Even though Chomsky's evidence shows that many
transformations do not apply in noun phrases, he does not state any definitive
condition on transformations that predicts that a certain class of transformations can apply to sentence but not to noun phrase structures. In this sense,
the lexicalist hypothesis does not predict, but is compatible with, the fact
that derived nominals do not exhibit structures that are the output of certain
transformations such as subject raising, object raising, indirect object
movement, etc. (The competing transformationalist hypothesis, given the

ordering principle of the transformational cycle, is not even compatible with these facts.) For discussion see Newmeyer (1971).[24]

In particular, there are three widely accepted transformations of English grammar that do apply in both noun phrase and sentence domains—agent postposing, extraposition, and equi-NP deletion. Examples of derived nominals in which these three rules apply in both types of structures are given in (84):

(84)   *The allegations of atrocities by the enemy (were false.)*
         Atrocities were alleged by the enemy.

         The certainty that we would lose (frightened us.)
         It was certain that we would lose.

         Your tendency to lie (is troublesome.)
         You tend to lie.

On the other hand, many transformations do apply only in the domain of sentences—NP preposing (cf. the preceding section), indirect object movement and postverbal particle movement (cf. Section III.3), subject raising, object raising, raising to object, and (optional) manner adverbial movement (cf. Section V.2). There are also transformations that apply only in the domain of noun phrases—the possessive transformation (cf. the preceding section) and the obligatory adjective-over-noun movement (cf. Section V.3).

The following principle of derived nominal structure predicts, under the lexicalist hypothesis, exactly which transformations will not apply in derived nominals:

(85) *Transformations that move material to the left in English cannot apply in the domain of both NP's and S's.*

It would be interesting to try to formulate a general condition on grammars so that (85) emerges automatically as a special case for English, but such an undertaking is beyond the scope of this study. For our purposes it suffices to note that the possibility of formulating a general principle such as (85) in the lexicalist framework both argues for this treatment of derived nominals and also suggests the lines of a particular alternative to the agent-postposing rule.

---

[24]The competing transformationalist hypothesis is not compatible with these facts because if subject raising, etc., are cyclic rules, they must apply before a "derived nominal transformation," which means that derived nominals should exhibit structures resulting from such rules (**John's appearance to be happy,* **The problem's difficulty to solve,* etc.). The only alternative left for the transformationalist hypothesis is to assign derived nominal formation to a class of "precyclic" transformations, as in Newmeyer (1974).

In the extended standard theory precyclic rules of this type are identified with rules of semantic interpretation that operate on deep structures. This is not to say that the "middle structures" of Newmeyer (1974) and the deep structures of the extended standard theory do not differ empirically; however, Newmeyer points out that they are in some ways similar.

This alternative is the following: The subject NP's of active constructions (both active sentences and active noun phrases) THAT ALTERNATE WITH PASSIVE CONSTRUCTIONS are taken to originate in deep structure in a *by* phrase.[25] In the domain of sentences ONLY, an agent-preposing rule optionally deletes *by* and replaces an (empty) subject NP with the agent phrase. By (85), this

[25]Since many active sentences and active noun phrases do not alternate with passive constructions, there is no reason to suppose that their surface order of subject NP—head differs from their deep structure order. This holds for any number of intransitive verbs (*tremble, die, blossom, rest, doze, wilt,* etc.) and for many transitive verbs and a great variety of derived nominals:

> *John became our doctor.*
> **Our doctor was become by John.*
>
> *Distant clouds often resemble the mountains.*
> **The mountains are often resembled by distant clouds.*
>
> *Bill has had this car for a long time.*
> **This car has been had by Bill for a long time.*
>
> *The suit fits Mary perfectly.*
> **Mary is fit by the suit perfectly.*
>
> *A better solution escapes us.*
> **We are escaped by a better solution.*
>
> *John should get the prize.*
> **The prize should be gotten by John.*
>
> *The gas entered the house.*
> **The house was entered by the gas.*
>
> *The Black Death never reached America.*
> **America was never reached by the Black Death.*
>
> *Tumbleweeds flew across the lakebed.*
> **The lakebed was flown across by tumbleweeds.*
>
> *The soap slipped into the closet.*
> **The closet was slipped into by the soap.*
>
> *John disappeared into the brush.*
> **The brush was disappeared into by John.*
>
> *John's resemblance to his father.*
> **the resemblance to his father by John*
>
> *Mary's lack of money*
> **the lack of money by Mary*
>
> *my family's friendliness toward strangers*
> **the friendliness toward strangers by my family*
>
> *women's entry into the movement*
> **the entry into the movement by women*
>
> *the corn's growth*
> **the growth by the corn*
>
> *John's stupidity*
> **the stupidity by John*
>
> *the table's length*
> **the length by the table*
>
> *John's strange beliefs about geometry*
> **the strange beliefs about geometry by John*

rule may not apply within noun phrases. Rather, the possessive transformation of NP domain (discussed in the preceding section) can, with a slight modification, effect the movement of agent phrases into the possessive NP position:

(86)   **Possessive:** $[_{NP} \Delta] - X - [_{PP} (by) - NP] - Y \Rightarrow 4-2-\emptyset-\emptyset-5$

Both alternatives we are considering, the "standard" analysis of the passive as in Section III.1.2 and the "agent-preposing" analysis given here, are consistent with (85), and both utilize the same number of structure-preserving rules. The standard analysis has a more restricted possessive transformation and an agent-POSTposing rule for both S's and NP's, while the alternative has an agent-PREposing rule for S's only and a generalized possessive transformation as in (86).

I now present three considerations that favor the agent-preposing analysis over the standard analysis of passive constructions in English.

The first consideration is the existence of full paradigms of determiners in "mixed noun phrases" of the type seen before in (74):

(87)   *each defeat of Germany by Russia*
                       those defeats of Germany by Russia
                       which defeats of Germany by Russia
                       any defeat of Germany by Russia

If the deep structure position of the NP object of *by* in (87) were in the DET position [i.e., were generated prenominally by (67) or (68)], then there would be no source for the noun phrases in (87). Various ad hoc output conditions might be found to incorporate the "exceptional" facts of (87) into a total analysis, but (87) is in fact just what we expect under the agent-preposing analysis of the passive.[26]

---

[26]Noam Chomsky has pointed out to me that some kind of output condition might be required in any case, although its nature is still obscure. The reasoning is thus: *The conclusion of John's* would seem to derive from *John's conclusion*, to explain the possessive marker; note also *that nose of John's*, which eliminates **that nose of John's noses* as a possible uniform source of the postposed possessive. But then *each conclusion of John's* would appear to derive from a structure in which *John's* and *each* both precede the head *conclusion* in deep structure. In turn, the exclusion of such surface structures (**John's each conclusion*, **Each John's conclusion*) means that an output constraint would be needed.

Inasmuch as there is no reason to choose either of the unacceptable orders (DET–NP–'s or NP–'s–DET) as the deep order, it would seem that these two constituents, the DET and the possessive NP, should be unordered in deep structure. We might then more generally permit unordered sets of constituents in deep structure in certain positions, provided that each element of the set appears in the given position in some surface structures, and require that a universal constraint on grammars exclude any surface structures in which such sets of constituents are not reduced to one. This would eliminate the statement of "output constraints" in particular grammars in many cases. There would be no complication in the base rules of particular grammars either, as each position specified in them would have to be justified in the same way as at present (cf. the discussion of base restrictions in Chapter I). Such a device was introduced in Emonds (1970) and termed DOUBLY FILLED NODES; in principle a node could be "multiply filled" in deep

A second consideration that favors the agent-preposing analysis is the fact that there are no "mixed" sentences of the form (*was*) *defeated Germany by Russia* that correspond to NP's of the form *the defeat of Germany by Russia*. In the agent-preposing analysis the convention that Δ is not permitted in well-formed surface structures combines with the fact that the base rule expanding S has an OBLIGATORY subject NP node (whereas the base rule expanding NP in English has an optional possessive NP node) to predict that such "mixed" sentences will be ill-formed. That is, the base rules can generate *defeat Germany by Russia* as an S ONLY IF there is an empty subject NP node, and either NP preposing or agent preposing must apply to remove $[_{NP}\ \Delta]$ in surface structure, yielding, respectively, the passive or the active sentence type.[27]

In the standard analysis, however, the fact that the agent-postposing rule MAY leave behind an empty NP in the subject position in sentences cannot be taken as an EXPLANATION (but only as a description) of the absence of "mixed" sentences; for ordinarily structure-preserving movement rules do not obligatorily leave behind a Δ that subsequently must be transformationally removed or replaced in order to obtain a well-formed surface structure.

A third consideration that favors the agent-preposing analysis over the standard analysis of the passive is the fact that the agent-postposing rule of the latter must be subject to a restriction, apparently semantic in nature, that can be eliminated in the agent-preposing analysis. Consider the following pairs of sentences, in which the verb is a motion verb:

(88)   *The thief (soap) slipped into the closet.*
         The closet was slipped into by the thief (*soap).

         The bird (dictionary) flew across the room.
         The room was flown across by the bird (*dictionary).

         The boy (gas) entered the house.
         The house was entered by the boy (*gas).

The absence of passive sentences with inanimate *by* phrase object NP's in (88) requires that a "semantic" restriction be put on the agent-postposing

---

Footnote 26 continued

structure by this device, although it would make no sense to speak of "doubly empty," since a null set cannot be doubly null.

Inasmuch as this extremely tentative device was mistakenly thought by some to be of crucial importance for establishing the structure-preserving constraint, I have eliminated its use in this study. In terms of the material discussed in this note, this means simply that I accept here the possibility of negative output constraints in particular grammars. This possibility also is accepted, to my knowledge, by all critics of "multiply filled nodes."

[27] If the insertion of the dummy subject *it* were permitted in English in transitive constructions, this would yield a variant **It was defeated Germany by Russia*. Even though an *it* insertion rule exists in English (for "weather verbs" such as *rain* and *snow*, for *seem* and *appear*, for cleft constructions, etc.), it does not apply in the context _____V—NP, where V $\neq$ *be*.

rule in the standard analysis of the passive. In accordance with the terminology in Jackendoff (1972), let us call the NP that undergoes the motion in a clause with a motional verb the THEME. We must then say that agent postposing cannot apply to a subject of a motional verb that is a theme but not an agent (i.e., is inanimate or dead).

However, in the agent-preposing analysis this restriction can be expressed in the base by analyzing nonagent themes of motional verbs as deep structure subjects and agent themes of motional verbs as deep structure objects of *by*. That is, a different deep structure grammatical relation is assigned to agent and nonagent themes of motional verbs. Since the grammatical relations of deep structure typically reflect different semantic relations between a verb and its "arguments" or "clausemates" while transformations are typically immune to such differences, the agent-preposing analysis is to be preferred.[28]

In this section, I have compared two analyses of the passive constructions of English that are equally consistent with the structure-preserving hypothesis and with what I take to be an important principle in the lexicalist framework of Chomsky (1970): the restriction on movement rules given as (85). Three arguments have been advanced that favor the second, nonstandard analysis of the passive.

III.6　CONSTRUCTIONS WITH THE EXPLETIVE SUBJECT THERE

III.6.1　*There* Insertion

A certain number of intransitive verbs in English may also occur with the "dummy" or "expletive" surface subject *there* and following noun phrases of the type that usually play the role of their subject:

(89)　　　　　　　*A hatless stranger appeared.*
　　　　　　　　There appeared a hatless stranger.

---

[28]Actually the observations concerning (88) are equivalent to the "first thematic hierarchy condition" in Jackendoff (1972): "The passive *by*-phrase must be higher on the Thematic Hierarchy than the derived subject [pp. 43–46]." (For terminology Jackendoff's discussion of "thematic relations" must be consulted.)

Given Jackendoff's thematic hierarchy, this condition can be violated only if (i) the passive *by* phrase contains the NP marked "theme" or (ii) the passive surface subject NP is the "agent." But as he points out (p. 42), an agent NP within the standard analysis must be a DEEP STRUCTURE SUBJECT (i.e., cannot be a deep structure object), so (ii) can never occur anyway.

In all the starred examples in (88), the problem is exactly that the *by* phrase does contain an NP that stands only in the thematic relation of "theme" to the main verb; in the acceptable examples, the *by* phrase NP is both theme and agent. Other examples given by Jackendoff where (i) is violated are:

　　　　　　　The car was hit by John with a thud.
　　　　　　　Five dollars are cost by the book.

A solution to this problem may not exist.
There may not exist a solution to this problem.

A catastrophe occurred in that century.
There occurred a catastrophe in that century.

Some problems remain in this regard.
There remain some problems in this regard.

This alternation can be accounted for by a structure-preserving movement of the subject NP into the NP position that follows the verb inside the VP, accompanied by the insertion of the pronoun form *there* into the subject NP.[29]

More controversial is the question of whether the same transformation relates the pairs of sentences in (90), in which the main verbal element is *be* rather than a lexical verb. Jenkins (1974) argues to the contrary, i.e., that the *there* noun phrases in (90) are either empty or exhibit some pronominal form in deep structure, and that the predicate attribute (postcopular) noun phrases are in their deep structure position:

(90)   *A small dog is in that room.*
        There is a small dog in that room.

        Several prizes are distributed on Saturday.
        There are several prizes distributed on Saturday.

        Some children have been playing in the yard.
        There have been some children playing in the yard.

        Few students are entirely without means of support.
        There are few students entirely without means of support.

Clearly, if Jenkins is correct, the *there—be* construction is not relevant for establishing the validity of the structure-preserving constraint. For the purposes of discussion I will assume that he is incorrect so as to show that the *there—be* construction in fact has properties of a base phrase structure configuration that can be accounted for by a structure-preserving formulation of *there* insertion. The arguments here do not choose between Jenkins' view and an analysis utilizing a structure-preserving operation, but they argue against an analysis that utilizes a non-structure-preserving transformation.

---

[29]The postverbal NP can sometimes be subsequently placed at the end of the VP by the "complex NP shift" rule discussed in Section III.7.

There can be no doubt about the NP status of the literal (locative) use of *there* elsewhere in the grammar, even though a preceding P is sometimes deleted: *Bill walked away from there, What's happening in there? Don't go near there,* etc. So we are not introducing any irregularity of category by inserting *there* in another NP position. Furthermore, subsequent rules treat this *there* as an NP: *There seems to remain a problem.*

A first agrument for the structure-preserving nature of *there* insertion can be made by examining the use of *be* as a modal (M) either of expectation or necessity or of futurity (in connection with *going* or *gonna*). These uses, exemplified in (91), are modal uses because they do not occur inside VP's (i.e., after other modals or in infinitives, gerunds, etc; I justify analyzing M as a sister to VP in Chapter VI):

(91)   *A demonstration is going to be held at six.*
        **A demonstration may be going to be held at six.*
        **They expect the demonstration to be going to be held at six.*

        Three senators are to be here for the conference.
        **The senators' being to be here surprises me.*

        You are to read one book every evening.
        **They insisted on your being to read one book every evening.*

If *there* insertion were not structure-preserving, a simple statement of it without ad hoc conditions concerning modals would place the subject NP after the first occurrence of *be*, as in (92):

(92)   *There is a new house being built next door.*
            **There is being a new house built next door.*

            There were only three students being obnoxious.
            **There were being only three students obnoxious.*

But when the first *be* is an M, such a statement of the rule yields the wrong results:

(93)   **There is a demonstration going to be held at six.*
            **There are three senators to be here for the conference.*

Rather, *there* insertion moves the subject NP to a position after the first *be* that is under the VP:

(94)   *There is going to be a demonstration held at six.*
            There are to be three senators here for the conference.

The structure-preserving constraint not only accounts for this but explains it, in the sense that another formulation of *there* insertion that would place the subject NP between M and V (when M is *be*) would be impossible, since the phrase structure rules do not provide an empty NP in that position.

The structure-preserving formulation of *there* insertion also predicts that *there* insertion should not be permitted in sentences in which *be* is followed by a nonempty (lexical) predicate attribute NP or AP. Such nodes do not have a source outside the lowest VP; so if they are present and filled in deep structure, no empty node onto which the subject NP can move is generable.

(95)   *Some graduate students are union members.
           *There are some graduate students union members.

           Few taxi drivers are rich.
           *There are few taxi drivers rich.

           One man was a pharmacist.
           *There was one man a pharmacist.

           Many homeowners are angry.
           *There are many homeowners angry.

           A few photographs were very dark.
           *There were a few photographs very dark.

           In this course, three books are important.
           *In this course, there are three books important.

These arguments lead to the same conclusion: If *there* insertion is a movement rule, it must substitute an NP for an empty predicate attribute NP generated by the base rule expanding VP.

A few adjectives appear to violate this claim; that is, *there* insertion can move subject NP's to a position before such adjectives:

(96)   There are probably a dozen people drunk.
                 ? There might be some students hungry.
                 ? There was a man very sick.

However, it is roughly these adjectives that sometimes appear in VP-final positions in certain other poorly understood constructions (i.e., the node AP does not appear in them freely):

(97)

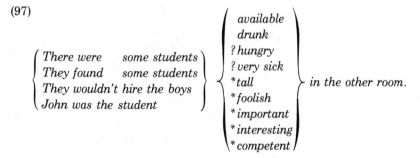

Certain properties and restrictions of such constructions are outlined in Green (1972). Although this might not be her conclusion, it seems to me that the properties that she describes indicate that there are essentially two adjective phrase positions for which verbs are subcategorized. The true predicate adjective AP, a base position, alternates with, but does not cooccur with, the predicate nominal NP. Such adjectives may be termed CHARACTERIZING adjectives, following Milsark (Temple University colloquim, 1974):

(98)   *Bill and Sue were (*the nonmembers) talkative.*
            The gold key is (*the key) octogonal.
            My kid is (*a terror) intelligent.
            John is (*a competent typist) tall.
            The man was (*pitiful) careless.
            Jane is (*very witty) Polish.

In (98) the characterizing adjectives cannot occur after another predicate attribute NP or AP.

On the other hand, English permits certain "circumstantial" or (following Milsark) "state-descriptive" adjectives to follow predicate attributes. Such adjectives seem to have the sense of circumstantial prepositional phrases, which may also occur in the same position:

(99) *Bill and Sue were the nonmembers present (available, in the other*
       room, etc.).
    The gold key is the key missing (available, on the table, etc.).
    My kid is a terror naked (drunk, without clothes, etc.).
    John is a competent typist sober.
    The man was pitiful undressed.
    Jane is very witty drunk.

If *there* insertion is a structure-preserving substitution of the predicate attribute NP, then we expect that the state-descriptive but not the characterizing adjectives in general appear after the sequence *there—be*—NP, as pointed out by Milsark:

(100)

$$\textit{There were quite a few nonmembers} \left\{ \begin{array}{l} \textit{present} \\ \textit{available} \\ \textit{drunk} \\ \textit{*talkative} \\ \textit{*tall} \\ \textit{*smart} \\ \textit{*witty} \end{array} \right\} .$$

$$\textit{There is a gold key} \left\{ \begin{array}{l} \textit{missing} \\ \textit{available} \\ \textit{*octogonal} \end{array} \right\} .$$

$$\textit{There were three kids} \left\{ \begin{array}{l} \textit{naked} \\ \textit{*intelligent} \end{array} \right\} .$$

$$\textit{Is there a competent typist} \left\{ \begin{array}{l} \textit{sober} \\ \textit{*tall} \end{array} \right\} .$$

$$\textit{There is a pitiful man} \left\{ \begin{array}{l} \textit{undressed} \\ \textit{*careless} \end{array} \right\} .$$

I conclude that a second AP position within the VP, the circumstantial AP position, is the source of any AP that follows postcopular NP's moved by *there* insertion. Hence, the examples in (96) are not counterexamples to the structure-preserving formulation of *there* insertion.

It is of interest to note that the two adjectival positions within the VP are not for the verb *be* only. Circumstantial AP's can follow predicate attributes after other linking verbs as well:

(101)   *He sounds intelligent drunk.*
               Rhubarb tastes bitter raw.
               Bill looks slim naked.
               She became a doctor young.
               She became intolerant young.
               I easily get very thirsty sober.

(Of course reversing the order of a characterizing and a state-descriptive adjective reverses the sense, in most cases leading to unacceptability: **He sounds drunk intelligent*, etc.)

Further, some transitive verbs can take a predicate attribute and some can take circumstantial AP's. A predicate attribute NP or AP after a direct object of a "change of state" verb has a "resultative" sense that modifies the direct object:

(102)   *They painted the house **red (another color**, etc.).*
               *Bill cooked the meat (until it was) **dry**.*
               *That made her **furious (a communist**, etc.).*
               *The intelligence agents beat us **bloody**.*
               *This will render the machine **useless**.*

(Cf. Green, 1972, for discussion of limitations on this construction.)

On the other hand, some of the verbs in (102) can also take a circumstantial AP: Hence, *They painted the house unsanded, Bill cooked the meat unsalted, Bill cooked the meat dry (without water)*. With these verbs, as with linking verbs, the predicate attribute (resultative) AP must precede the circumstantial AP when the two cooccur [cf. (101)]:

(103)   *They painted the house red unsanded.*
             *They painted the house unsanded red.
               Bill cooked the meat dry unsalted.
             *Bill cooked the meat unsalted dry.

A final note is in order. The analysis of *there* insertion given here, as well as that in Jenkins (1974), is not compatible with the claim that the sentences in (105) are derived directly from those in (104) by movement of the subject NP into the auxiliary (there is no deep structure NP generable inside the auxiliary):

(104)   *Several prizes are distributed on Saturday.*
          Some children have been playing in the yard.
          ?A lot of evidence is indicating his guilt.
          Only three students were being obnoxious.

(105)   *There are several prizes distributed on Saturday.*
          There have been some children playing in the yard.
          There is a lot of evidence indicating his guilt.
          There were only three students being obnoxious.

Rather, these analyses relate the sentences in (105) to those in (106):

(106) *There are several prizes that are distributed on Saturday.*
      There have been some children who were (?have been) playing
          in the yard.
      There is a lot of evidence that indicates his guilt.[30]
      There were only three students who were being obnoxious.

Of course the sentences in (106) are, in turn, open to alternative analyses; Jenkins (1974) claims that they are variants of the cleft construction and that a rule very similar to relative clause reduction effects the change to the sentences in (105).

III.6.2   *There* Replacement

Consider the pairs of sentences in

(107) a.   *There are some pine trees behind that barn.*
      b.   *That barn has some pine trees behind it.*

(108) a.   *There will be a hole in Jack's pocket.*
      b.   *Jack's pocket will have a hole in it. (or Jack will have a hole*
              in his pocket.)

(109) a.   *There are some paintings hanging on the wall.*
      b.   *The wall has some paintings hanging on it.*

Ross (1967a) argues that the (b) sentences in (107)—(109) should be derived from the (a) sentences by a rule he calls "*there* replacement." [Ross does not explicitly mention sentences like those in (109), however.] The movement part of this rule, which has the effect indicated in (110), is clearly structure-preserv-

---

[30]The rules of reduced relative clauses given in Chapter V relate this source sentence in perfectly regular fashion to the corresponding sentence in (105). The questionable acceptability of the corresponding sentence in (104) could not be explained so easily, which supports the conclusion in the text. Sentences of this type and their relevance were pointed out to me by Sharon Sabsay.

ing. It should be stated so that either of the boxed NP's in a tree like (110) can be moved by it:

(110)

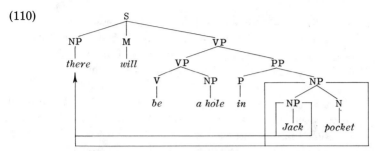

(I assume that this rule applies before *'s* insertion. We could think of it as leaving behind a pronoun copy of the original NP that is subsequently not reflexivized.)

   If a rule like *there* replacement is correct, it suggests that *have* and *be* are inserted transformationally (under empty V's, in the structure-preserving framework), as suggested by Bach (1967). *There* replacement would be one of the rules that inserts *have*. Most probably, *be* would be inserted only later in the derivation. Perhaps many of the nonverblike properties of *be* could be reconciled with its verblike properties in this way; the topic deserves detailed study of a kind I cannot enter into here.

III.7 COMPLEX NP SHIFT

   A counterexample to the structure-preserving constraint at this point is the rule of COMPLEX NP SHIFT discussed in Ross (1967a). This rule relates the pairs in (111).

(111) *I've sent every letter I ever received to my lawyer.*
I've sent to my lawyer every letter I ever received.

They brought the robe I had asked for into my room.
They brought into my room the robe I had asked for.

She presented a plan for redistributing the land before the council.
She presented before the council a plan for redistributing the land.

This rule moves object NP's to the end of the verb phrase if they dominate an S. In some cases it is sufficient that the NP dominate a PP. (When, if ever, the rule is obligatory is not of interest here.) The structure in a typical example in (111) after this rule has applied is as in (112):

(112)

$$\underset{\text{V} \quad \text{PP} \quad \text{NP}}{\overset{\text{VP}}{\diagup\mid\diagdown}}$$

Since the sequence V—PP—NP is not generable by the phrase structure rules of English (i.e., since no empty NP is generable after PP's in a VP), this rule is not structure-preserving according to our definition in Chapter I.

On the other hand, it does not seem to be an accident that the condition on complex NP shift is that the NP dominate an S or a PP, and that the NP in question is moved to the S or PP position at the end of the VP. In more general terms what seems to be happening is the following: Ordinarily a transformational operation that substitutes a constituent B for a constituent A is structure-preserving if and only if B and A are of the same category. But complex NP shift is a transformational operation that may substitute a constituent B (an NP) for a constituent A (an empty PP or S in VP-final position) whenever B DOMINATES A.

Thus we must weaken somewhat the structure-preserving constraint to allow for this variation on it, but we should weaken it under as restrictive a condition as possible. One such condition would be a requirement that this weakening of the structure-preserving constraint can take place only if A is a rightmost or leftmost constituent of an S.

In fact there is good evidence that this is nearly the correct version of the condition under which rules are required to preserve structure only in a weaker sense: The WH-fronting rule substitutes phrase nodes for the sentence-initial COMP node with the feature WH whenever these phrase nodes DOMINATE WH. In the course of this study, the mechanisms underlying WH fronting are examined in the appropriate sections, but full attention is turned to this rule only in Chapter V; we will see then that this initial observation holds true: WH fronting may effect the movement of a phrase node just in case that phrase node dominates (or is) a category in the feature complex of COMP.

I therefore propose extending the notion of structure-preserving operations to those that satisfy the following condition:

(113) **The Sentence Boundary Condition:** *If* A_j *is a rightmost or leftmost constituent of an* S, *a transformational operation that substitutes* B *for* A_j *is structure-preserving if* B *dominates* A_i, *provided that there is no* S *such that* $B = X \left[{}_S Y A_i Z_S \right] W$.[31]

---

[31] The fact that a rightward movement of an S (= B) that might contain an S (= A) to an S position does not qualify as structure-preserving by (113) does not nullify the fact that such a movement is structure-preserving by the definition in Section I.1.

In Chapter V we will see that perhaps (113) should be extended to NP boundaries as well, to explain why an AP that dominates a PP or an S (and only such AP's) can follow a head noun within the NP. Such an extension then suggests that possessive NP's might be derived from postnominal *of* phrases by an application of (113) properly generalized in which A = DET and B = NP. However, it still seems more plausible to me that possessive NP's are in the base, because of the arguments of Section III.5.

The last requirement in (113) ensures that no rule will substitute an S or any other constituent for COMP just because that constituent contains a COMP in an embedded sentence. Note that if the leftmost constituent of an S is COMP, and if the only feature that appears with COMP and also in other positions is WH, it follows that the ONLY fronting rules permitted by (113) that are not structure-preserving in the sense of Section III.1.2 are WH fronting rules.

For our purposes in this chapter, it is sufficient to note that while (113) permits the rule of complex NP shift, with A = S or PP and B = NP, it does not permit non-structure-preserving rules (in the sense of Section III.1) to apply in sentence-internal positions at all or even at sentence boundaries except under very special conditions.

The analysis of complex NP shift permitted by the sentence boundary condition predicts that the rule can apply only if the NP moved substitutes for a VP-final (empty) S node. In fact Ross (1967a, pp. 30–34) must impose a very complicated ad hoc condition on this rule (which in part involves his view that adjectives are verbs, since refuted in Chomsky, 1970, and not held here) to ensure that the rule does not apply if the VP terminates in a (nonempty) S. The following examples and judgments are from Ross.[32] The VP-final S constituents that block complex NP shift are in boldface:

(114) *I forced (wanted) **to eat hot soup** all the children who were
          swimming.
       *I told **that we were in trouble** a man who had a kind face.
       *I watched **talk (ing)** all the children who had never seen the sea.
       ?*I found **to be delicious** some fruit that I picked up on the way
          home.
       ?*The major regarded **as being absurd** the proposal to build a
          sidewalk from Dartmouth to Smith.
       *I consider **to be a fool** the senator who made the opening
          speech.
       *She asked **whether it looked like rain** a man who was near
          the window.

The structure-preserving formulation of complex NP shift automatically predicts that the examples in (114) are ungrammatical, since there is no empty S (or PP) node under the VP to the right of the VP-final S constituents in (114). The structure-preserving constraint therefore not only permits the description of the facts in (114) but explains WHY such facts exist.[33]

---

[32] I assume with Ross (1968) that the S node over infinitives does not "prune," although it does prune if only an AP remains after deletions.

[33] There are still unexplained cases, both here and in the final formulation of the rule (with two special conditions) given by Ross. For example, Ross notes the contrast *We elected President the man who was sixty* versus *We gave money the man who was sixty.* It seems to me that a promising line of research in this regard is that being followed in Culicover and Wexler (1973).

IV

Root and Structure-Preserving Movements of Sentences and Verb Phrases

In this chapter, I argue that the rules that move S and VP constituents in English are root or structure-preserving operations.[1] We are concerned almost exclusively with rules that move S's, and perhaps should be formulated to move VP's also, simply because few rules that move VP's but not S's have been proposed in the literature. Three rules of this type have, however, been justified.

IV.1 VP MOVEMENT RULES

In Sections II.5.2 and II.7 two root transformations that move VP's are described—VP preposing and participle preposing. They are exemplified again here:

(1)   **VP *Preposing:***
    *We thought she would lose her temper, and **lose it** she has.*
    *They said we shouldn't buy gold, but **buy gold** we will.*
    *We thought that she would lose her temper, and he writes that
        ***lose it** she did.*

---

[1] It seems possible that in Dutch and/or German there is a local movement rule involving S. H. van Riemsdijk has pointed out to me that such a rule might interchange an S—V input sequence. Thus I do not mean to imply by the title of this chapter that S and VP nodes cannot take part in local rules in the way other phrasal categories can. Such a rule for German would cancel the argumentation of Higgins (1973) that leads to his conclusion that "it is, prima facie, unlikely that the sentential extraposition rules of German can be fitted into the structure-preserving framework [p. 183]."

*They are saying that we didn't hate Capetown, even though **hate it**
we did.

Participle Preposing:
Fouling up their plans now *is the new demand to abolish
profit increases.*

I hope that **fouling up their plans now *is the new demand to
abolish profit increases.*

An example of a structure-preserving VP movement rule for English is
Dougherty's (1970a) "conjunction reduction" movement transformation, which
performs the operation indicated in (2). Dougherty's discussion of the need for
this rule seems convincing to me, at least in light of previous analyses of the
same material; I have no additional supporting arguments.[2]

(2)

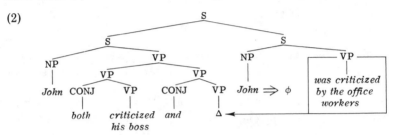

To my knowledge, these are the only VP movement rules that have been
proposed for English in the literature with supporting argumentation, and they
present no counterevidence to the structure-preserving constraint.

IV.2   CLAUSAL SUBJECTS AND OBJECTS: EXTRAPOSITION

IV.2.1   Deep Structure Sources of Complement Clauses

In examples (3) and (4) the constituents in boldface have the internal
structure of sentences (S) but appear to take the positions of NP's; that is, the
sentences appear in the positions of direct object, subject, and object of a
preposition:

---

[2]It is true that Dougherty's rule as formulated violates the prohibition on transformationally inserting
material into a clause S_i [the leftmost S in (2)] on a transformational cycle of a clause higher than S_i
[in this case, the cycle of the top S in (2)]. However, since this constraint could easily be amended to
exceptionally allow such insertion into conjoined S's on the cycle of the conjoining S (i.e., such an addendum
could be stated in terms of well-motivated constructs in universal grammar such as conjoined and conjoining S's), this consideration alone does not seem to me to invalidate Dougherty's proposal.

(3)   *John believed **(that) Mary was a foreign agent**.*
   *John will see to it **that you have a reservation**.*
   *Bill would prefer **for Mary to stay awhile**.*
   *Barbara decided **to buy a car**.*
   ***That Bill knows German thoroughly** is obvious to all.*
   ***To read so many magazines** is a waste of time.*
   ***For the house to be painted** would irritate him.*

(4)   *John regretted **stealing Mary's book**.*
   *John will see to **your getting a ticket in time**.*
   *Bill would prefer **buying fewer foreign books**.*
   ***Your being able to find a new job** would be surprising.*
   ***Reading so many magazines** seems a waste of time.*
   ***Mary's having so many books** surprised him.*
   *John just came back from **driving his cab**.*
   *She blamed it on **Bill's being too strict**.*
   *Because of **John's being so old**, Mary gets a pension.*
   *Your explanation for **the table's being badly scratched** sounds
   suspicious.*

Following widely accepted terminology, I call the infinitives and *that* clauses in boldface in (3) "(nongerund) complement clauses" and the clauses in boldface introduced by V—*ing* in (4) "gerund complements" or "gerunds."[3]

---

[3] Subordinate clauses introduced by V + *ing* that are NOT subjects or objects of verbs or objects of prepositions are termed not GERUNDS but, rather, PARTICIPLES.

An alternative to the analysis of extraposed complement clauses of Rosenbaum (1967) is to be found in Emonds (1972b), in which complement clauses are generated in VP-final position and moved into subject position by a root transformation called SUBJECT REPLACEMENT. This analysis here is formally similar to Rosenbaum's and quite different from Emonds (1972b). But empirically speaking I am not sure that my own two proposals can be clearly differentiated one from the other, whereas both make quite different (and I think better) predictions than Rosenbaum's does.

I received an analysis of extraposition for Dutch (de Haan, 1974) that is very similar to the analysis for English given here just before sending the manuscript to press. De Haan includes a critical appraisal of Rosenbaum (1967) and Emonds (1972b).

Higgins (1973) gives a detailed criticism of Emonds (1972b) and purports to refute that analysis. Almost all of his arguments seem to me to be flawed or based on misunderstandings of my original proposals (the latter due in some cases to my own lack of explicitness or clarity). I might make exception when it comes to arguments Higgins proposes based on the pseudo-cleft construction, since I have a poor understanding of that construction (especially of the mechanism that "matches" the two sides of the copula). On the other hand, formal differences between the present analysis and Rosenbaum's are so few that I doubt that one could base an argument on the pseudo-cleft construction that would convincingly differentiate or choose between them.

Similarly, Nagahara (1974) presents arguments against Emonds (1972b). In this study, I am not trying to compare the analysis of Emonds (1972b) to that given here. Thus the question of whether Higgins or Nagahara has effectively refuted my previous analysis is not really relevant to the development. I would hope that a comparison between a "perfected" subject replacement analysis and my extraposition analysis could appear in the literature in the future. However, since I understand that in Higgins' dis-

In an important study of complement clauses in a generative framework, Rosenbaum (1967) proposes that all the clauses in boldface in (3) and (4) are instances of the following deep structure:

(5)

Rosenbaum points out that the deep structure in (5) requires that the lexical proform be strictly subcategorized for the frame +_____S, since we cannot allow *it* to appear freely in the N position. This is necessary to ensure that determiners do not appear to the left of *it* or PP to the right of *it*. The ad hoc nature of this subcategorization feature can be seen by noting that *it* belongs to a class of "proforms" (in traditional terms, the "personal pronouns": *it, he, she, they, we, you, I,* and perhaps *who*), which otherwise share the property that they occur ONLY in the context $_{NP}$[_____].[4]

This class is defined in other ways also: Only personal pronouns show subject—object "case" differences in English. (Cf. Section V.9. Of course such case differences are not required; e.g., *you*.) Only personal pronouns cannot as objects be separated in surface structure from a preceding verb in a non-contrastive context (as discussed in Ross, 1967a, and Fischer, 1971):

(6)   **John brought out it.*
        *John brought Mary it.
        *She gave the boys them.
        *Please run off them quickly. (meaning "run them off")
        *They have divided up us according to age.
        (*Here's my pet cat.*) **Why don't you show the kids her?*
        John brought out some.
        John brought Mary this.
        She gave the boys several.
        Please run off three quickly.

Footnote 3 continued

sertation the analysis of the pseudo-cleft presupposed in his original criticisms has been abandoned, one might omit discussion of that construction.

Throughout this chapter (especially in the notes), I do try to answer whatever arguments of Higgins' and Nagahara's would apply to my analysis here.

[4]I assume that various modifying relative clauses, reduced relatives, and appositives are SISTER constituents to the modified NP: *we the doctors, he who knows best, you from St. Louis,* etc. For discussion of appositives see Delorme and Dougherty (1972). Hence the claim in the text.

Proper nouns may appear without determiners but may also appear with them. Note the contrast with personal pronouns: *the three Susans, young John* versus **the three yous, *young she.*

They have divided up many according to age.
Here's my pet cat. Why don't you show the kids yours? (**yours**
is a possessive, not a direct object)

We see, then, that *it* belongs to a well-delineated class of proforms, and that
an .analysis that assigns it a special subcategorization feature + _____S is
utilizing an ad hoc (exceptional) device. That is, a grammar that expresses the
stated generalizations about English personal pronouns would automatically
predict that *it* does NOT occur in the context + _____S.

As a means of eliminating this subcategorization feature, I propose to
replace the deep structure for gerund and nongerund complement clauses
proposed by Rosenbaum (5), with a deep structure that utilizes an empty node
(7):

(7)

Clearly no strict subcategorization feature is needed (or in fact possible) in this
framework for Δ, which is not a lexical item.

Beyond this simplification, however, there are far-reaching consequences
associated with the choice between the minimally differentiated deep structures
in (5) and (7). Rosenbaum's deep structure will always give rise to a WELL-
FORMED surface structure if no transformation applies to it. By contrast, the
deep structure in (7) WILL ALWAYS GIVE RISE TO AN ILL-FORMED SURFACE
STRUCTURE (because of Δ), unless some (well-motivated) transformation deletes
or replaces Δ. As we proceed it will be argued that a wide range of facts about
English clausal complements force the choice of (7) over (5). This choice is
further supported by the fact that it allows the elimination of the subcategorization of *it* in the lexicon.[5]

Before comparing the analyses that follow from choosing (5) or (7), we must
consider another source for complement clauses in deep structure proposed by
Rosenbaum: that given by a VP expansion rule such as (8):

(8)   VP → . . . V . . . (S)

---

[5] It might be preferable to add to a deep structure like (7) a feature on the head N such as + ABSTRACT
[i.e., any transformation that applies to (7) to delete Δ and derive a well-formed surface structure should
perhaps apply only to structures in which the empty N has such a feature value]. This feature could then
serve in the selectional restriction mechanisms that match verbs with appropriate subjects and objects. Such
a feature does not affect the lines of the transformational analysis given here. At worst it can be identified
with Rosenbaum's arbitrary "complementizer" features, $\pm$D and $\pm$E, which differentiate among the deep
structure sources of gerunds, infinitives, and *that* clauses in his system.

Rosenbaum presents certain arguments for deriving certain clausal complements from deep structures provided by this rule, but my own views are only partly in accord with his. For an exposition of what I take to be valid arguments in favor of analyzing certain clausal complements of verbs as deep structure sisters to V [i.e., as generated by (8)], see Sections 1.1 and 2.2 of Emonds (1972b) and also Kajita (1967).

Typical examples of the various verb complement constructions that are argued to be deep structure sisters to their governing verbs in the works cited are in boldface in (9):

(9)   *It appeared to us **that the motion would pass**.*
      *John started **telling us we would lose**.*
      *The woman heard us **doing the laundry**.*
      *We hesitated **to voice our ideas publicly**.*
      *The teacher admonished his best students **to take the course
          seriously**.*

At least one other type of verb that I claim takes an S sister in deep structure is the "manner of speaking" verb in its "understood communicatively" sense. The definition and explication of these terms, and examples and properties of this class of verb are given in Zwicky (1971). Examples:

(10)   *Morris whined that night was falling.*
       A kid shrieked that Baltimore had just gone ahead.
       One guest growled to the waiter that an hour was long enough.
       Several people mumbled to Harry that he'd better leave.

In Emonds (1970) I used *quip* and *guess* as verbs of this type, though I was not aware of all the properties of the class. Because *guess* has several related but different uses, I omit it here.

(11)   *John quipped that he could pass without trying.*

As Zwicky notes, these verbs in the sense indicated (where the complement S is understood as carrying the meaning of a proposition and not just the representation of a sound sequence) cannot be found in the passive:

(12)   * *It was whined by Morris that night was falling.*
       * *That night was falling was whined by Morris.*
       * *It was shrieked by a kid that Baltimore had just gone ahead.*
       * *It was growled to the waiter by one guest that an hour was long
          enough.*
       * *That an hour was long enough was growled to the waiter by one
          guest.*
       * *It was mumbled to Harry (by several people) that he'd better leave.*

> *That he could pass without trying was quipped by John.*
> *It was quipped by John that he could pass without trying.*

This fact is accounted for by generating the complement clause S's as sister constituents to the verbs rather than as NP's.

According to the analysis to follow, gerunds that may have a surface subject expressed as a possessive NP are themselves in NP positions THROUGHOUT their transformational derivation. This, together with the fact that "manner of speaking verbs understood communicatively" have S but not object NP complement clauses, explains why such verbs cannot have gerund objects (as pointed out by Zwicky):

(13)   *John quipped his being able to pass without trying.*
        Morris whined night's being about to fall.
        A kid shrieked Baltimore's having just gone ahead.
        A guest growled an hour's being long enough to the waiter.

A third test that such complement clauses are not NP's is that they cannot undergo object raising:

(14)   *It was easy to growl that the food was late; why didn't you refuse to pay?*
        **That the food was late was easy to growl; why didn't you refuse to pay?*
        It would be interesting to shriek that Baltimore has gone ahead.
        **That Baltimore has gone ahead would be interesting to shriek.*
        It must be tough for him to quip that half a leg is better than none.
        **That half a leg is better than none must be tough for him to quip.*

Thus Zwicky's "manner of speaking verbs understood communicatively" and the classes of verbs discussed in Sections 1.1 and 2.2 of Emonds (1972b) take S complements in deep structure. Besides these, a sizable class of verbs that take an object NP and a following complement clause are those given in Rosenbaum (1967) as list A.6.1 in the Appendix: *admonish, appoint, command,* etc. In most cases I agree with this classification. Taken together, these classes of verbs amply justify the phrase structure rule in (8).

IV.2.2   Extraposition

The central transformation in Rosenbaum's analysis of clausal complements is the optional extraposition transformation; by means of this rule, a nongerund clause in the context $[_{NP} it + \underline{\hspace{1cm}}]$ is moved to VP-final position. In my terms, this rule moves a nongerund clause in the context $[_{NP} \Delta + \underline{\hspace{1cm}}]$ to VP-final position, replacing Δ with *it*:

(15)   ***Extraposition***: $X-[_{NP} \Delta-S]-Y \Rightarrow 1-it-\emptyset-4+3$

(A formal revision in the rule is made below.)

The extraposition transformation yields the sentences in (16), which correspond to the sentences with nongerund subject clauses in (3); "extraposed" clauses are in boldface:

(16)   *It is obvious to all **that Bill knows German thoroughly**.*
         *It is a waste of time **to read so many magazines**.*
         *It would irritate him **for the house to be painted**.*

It should be kept in mind that additional transformations must apply to either Rosenbaum's deep structure or mine if the original examples in (3)—(4) (which contain no surface *its*) are to be generated. I return to these crucially important rules later.

We have seen that the phrase structure rule for expanding VP in English can generate an S in VP-final position. This means that extraposition can be formulated as a structure-preserving rule:

(17) ***Extraposition***: $X-[_{NP} \Delta-S]-Y-[_S \Delta]-Z \Rightarrow 1-it-\emptyset-4-3-6$

[Of course the notation of (17) may be redundant, since the structure-preserving hypothesis may permit conventions on the formal statement of rules that ensure that the previous formulation of extraposition, (15), is automatically interpreted as (17).]

This structure-preserving effect of extraposition can be illustrated as follows:

(18)

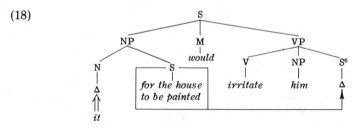

Such a formulation predicts correctly that adverbs generated "outside the VP"—cf. Chomsky (1965, Chapter 2) and Section V.4 of this study—can FOLLOW extraposed subject clauses; each of the following examples has a clear reading in which the postposed adverb modifies the main verb:

---

[6]Formally, an empty S dominates a string of Δ's—those under categories generated by the obligatory base rule choices such as the subject N, the main verb, and perhaps TENSE.

(19) *It seems conceivable **that our long-term goals will be achieved** today.*

*It means nothing **to speak of simultaneity** in Einstein's framework.*

*It isn't required **that the players be tall** in this school.*

*It pleased me **that they played those records** very much.*

*It doesn't frighten me **to watch horror movies** anymore.*

*It isn't necessary **to be smart** on this campus.*

Time and place adverbials, and less generally causal adverbials, can also precede extraposed subject clauses; any grammatical analysis of English using the extraposition rule must account for this alternation. In Section V.4 I propose a structure-preserving rule that optionally moves such adverbials inside the verb phrase which immediately dominates the main verb; this rule yields the following variants of the examples in (19):

(20) *It seems conceivable today that our long-term goals will be achieved.*

It means nothing in Einstein's framework to speak of simultaneity.

It isn't required in this school that the players be tall.

It pleased me very much that they played those records.

It doesn't frighten me anymore to watch horror movies.

It isn't necessary on this campus to be smart.

An interesting confirmation of the fact that extraposition is structure-preserving is that such a formulation predicts that two separate sentence complements cannot be extraposed from subject and object positions to the same VP-final S position. (We will see later that extraposition is in effect obligatory from object position.) The unacceptable examples in (21) are predicted by the joint effects of the structure-preserving hypothesis and the requirement that a base rule like (8) not provide nodes, such as two VP-final S's, that are not utilized in a productive class of deep structures:

(21) *That John has blood on his hands proves (that) Mary is innocent.*

* It proves (that) Mary is innocent that John has blood on his hands.

To see this movie is to relive the past.

* It is to relive the past to see this movie.

That John is late persuades me that the train was delayed.

*It persuades me that the train was delayed that John is late.

Examples of this type and their possible significance were first pointed out to me by Edward Klima.

In both Rosenbaum's analysis and this study, the extraposition of a clause from an NP position leaves an *it* in that position. Therefore both equally require a further rule to delete this *it* in direct object position after certain verbs, whether or not a PP (or other adverbial) intervenes between this *it* and the extraposed S:

(22)   *John said (*it) (to his friends) that we had betrayed him.*
        That suggests (?it) (to us) that he was correct.
        Several people explained (*it) to her how it should be done.[7]

Further, this direct object *it* in the clauses with extraposed object clauses gives rise to the following passives [cf. the lack of such passives with "manner of speaking verbs communicatively understood" in (12)]:

(23)   *It was said by John that we had betrayed him.*
        It was suggested to us that he was correct.
        It was explained to her by several people how it should be done.

This rule, common to both analyses, is roughly as follows; with Rosenbaum, I limit myself to saying only that it is "usually optional":

(24) **Pronoun Deletion**: $X + V - [_{\text{NP}} it] - \left(\begin{Bmatrix} \text{PP} \\ \text{AP} \end{Bmatrix} \right) - \text{S} - Z \;\Rightarrow\; 1 - \emptyset - 3 - 4 - 5$

IV.2.3 Gerund Formation

Rosenbaum observers that extraposition does not apply to gerund clauses (save in a few exceptional cases):[8]

---

[7] Higgins (1973, pp. 184—185) gives several examples with passive counterparts to (22) that emphasize the need for an NP (= *it*) in direct object position with these verbs, so that the passive transformation does not apply incorrectly to yield:

> **His friends were said to that we had betrayed him.*
> **We were suggested to that he was correct.*
> **She was explained to by several people how it should be done.*

These facts are perfectly consistent with my analysis and also with that in Emonds (1970) because of the direct object *it* (deleted in surface structure) that intervenes between the verb and the indirect object when the passive rule applies to the strings underlying the examples in (22). Higgins, in the passage under discussion, refers to my "cavalier treatment of the *it*" in comparing the analysis of Emonds (1970) to that of Rosenbaum, and claims that the preceding examples support Rosenbaum's analysis. My treatment of *it* was exactly as cavalier as Rosenbaum's, for as pointed out in Emonds (1970), "the theory of verb complementation I am proposing agrees with that of Rosenbaum in that the distribution of the deep structure *it*'s whose antecedents are sentence and infinitive (but not gerund) complements is essentially the same in both theories." Thus the examples under discussion are not generable in all three theories for exactly the same reason——there is a (nonempty) direct object NP between the verb and the indirect object when the passive rule applies.

[8] Embedded sentence contexts are chosen in (25) so as to avoid confusion with the possibility of sentences in which right dislocation applies to gerund (NP) subjects:

> *It would be surprising, your being able to find a new job.*
> *It irritated him, Mary's having so many books.*
> *?It seems to satisfy him, reading magazines.*

(25)   **The thought that it would be surprising your being able to find a
new job never occurred to me.*
   **The times that it irritated him Mary's having so many books were
few.*
   ** He admits that it seems to satisfy him reading magazines if you
ask.*

Nothing in this analysis crucially depends on the following proposal for the
derivation of gerunds from a deep structure $[_{NP} \Delta + S]$; the arguments favoring
$\Delta + S$ over $it + S$ as a deep structure for infinitives and *that* clauses in English
could be made even if gerunds did not exist. However, since gerunds will be seen
to be in interesting distributional contrast to nongerund clauses (i.e., gerunds
pattern like NPs with head nouns), I give the rule that can account for this
contrast.

Any analysis that includes the extraposition rule must account for the
fact, noted by Rosenbaum, that gerunds do not freely undergo this rule. This
can be done ad hoc by specifying some feature characteristic of gerunds in the
extraposition rule itself; such is Rosenbaum's mechanism. But one might also
suppose that the transformation that creates gerunds (i.e., either adds the
markers *'s* and *ing* or creates contexts so that subsequent rules automatically
add *'s* and *ing*) precedes extraposition and destroys the context on which
extraposition is defined. This is what I propose, although Rosenbaum could have
taken this course as well. In subsequent discussion many distributional contrasts
between gerunds and other complement clauses (besides that concerning extraposition) are shown to follow from ordering and formulating gerund formation
in this way:

(26)   **Gerund Formation:** $[_{NP} \Delta - [_{S} NP - TENSE - VP]] \Rightarrow 2 - \emptyset - \emptyset - 4$

The replacement of Δ by the subject NP in (26) destroys the context (Δ)
on which extraposition as in (15) can operate, accounting for the fact that
gerunds cannot extrapose. This also predicts that gerunds will appear in surface
structure in any NP position where they can appear in deep structure, which is
borne out in the next section.

Rule (26) also creates the context for adding *'s* transformationally

---

Footnote 8 continued

Most speakers agree, however, that the lack of comma intonation in such sentences is unacceptable (i.e.,
extraposition, which does not induce such intonation, is not grammatical):

   *It would be surprising your being able to find a new job.
   *It irritated him Mary's having so many books.
   *It seems to satisfy him reading magazines.

(i.e., $\left[_{\text{NP}} \text{NP}\underline{\hspace{2em}}X\right]$);[9] alternatively, it may be that *'s* is a grammatical formative obligatorily generated in the base with a prenominal NP, and that (26) is a replacement of an empty NP from this source; this would necessitate mentioning *'s* in (26).

The effect of (26), apparently an amalgam of two local transformational operations, is represented in (27):

(27)

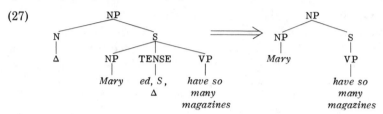

We could revise (26) so that it adds *ing* to the VP, but it seems more likely that *ing* is added by a more general rule to a wide range of structures of the form $\left[_{\text{S}} \text{VP}\right]$. Such a rule would add *ing* to various reduced relative and sentence-modifying participles as well.

IV.2.4 Comparison of $\Delta + \text{S}$ and *it* + S as Clause Sources

This analysis of clausal complements and Rosenbaum's analysis differ empirically not in what they say about clauses that are extraposed but in what they say about distribution of clauses that remain in their deep structure NP positions. The result of NOT applying optional extraposition in Rosenbaum's framework is $\left[_{\text{NP}} it + \text{S}\right]$; in mine, it is $\left[_{\text{NP}} \Delta + \text{S}\right]$. Both analyses require a further deletion rule in order to generate, for example, the subject clauses in (3).

For Rosenbaum, a second case of pronoun deletion that has no term intervening between *it* and S [cf. (24)] is required; no V occurs in the left context, and it is obligatory:

(28) $$X - \left[_{\text{NP}} it - \text{S}\right] + Y \Rightarrow 1 - \emptyset - 3$$

[9] If *'s* is added transformationally in this context, the inside NP cannot also be inside an S (as is the case prior to gerund formation), owing to Chomsky's (1965, Chapter 3) "lower-S insertion prohibition."

Higgins (1973) points out that some condition must ensure that X is not a relative clause in the context for *'s* insertion. If such a condition is not ensured by some factor of universal grammar (what must be blocked is adding *'s* to the head NP of a larger NP), this might be taken as an argument for generating *'s* in the base with a (filled or empty) prenominal NP.

Nagahara (1974) points out that an *'s* insertion could not be structure-preserving. Doubtless it should be classed as local. For discussion of a formally similar rule, see the last note of Chapter VI.

I counterpose to this a rule deleting Δ just in case the NP of the form $[_{NP} \Delta + S]$ is TOPICALIZED, i.e., placed in the COMP position. See Sections II.5 and II.8 for a discussion of topicalization, a root transformation affecting NP's; the deep structure VP-final clauses of (9)−(10) cannot topicalize, and neither can extraposed clauses (see Higgins, 1973, for many examples), because these constituents are not NP's:

(29)   ***Clausal Topicalization:*** $X-[_{COMP} \Delta-S] + Y \Rightarrow 1-\emptyset-3$[10]

Rosenbaum's *it* deletion, (28), claims that clausal complements can appear in all NP positions, whereas clausal topicalization, (29), claims that nongerund clauses will appear only in extraposition and in topicalized NP positions. In all other NP positions the Δ that accompanies such clauses ensures an ill-formed surface structure. [Gerund formation, (26), of course means that gerunds will appear freely in all NP positions, other things being equal.]

When we examine various NP contexts, we find in fact that (nongerund) clauses are excluded in all nontopicalized positions, just as (29) predicts. Exclusion of nongerund clauses in direct and indirect object position (i.e., preceding the boldface constituents that are SISTERS to the main verb) is shown in (30):

(30)   *Bill preferred riding a bicycle **to hitchhiking**.*
  Bill preferred to ride a bicycle **to hitchhiking.*
  Bill prefers that we ride bikes **to our hitchhiking.*
  *Bill prefers our riding bikes **to our hitchhiking**.*
  Bill prefers that we ride bikes.
  Bill preferred to ride a bicycle.

  Writing out their grievances is silly.
  To write out their grievances is silly. (topicalized nongerund clause)
  *The women consider writing out their grievances **silly***
  ** The women consider to write out their grievances **silly**.*

---

[10] The left context X is not necessary in my view, since I do not think that topicalized NP's are strictly grammatical except initially, but this is a separate issue, discussed in Section II.7.

One could state topicalization so that this rule deleted Δ directly:

$$\text{COMP}-X-\left[_{NP}\begin{Bmatrix} \emptyset-Y \\ \Delta-S \end{Bmatrix} \right]-Z \Rightarrow 4-2-\emptyset-\emptyset-5.$$

This formulation would be attractive if it were necessary both (i) not to retain the node COMP after a COMP substitution transformation and (ii) to allow root transformations to apply in certain embedded sentences in English.

If the node COMP is not retained after COMP substitution, and if root transformations are NOT grammatical in embedded sentences, then (29) can be equivalently restated as follows:

$$X-[_{NP} \Delta-S] + Y \Rightarrow 1-\emptyset-3$$

where $X = \emptyset$.

*I take this responsibility **upon myself**.*
*I take fixing the lamp **upon myself**.*
I take to fix the lamp **upon myself.*
*I take it **upon myself** to fix the lamp.* (infinitive in extraposition)

*They told a fairy tale **to the children**.*
*They told **the children** a fairy tale.*
They told how to build a kite **to the children.*
*They told **the children** how to build a kite.*

She won't tell she is sick **to the doctor.*
*She won't tell **the doctor** she is sick.*

*You promised a new hat **to Mary**.*
*You promised **Mary** a new hat.*

You promised to be quiet **to Mary.*
*You promised **Mary** to be quiet.*
You promised you would do the wash **to Mary.*
*You promised **Mary** you would do the wash.*

*The man taught the importance of books **to his sons**.*
*The man taught **his sons** the importance of books.*
The man taught that books were important **to his sons.*
*The man taught **his sons** that books were important.*

*John reported having seen the fight **to the press**.*
John reported that he had seen the fight **to the press.*
*It was reported **to the press** that a fight had occurred.*
It was reported that a fight had occurred **to the press.*
A fight was reported to have occurred **to the press.*

*They expect some cooperation **of (from) you**.*
They expect that you cooperate **of you.*
*They expect it **of you** that you cooperate.*

*John said something nasty **to Mary**.*
John said to leave him alone **to Mary.*
*John said **to Mary** to leave him alone.*

Exclusion of nongerund clauses after prepositions that take NP objects is demonstrated in (31). (Note the acceptability of gerunds in all these contexts):

(31)   *John just came back from his job.*
           John just came back from driving a cab.
           **John just came back from to drive a cab.*
           **John just came back from that he drove a cab.*

           He blamed it on Bill's strictness.
           He blamed it on Bill's being too strict.

*He blamed it on for Bill to be too strict.
*He blamed it on that Bill was too strict.

Because of John's age, Mary gets a pension.
Because of John's being so old, Mary gets a pension.

*Because of for John to be so old, Mary gets a pension.
*Because of that John is so old, Mary gets a pension.

*Because John's age, Mary gets a pension.
*Because John's being so old, Mary gets a pension.
Because John is so old, Mary gets a pension.

Exclusion of nongerund clauses in the passive *by* phrase is shown in (32):[11]

(32)   *That the boys were dancing together was amusing John.*
       For John to arrive would cause embarrassment.
       That the children are always late shows the necessity of discipline.
       That you spoke out of turn didn't help the situation.
       To suggest devaluation would anger the bankers.

       *John was being amused (by) that the boys were dancing together.
       *Embarrassment would be caused (by) for John to arrive.
       **The necessity of discipline is shown (by) that the children are
           always late.*
       *The situation wasn't helped (by) that you spoke out of turn.
       *The bankers would be angered (by) to suggest devaluation.

Nongerund clauses in possessive NP position are less acceptable than gerunds
or derived nominals (the marginal status of gerunds is due to the restriction
on embedded S's in this position):

(33)   **Does he know about smoking pot's being illegal?*
       *(Worse) Does he know about to smoke pot's being illegal?

       Does he know about smoking pot being illegal?
       **Does he know about to smoke pot being illegal? (cf. Does he know
           about it being illegal to smoke pot?*

       We agree about shoveling snow being ridiculous.
       **We agree about to shovel snow being ridiculous. (cf. We agree
           about it being ridiculous to shovel snow.)*

---

[11]Several arguments are given in Emonds (1972b, pp. 44—45) that the forms in boldface in the following examples are adjectives and not passive verb forms; hence, no passive *by* phrase is involved:

   *John was **disturbed** (*by) that the neighbors were so noisy.*
   *Mary was **pleased** (*by) that she had found a job.*

Exclusion of nongerund clauses in the subject NP position of embedded clauses (i.e., wherever the subject NP cannot be topicalized) is shown in (34):[12]

(34)   *That for Bill to smoke bothers the teacher is quite possible.*
        That it bothers the teacher for Bill to smoke is quite possible.
        That Bill's smoking cigarettes bothers the teacher is quite possible.
        **It is quite possible that for Bill to smoke bothers the teacher.*

        **For that you pay that tax to be necessary would be an inconvenience.*
        For it to be necessary that you pay that tax would be an inconvenience.
        **It would be 'an inconvenience for that you pay that tax to be necessary.*

        **He protested the decision that for the bill to be marked "paid" meant nothing.*
        He protested the decision that it meant nothing for the bill to be marked "paid".
        He protested the decision that the bill's being marked "paid" meant nothing.

        **John was happy that to own a car didn't disqualify you.*
        John was happy that it didn't disqualify you to own a car.
        John was happy that owning a car didn't disqualify you.

        **I don't believe for you to study history hurts you.*
        **I don't believe that you study history hurts you.*
        I don't believe your studying history hurts you.

        **A day at the beach is more fun than to play golf is.*
        A day at the beach is more fun than playing golf is.

        **To go by car doesn't seem as rewarding as to ride a horse used to seem.*
        Going by car doesn't seem as rewarding as riding a horse used to seem.

        **Although that the house is empty may depress you, it pleases me.*
        **Although for the house to be empty may depress you, it pleases me.*
        Although the house's being empty may depress you, it pleases me.

---

[12]The claim here is that nongerund clauses appear in subject (preverbal) position only if topicalized. For those who feel that (non-WH) topicalized NP's are acceptable in some range of embedded clauses, the claim here is that nongerund clauses will have the same range of acceptability. Cf. Hooper and Thompson (1973).

The analysis of extraposition given here does not depend on what the structure-preserving constraint says about topicalization, but only on the fact that some device in the grammar prevents free application of (non-WH) topicalization in embedded clauses. It is, of course, my further contention that this device is the structure-preserving constraint.

*He exercises so rarely that to lift those bricks is bad for his heart.
He exercises so rarely that lifting those bricks is bad for his heart.*

*The children for whom to diagram sentences is easy often become
    mathematicians.
The children for whom it is easy to diagram sentences often become
    mathematicians.
The children for whom diagraming sentences is easy often become
    mathematicians.*

*She forgets how expensive to go to the dentist is.
She forgets how expensive going to the dentist is.*

*The reason why that you have insurance doesn't protect you is that
    you're a foreigner.*

*The reason why for you to have insurance doesn't protect you is
    that you're a foreigner.
The reason why your having insurance doesn't protect you is that
    you're a foreigner.*

*Situations in which to write out a check is necessary should be
    avoided.
Situations in which writing out a check is necessary should be
    avoided.*

*The salesman who that I bought a car seemed most important to
    was a southerner.*

*The salesman who for me to buy a car seemed most important to
    was a southerner.
The salesman who my buying a car seemed most important to was
    a southerner.*

*She likes the kind of man that to see a few movies a year will satisfy.
She likes the kind of man that it will satisfy to see a few movies
    a year.
She likes the kind of man that seeing a few movies a year will
    satisfy.*

Exclusion of nongerund clauses in subject position when some other NP is in
the COMP position, by virtue of WH fronting or topicalization, is demonstrated
in (35):

(35)   *Why did* $\begin{Bmatrix} \text{*that Mary liked old records} \\ \text{Mary's liking old records} \end{Bmatrix}$ *irritate him?*

      When was $\begin{Bmatrix} \text{*to arrive an hour early} \\ \text{arriving an hour early} \end{Bmatrix}$ *a requirement?*

   Never will for us to be comfortable be possible in this climate.

Never will it be possible for us to be comfortable in this climate.

$$A \text{ disease like that} \left\{ \begin{array}{l} {}^*\text{to take a lot of pills} \\ \text{taking a lot of pills} \\ \text{frequent exercise} \end{array} \right\} \text{won't cure.}$$

"Categorial identity may be a necessary condition for conjunction, but it is rarely a sufficient one [Higgins, 1973, p. 191]." From this, we expect that some but not all gerunds conjoin with NP's with heads, and that NO other complement clauses do:

(36) *She once liked watching television and physical exercise both.*
      *She once liked watching television and to play volleyball both.
      *She once liked to watch television and physical exercise both.
         (where *physical exercise* is object of *like*.)
      *She once liked physical exercise and to watch television both.

   Outdoor bathrooms and pitching a tent every day would bother me.
   *To pitch a tent every day and outdoor bathrooms would bother me.

   *Eating canned foods and to pitch a tent every day would bother me.

   He proposed a 20% reduction for the elderly and discontinuing the translation service.
   *He proposed a 20% reduction for the elderly and that the office be moved to the suburbs.
   *He proposed discontinuing the translation service and that the office be moved to the suburbs.

In Section IV.3.1, the cleft construction (e.g., *It—is*—focus constituent—*that*—S, where the focus constituent receives the main sentence stress) is analyzed in some detail. Here, it suffices to establish that cleft focus position is in fact a diagnostic in English for the categories NP and PP, and then to examine the distribution of clausal complements in this position. In Section IV.3.1, an explanation for why this position excludes other phrasal categories is given.

In (37) we see that NP's with lexical heads and PP's do occur in cleft focus position, and that AP's (whether adverbial or adjectival) and S's and VP's of the type that are quite clearly not NP's do not appear in this position:

(37)   *It's the custard pie that I disliked.*
          It was a tax break that was counted on.
          Was it John that broke the window?
          It was to John that she spoke.
          It's because of the flood that they are leaving.
          It is with great pleasure that I present our speaker.
          It was because it was raining that they left.
          It isn't John that you're speaking to, is it?

*It's very unhappy that Bill is.
*It was useless that the meeting seemed.
*It was explicitly that he rejected our assumptions.
*It was too carefully that she spoke.
*It's dark that he likes his study.
*It is blow up some buildings that you should.
*It may be playing for time that Bill is.
*It was ask John for money that I heard you.
*It was to report on time that we failed.
*It was that the guests left that John drank so much.
*Isn't it for industrialists to take action that safe working conditions
   are too unprofitable?*

In fact infinitive and *that* clauses are also generally excluded in this position:

(38)   *It is blow up some buildings that you should do. (cf. What you
          should do is blow up some buildings.)
       *It is playing for time that Bill is doing. (cf. What Bill is doing is
          playing for time.)
       *It was to buy a new hat that I wanted.
       *It's for Mary to drive carelessly that upsets Ann.
       *It is to always be on time that you should decide.
       *It was that you explain your motives that was important.
       *It's that John has come too late that Bill realizes.
       Was it that Mary had cashed the check that Bill regretted?

Further, the two classes of verb phrases introduced by V—*ing* shown in Rosenbaum (1967) and Emonds (1973a) NOT to be NP's like other gerunds do not
appear in cleft focus position, again as expected (the verb phrase classes in
question are the complements to verbs of temporal aspect and the complements
to transitive verbs of perception):

(39)   *It was throwing away some letters that John noticed Bill.
          *It was stealing my money that she caught him.
          *It is drinking beer from the bottle that she keeps.
          Is it painting the house that you've finished?

By contrast, gerund clauses appear freely in cleft focus position, a final
confirmation of their membership in the category NP:

(40)   It was buying a new hat that I enjoyed.
       It was John's knowing the location of the mailbox that surprised
          her.
       It's driving carelessly that upsets me.
       It was explaining your motives that was important.
       Was it Mary's having cashed the check that Bill regretted?

The data in (30)—(40) indicate clearly that nongerund complement clauses cannot appear as NP's (i.e., they must be extraposed) if the NP in question has not undergone the root transformation of topicalization. Equivalently when we ASSUME with Rosenbaum that clausal complements (subjects or objects) to verbs are sisters to nonlexical nouns in deep structure, we find that such complements appear in surface structure ONLY IF THEY HAVE BEEN TRANSFORMED (by gerund formation, extraposition, or topicalization).[13]

This generalization about the distribution of clausal complements is predicted automatically by an analysis that assigns them a deep structure configuration that is filtered out in surface structure (i.e., is malformed) if not transformed. Such a configuration is provided by taking the nonlexical deep structure sister to such clauses as $[_N \Delta]$, as in (7), rather than as $[_N it]$, as in (5).[14]

---

[13]The alternative to such an assumption is to generate some or all of these clausal complements as sisters to the verb (i.e., to generate them in extraposition in deep structure). This approach is taken in Emonds (1970, 1972b). As noted earlier, I am not comparing that analysis with that being presented in the text.

[14]If *it* is taken as the deep structure sister of clausal complements to verbs, the facts in (30)—(40) cannot be handled just by restricting *it* deletion to topicalized NP's, because this will leave *it*—S sequences in all those NP positions where only gerund clauses are allowed (including complements with modals). Such sequences are even less acceptable than nongerund clauses:

> *The women considered it that we wrote out our grievances silly.
> *They would blame the affair on it for Bill to be too strict.
> *Because of it that John is so old, Mary gets a pension.
> *We agreed about it to shovel snow being ridiculous.
> *I don't believe that it that you study history hurts you.
> *Why did it that Mary liked old records irritate him?
> *She used to like watching television and it to play volleyball both.
> *It was it that you explain your motives that was important.

Another possibility open to Rosenbaum is to impose an ad hoc condition that extraposition is obligatory in nontopicalized position, but such a special condition can be dispensed with in my analysis. Ross (1967a) claims that this condition is a special case of an output prohibition (exception-laden, by his own account) on sentence-internal $[_{NP} S]$ configurations; for arguments against this, see Emonds (1970, Chapter 3). Essentially these arguments state the obvious: that free relatives, indirect questions, and gerunds are examples of the "forbidden" configuration that appear freely in sentence-internal position. Higgins (1973) tries to justify the existence of underlying heads of phrases for the first two constructions mentioned, but this is irrelevant, since an OUTPUT constraint is in question. In fact Higgins gives further counterexamples to Ross's output constraint that falsify it in the other direction. While the constraint purportedly excludes (i), it does not exclude (ii):

(i)   *How obvious does that John is unqualified seem?
                 *How easy would to please John be?

(ii)   *How likely is that John will come?
                 *How easy is to please John?

The examples in (i) and (ii) are excluded for exactly the same reason in the analysis given here (they can result only from a surface occurrence of $[_{NP} \Delta - S]$).

I do claim here that an "input" constraint against $[_{NP} S]$ is involved, namely, the universal conditions on base rules embodied in Base Restrictions II and III of Chapter I. The following discussion in the text takes up this point.

The ability of this analysis to predict that clausal complements are ill-formed in NP positions when untransformed confirms the choice of the convention that empty nodes are permitted in deep structure but not throughout an entire transformational derivation. But actually we are forced to use this device [i.e., to derive deep structure clauses that are NP's from (41) rather than from (42)] only by the requirement that all phrasal nodes have obligatory lexical heads in the base (Base Restrictions II and III in Chapter I):

(41)

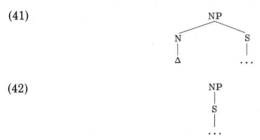

(42)   NP
                                        |
                                        S
                                        |
                                       ...

That is, the Base Restrictions (Harris' endocentricity claim) are responsible for the choice of (41) and not (42) as the simplest possible representation in deep structure for clauses that are NP's. Because such a representation necessarily and correctly predicts that clauses in NP positions that do not undergo independently motivated transformations are ill-formed surface structures, we have further evidence for excluding base rules of the form A → B, where A and B are phrase nodes corresponding to different lexical categories.[15]

I conclude, then, that clausal complements, if they are generated as NP's, are in fact sisters to empty head N's. Further, the transformations that apply to these complements are the local rule of gerund formation in (26), the structure-preserving rule of extraposition in (17) (formulated as optional without conditions), and the root transformation of (NP) topicalization, which is followed by or collapsed with the deletion of an empty sister head N [(29) and note 10]. The convention on empty nodes guarantees that if none of these rules apply to deep structure NP clausal complements, an ill-formed surface structure results. Each step of the analysis has been amply supported empirically.

IV.2.5   Free Relatives and Indirect Questions

In Emonds (1970) I show that free (= "headless" = "independent") relative clauses have the distribution of noun phrases and not of clausal complements with respect to the various tests given in (30)—(40). Examples:

---

[15]Interestingly, the rule NP → S, which the arguments and data of this and preceding sections indicate is incorrect for English, is one of the few of the form A → B (B is a phrase node) that seem even superficially plausible. Rules such as S → AP, NP → PP, PP → VP, VP → NP, VP → S, etc. are also ruled out by Base Restrictions II and III, and these exclusions do not seem controversial.

(43)   *Bill preferred what she had said to his own previous statement.*
       The women considered what was being argued silly.

       I'll take what needs to be done upon myself.
       Any claim that what he bought was necessary can easily be refuted.
       How could what I say about it influence her?
       It's what they stand for that we are opposed to.
       They are looking at what we bought.

However, in the analysis of such constructions in Kuroda (1968) we find a rule
that deletes an underlying head N of a noun phrase; thus only in surface structure is there no head as a sister to the free relatives. We therefore expect to
find them in NP positions, as in (43). Once again, a construction (the free
relative, in this case) can have the surface form $[_{NP} S]$ only if it is a transform
of a deep structure $[_{NP} N + S]$.

In the case of indirect questions, it seems probable that a nonempty deep
structure head of an NP cannot be motivated in the contexts of (44):

(44)   *The question of* $[_{NP}$————$[_{S}$ *whether he will be hired*$]]$ *is being
       debated.*

       We questioned (asked) them about $[_{NP}$————$[_{S}$ *how often they
       would visit*$]]$.

Must we assume, then, that there are deep structures of the form $[_{NP}S]$ only
in some positions, and then only for indirect questions?

As noted in (31) and (32), *that* clauses are excluded in just such post-
prepositional contexts as (44):

(45)   **The question (of) that he will be hired is being debated.* (cf. *The
       question of his being hired is being debated.*)
       *The reaction against that they visit so often is irrational. (cf.
       The reaction against their visiting so often is irrational.)
       *We asked them about (that) the boys were so aggressive. (cf. *We
       asked them about the boys' being so aggressive.*)

In any analysis, then, some rule must permit indirect questions in some
of the contexts in which *that* clauses and infinitives are excluded. It does not
seem that the head deletion rule proposed by Kuroda for free relatives should
be extended to delete a dummy (empty) head Δ for indirect questions, since
there are many contexts in which indirect questions are excluded while free
relatives are not. See, for instance, the examples in (30), which deal with the
context $[_{VP} V$————$PP]$; in this position, free relatives but not indirect questions are allowed. I conclude that some special rule dealing with indirect questions produces the contrasts between (44) and (45).

The following rule provides for such a contrast after prepositions, based on the assumption that indirect questions have the same status as other complement clauses in deep structure:

(46)   ***Indirect* Q:** $X + P - [_N \Delta] - \begin{bmatrix} \text{COMP} \\ \text{WH} \end{bmatrix} + Z \Rightarrow 1 - \emptyset - 3$

In (46) the P must be a sister to the NP of which the N is the head, and the N must be the sister of the S introduced by the WH. These conditions are necessarily satisfied by adjacent terms in local rules, and in Chapter VI I in fact propose extending the definition of this class of rules to deletions of specified formatives. Hence, I feel justified in not specifying such conditions here as part of the rule itself; see Section VI.4.

If (46) is formulated as obligatory and is ordered before extraposition, it removes the context for it by deleting Δ. This then correctly predicts the unacceptability of (47):

(47)   **He spoke about it with Bill why he had left town.*
         *She talked on it to us whether the virus had been isolated.

The lack of a preposition between the second and third terms of (46) means that the rule will rightly not apply when an indirect question begins with a fronted PP (i.e., P + WH):

(48)   **The question of for whom you should work is being debated.*
       *We asked them about with whom they wanted to visit.
       *They agreed on at what time the others should leave.
       *Susan spoke about to which towns her friends would drive.
       *She talked on in what theories such equations could be useful.

There are, however, problems with this; extraposition is not allowed here either: **They agreed on it at what time the others should leave.* I have not been able to investigate the full range of differences between indirect question distribution and nongerund complement clause distribution, or between indirect questions with fronted PP's and indirect questions with other fronted constituents. Some further generalizations on these questions are given in Bresnan (1970). For the moment I can only offer (46) as a first step toward formulating the rule(s) that accounts for these differences adequately.

The general claim that a clausal complement must undergo some transformation in order to become a well-formed surface structure does not seem to me to be seriously undermined by this inconclusive discussion, because it seems plausible that some transformation such as (46) is needed in the grammar in any case to differentiate indirect question contexts from nongerund complement clause contexts.

IV.3   *FURTHER STRUCTURE-PRESERVING RULES THAT MOVE* S *NODES*

IV.3.1   Cleft Sentences: Cleft Extraposition and Focus Placement

The following are examples of cleft sentences with the focus constituent in boldface and the extraposed S, which is characteristic of this construction, in parentheses:

(49)   *It was **buying a new hat** (that I enjoyed).*
           *It was **a tax break** (I counted on).*
           *It was **the custard pie** (that I disliked).*

(50)   *It was **to John** (that I spoke).*

(51)   *It was **because it was raining** (that I left).*

In cleft sentences only NP's and PP's can appear in focus position. Excluded are full sentences, infinitives, adjective phrases, and other verb phrases. Many examples of these contrasts are given in (37)−(40).

The cleft construction has been a source of confusion to grammarians, since the extraposed S has many but not all of the characteristics of a relative clause. For example, the relative clause introductory *that* as well as WH words may appear, while words like *why* and *how*, excluded in ordinary relative clauses, cannot. Thus *why* cannot replace *that* in (51). There are other factors favoring deriving the extraposed S from a relative clause source; these are set down in a transformational framework in a study by Akmajian (1970). According to his analysis, the examples in (49)−(51) are derived (roughly) from the structures in (52)−(54), respectively. (Since the focus constituent can be a proper noun, the extraposed S must be a relative clause in the SUBJECT NP in deep structure.)

TENSE is omitted in (52)−(54) for simplicity of exposition:

(52)

(53)

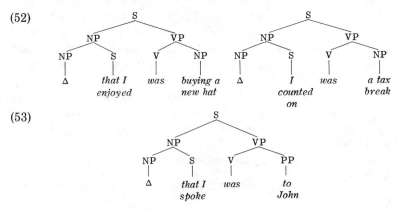

(54)

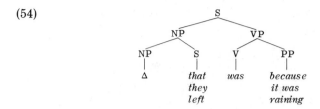

Akmajian assumes that the S's in the deep structure subjects in (52)—(54) are like "headless" or "independent" relative clauses of the type discussed in Kuroda (1968).[16]

It should be noted that the gender of the subject NP of a cleft sentence does not agree with that of the predicate nominative: *It (*he) was John with whom I was speaking.* In this, cleft sentences resemble answers to the question *Who's there?* These answers are of the form *It's me* and *It's John* rather than **He's me* or **He's John*; I take such sentences to indicate an empty subject NP in deep structure.

The principal difficulty with Akmajian's analysis, which has been noted by several grammarians, is the unlikely deep structure, such as (53), in which the preposition that appears in the focus PP is (and must be) missing in the relative clause: *It was to John that I spoke (*to).* Let us accept this defect for the moment, returning to a solution later. This problem is bound up with the question of whether the focus constituent in a cleft construction is in focus position in deep structure or is moved to focus position by another transformation, and for the moment I take no stand on this issue.

In Akmajian's analysis the cleft construction is due to a transformation that moves the relative clause S to a position at the end of the VP in the highest S, CLEFT EXTRAPOSITION.

Such a transformation is structure-preserving, because an S is generable by the phrase structure rules at the end of a VP. If the cleft transformation moved an S to a position where S cannot be generated by an independently motivated phrase structure rule, such as before the predicate nominative NP (yielding, say, **It may be that owns this car John* rather than *It may be John that owns this car*), then it would not be a structure-preserving rule.

Thus, viewed as a structure-preserving rule, cleft extraposition moves an S constituent according to the arrow in (55) (recall that empty nodes are ignored by subcategorization conditions):

---

[16]In fact it may be a characteristic of cleft sentences that everything except the embedded relative S is (or may be, since various modals may appear in the highest S) empty in deep structure. The pronoun (*it*) is inserted into certain empty subject NP's; the *be* in the highest S may be due to an insertion rule; and the constituent in focus position in a cleft sentence may be empty in deep structure (this matter is taken up later in this section). However, I will not pursue this possible characterization of the deep structure of a cleft sentence in detail.

(55)

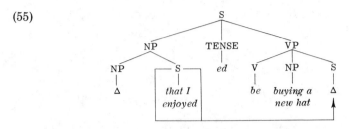

We are now in a position to explain why sentences, infinitives, and other verb phrases cannot appear in focus position in cleft sentences. In (37)–(40) we saw that, although in some cases intuitions of grammaticality are somewhat unclear, such constituents are generally unacceptable in this position. Typical examples are as in (56):

(56)   *It is **that we are careless** that we should admit.
        *It was **that they all leave early** that the teacher required.
        *It was **that Mary came home early** that John was happy (about).
        *It would be **for her to be late** that would upset me now.
        *It is **blow up some buildings** that you should do.
        *It is **playing for time** that they are doing.
        *It was **to buy a new house** that I wanted.

In order to obtain the nonsentences in (56) with a structure-preserving cleft transformation, at least one of the following phrase structures would have to be generable by the phrase structure rules:

(57)

                    VP   VP
                 ／ | ＼   ／ | ＼
                V   S   S   V   VP   S

But the impossibility of more than one clausal complement at the end of the VP in surface structure is the reason why extraposition is blocked with a verb like *prove* when it has both (non-NP) subject and object clauses (see Section IV.2.2). Thus the VP expansion rule does not provide the structures in (57); this means that the cleft transformation cannot move VP's and S's so as to generate the nonsentences in (56). (When the cleft transformation does not apply, Δ cannot be replaced by *it*, and an ungrammatical surface structure also results.)

Consider now the fact that predicate nominatives and predicate adjectives do not appear in focus position in the cleft construction:

(58)   *It is **quite unhappy** that Bill is.
            *It was **impudent** that Mary seemed.
            *It was **very sick** that the children became.
            *It is **the football coach** that John is.

>*It was **an interesting lecturer** that John remained.*
>*It was **tired** that John grew.*

The ungrammaticality of (58) is not due to the structure-preserving constraint on transformations but is, rather, simply further evidence in favor of Akmajian's derivation of extraposed clauses in cleft sentences from deep structure relative clauses. For it is known that predicate nominative NP's cannot generally be relativized, except when the relative clause modifies a predicate nominative (for discussion see Chiba, 1974 and Kuno, 1970):

(59)   *The football coach that John was lost the game.*
       I saw a German teacher that Harry was.
       Mary was listening to the interesting lecturer that John remained.
       The incompetent fool that the doctor seemed lost the patient.

Since in Akmajian's analysis the extraposed relative has its source in the SUBJECT NP, the ungrammaticality of (58) is attributable to the prohibition on relative clauses formed with a relative pronoun that replaces a predicate nominative NP, but does not modify a predicate nominative.

Let us now return to the problem of finding a deep structure source for (50). Akmajian in fact points out in his study that a structure like (53) is a dubious deep structure for (50). [Cleft extraposition applied to (53) yields (50).] The reason for this, of course, is that a relative clause of the type *that I spoke* cannot be generated from a deep structure clause in any natural way:

(60)

This problem is not directly related to the structure-preserving framework. However, inasmuch as Akmajian's analysis of cleft sentences provides additional evidence for the structure-preserving hypothesis, it would be helpful if we could eliminate a weakness in this analysis.

The impossibility of generating relative clauses of the type *that I spoke*, as in (53), by normal rules for relative clauses indicates that (53) itself may be transformationally derived from another source. An obvious candidate for this source is one in which the focus constituent is empty in deep structure. In this view, (53) would be derived from (61) by a movement rule (FOCUS PLACE-MENT) that has the effect indicated in (61) (focus placement would precede cleft extraposition):

(61)

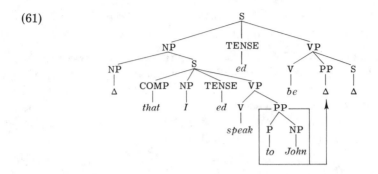

An important general observation about focus placement is that it would play a role analogous to the relativization rule in removing a fully specified NP from a relative clause structure. To see how this is so, we must digress to discuss the derivation of ordinary relative clauses.

E. Klima has suggested to me that *that* is not a relative pronoun when it introduces relative clauses but, rather, the same particle that introduces other (nonrelative) dependent clauses. In this view, a relativized NP or PP replaces COMP (the morpheme *that* in most clauses) only by means of the WH fronting rule. Such an analysis accords the same status to all S-introductory *that*s, explains why prepositions never precede *that* even though they precede other relative pronouns, and limits relative pronouns to being a subset of the WH question words. I accept this position for the present, amplifying it (but not crucially changing it) in Chapter V.

Furthermore, I assume that relativization either is accomplished in steps, the first step being ordinary pronominalization, or is an operation on base pronouns. This means that an underlying pronoun that is to be relativized either is moved to the front of its clause and changed to a relative pronoun by WH fronting or is deleted without being moved. Thus a typical relative clause can be derived through the steps outlined in (62):

(62)   Prerelativized structure:

The friend (that I spoke to him) drove away.

Removal of NP by relative deletion; optionally a pronoun is left behind:

A.   *The friend (that I spoke to him) drove away.*

B.   *The friend (that I spoke to) drove away.*

WH fronting in A of either NP or PP dominating coreferential pronoun (obligatory):[17]

---

[17] Two steps appear involved; the first is the attachment of the WH feature to the pronoun coreferential with the head of the relative clause. (Hence, no WH word *how* ever appears in relative clauses.) The second is WH fronting, as in questions.

A.   *The friend (who I spoke to) drove away.*
A.   *The friend (to whom I spoke) drove away.*

Optional *that* deletion in B when *that* precedes NP:
B.   *The friend ((that) I spoke to) drove away.*

A similar derivation of cleft sentences is given in (63); notice the analogous roles of relative deletion and focus placement:

(63)   Deep structure:
Δ —*(that I spoke to a friend) was*—Δ.

Removal of NP or PP by focus placement; optionally a pronoun is left behind if NP is removed:
A. Δ —*(that I spoke to him) was a friend.*
B. Δ —*(that I spoke to   ) was a friend.*
C. Δ —*(that I spoke   ) was to a friend.*

WH fronting in A of either NP or PP dominating pronoun (obligatory):
A. Δ —*(who I spoke to) was a friend.*
A. Δ —*(to whom I spoke) was a friend.*

Optional *that* deletion in B or C in _____NP:
B. Δ —*((that) I spoke to) was a friend.*
C. Δ —*((that) I spoke) was to a friend.*

Cleft extraposition (obligatory):
A.   *It was a friend who I spoke to.*
A.   *It was a friend to whom I spoke.*
B.   *It was a friend (that) I spoke to.*
C.   *It was to a friend (that) I spoke.*

This analysis correctly predicts the ungrammaticality of **It was to a friend who I spoke*, because WH fronting can apply only if focus placement leaves a pronoun behind [in the A structure of (63)].

The addition of the focus placement rule to Akmajian's analysis provides a plausible deep structure source for (53). Thus it appears that cleft extraposition as originally formulated by Akmajian is essentially correct, so that the argument for the structure-preserving hypothesis, presented as an explanation for the examples in (56), can stand.

Any thorough investigation of the focus placement rule would have to consider the pseudo-cleft construction in detail. The pseudo-cleft construction resembles the cleft construction in that it has a headless or independent relative clause as a deep structure subject and a *be* plus predicate attribute; typical examples are given in (64), with the focus constituent in boldface:

(64)   *What I enjoyed was **buying a new hat**.*
         *What I counted on was **a tax break**.*
         *What I did to Bill was **twist his wrist**.*
         *What they are doing is **painting the house**.*
         *What the teacher requires is **that they all leave early**.*
         *What would upset me now would be **for her to be late**.*
         *What John is is **stupid**.*
         *What these requirements are are **harassment techniques**.*
         What John spoke was **to a friend.*

Whatever the correct analysis of the pseudo-cleft construction, and whatever the relation between the pseudo-cleft and cleft constructions, it is doubtful that they would lead to any crucial new evidence for or against the structure-preserving hypothesis. In the first place, if no movement rule such as focus placement is involved in forming the pseudo-cleft construction[18] (i.e., if focus placement is limited to the cleft construction), then the structure-preserving hypothesis, concerned principally with movement rules, is not affected.

In the second place, if the correct analysis of the pseudo-cleft construction DOES involve a movement rule like focus placement, there is no reason to suspect that the rule could not be formulated in a structure-preserving manner without changing the rest of the grammar (in particular, without changing the phrase structure rule for expanding VP). For focus placement, if used in deriving pseudo-cleft sentences, would move constituents out of the relative clause dominated by the subject NP into positions immediately dominated by the highest VP, which would dominate only *be* and empty nodes in deep structure. Since the VP expansion rule provides for every type of major constituent under it (NP's, PP's, S's, VP's, and predicate NP's and AP's), focus placement would be structure-preserving.

Since an exact analysis of the pseudo-cleft construction and of the focus placement rule would seem not to affect the structure-preserving hypothesis, I omit discussion of them. The important point of this section concerns not focus placement, which I have introduced only as a possible solution for a problem in Akmajian's cleft analysis, but, rather, Akmajian's cleft extraposition rule itself. As explained earlier, the fact that the latter rule does not move a clause (VP or S) around a clause already in focus position is independent evidence for the structure-preserving framework, which allows but one (non-NP) clause complement per VP.

---

[18]Bach and Peters (1968) suggest an analysis involving only deletions under identity. Another possibility, suggested by Akmajian (personal communication) is that no transformations are involved at all; rather, some principle yet to be made precise would allow predicate attributes to match not only an NP but also, under certain conditions, larger deep structure constituents such as *do something to someone*. I understand that this position is argued for extensively and convincingly in Higgins (1974).

IV.3.2   Extraposition from Noun Phrase

Besides the cleft transformation, another rule that moves S's from subject NP's to the end of the following VP is EXTRAPOSITION FROM NP. It derives the relative clauses in boldface in (65) from a position of being immediately dominated by the subject NP:

(65) *A student was speaking **who knew very little about politics**.*
      (A student who knew very little about politics was speaking.)

      *A person has arrived **who we all like very much**.*
      (A person who we all like very much has arrived.)

The conditions for the application of this rule are discussed in some detail in Akmajian (1970). Similar rules or an extension of the same rule probably also move relative clauses to the end of an NP and from inside an object NP to the end of the VP, as suggested in Ross (1967a):

(66) *The donation of money to the party **that had been stolen** caused trouble.*
      (The donation of money that had been stolen to the party caused trouble.)

      *They brought a boy into the room **who looked hungry**.*
      (They brought a boy who looked hungry into the room.)

      *Mary typed out a letter to her brother **that didn't make sense**.*
      (Mary typed out a letter that didn't make sense to her brother.)

Whatever the details of the conditions on this rule, it is clearly structure-preserving, since it moves S's to the end of the VP or NP, where S complements are generable by the phrase structure rules:

(67)

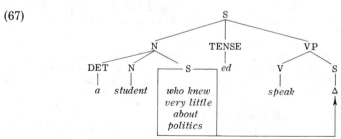

(Compare the "sentential relative" construction in *Mary typed out a letter to her brother, which didn't make sense*, where we can assume that the WH clause is not dominated by VP of the main clause; cf. note 16, Chapter II.)

It is important to see how the structure-preserving hypothesis explains rather than simply describes this extraposition rule (or the cleft extraposition).

GIVEN THE PHRASE STRUCTURE RULES OF ENGLISH, this hypothesis claims that extraposition rules with outputs like the examples in (68) are impossible. Without the hypothesis such rules would have the same status as the existing English extraposition rules, a counterintuitive result: [19]

(68)   **A student was speaking **who knew very little about politics** to John.*
    A man entered **who was from Philadelphia the room.*
    A person has **who we all like very much arrived.*

[19] The following observations summarize the commentary of Nagahara (1974) on this rule of extraposition from NP and on the structure-preserving nature of extraposition of clausal subjects: Some native speakers find extraposed clauses in sequence unacceptable, and others find extraposed clauses in sequence unacceptable when "short" and acceptable when "long." Judging from my own experience, it is also the case with sentences of this type that judgments of a single speaker with a single sentence can vary with time. Relevant examples with "long" extraposed clauses that cannot be placed within the VP are as follows:

> ?*Nobody thought that the movie was good who had good sense and knew that it would have an undesirable influence on young people.*

> ?*It was preferred by those people to remain silent who had not been at such a place before and, therefore, did not know what to talk about.*

> ?*A girl tried to lift up a heavy stone who was slim, looked pale and, therefore, could hardly be expected to be able to do it.*

> ?*It proves that Mary is innocent that John has gone to all the trouble to alert the press that she was in town at the time of the crime.*

(Nagahara elicited mixed judgments on the first three of these examples.)

What does all this variation in acceptability judgments indicate? It establishes a point emphasized repeatedly, for example, in articles by Otero (1972, 1973), namely, that acceptability judgments cannot be taken as an operational test for grammaticality. In the cases Otero discusses, the acceptability judgments in fact systematically run counter to what he argues are the grammaticality values. In the examples just given, the more usual case of unreliable and vacillating acceptability judgments is exemplified.

What, then, can we propose to account for the judgments, if not a strict correspondence to the grammar? As Nagahara indicates, "since the length of the extraposed relative clause changes the acceptability of the sentence, we may suspect that factors having to do with performance are of relevance [1974, p. 37]." I might add that since variations among speakers of the same speech community and variations with the same speaker over time are involved, the conclusion seems even more strongly warranted.

But what kind of performance factor would make sentences of a given structural pattern including a short constituent of type A LESS acceptable than sentences of the same pattern that include a long constituent of type A? We do not have a general heuristic that complication along various parameters ordinarily makes sentences MORE acceptable; rather, we expect unchanged or diminished acceptability in such a case. Yet Nagahara seems to imply that certain SHORT extraposed relatives are unacceptable due to performance, rather than due to their ungrammaticality.

By contrast to this bizarre role for performance invoked by Nagahara (and by many others in personal discussions), it seems more reasonable to repeat here an argument that I have never heard answered, although it rarely seems to be assimilated—that of Emonds (1970) and of Chapter II note 6: "It would be hard to explain even slight unacceptability for sentences that are relatively short and simple, semantically clear, and perfectly grammatical. But it is to be expected that intelligent language users [i.e., people who have other, nonsyntactic cognitive capacities, such as being able to recognize a long musical phrase more easily than a short one, even when played out of proper musical context] would possess strategies of interpretation to render certain types of sentences that are relatively simple, semantically clear, and slightly ungrammatical perfectly understandable and perfectly acceptable."

IV.3.3   Complement Extraposition

In this section, I describe a rule that produces sentences that may not be fully grammatical. It is nonetheless important, because it distinguishes two sets of examples, one of which has totally unacceptable members and the other of which has acceptable or marginally acceptable members, depending on the meanings involved, etc. The transformation that produces these differences, COMPLEMENT EXTRAPOSITION, may therefore be an extragrammatical device, but there is no doubt as to its being part of English usage. It is of interest here because it is a structure-preserving rule.

Of course complement extraposition may be totally grammatical in some dialects, but the more complex constructions in which it plays a part seem only marginally acceptable to most speakers. The main point is that for any given level of complexity the sentences that do not involve complement extraposition do not permit, with the same degree of acceptability, certain operations that sentences that do involve it permit. Thus the reader should lower his "acceptability threshold" in this section, paying attention to the differences in acceptability that the paired starred—unstarred examples exhibit.

In (69) the head nouns of the deep structure objects have S complements:

(69)   *John made the claim that the rain was causing the accidents.*
  The claim that the rain was causing the accidents was made by John.

  Susan made the assumption that Mary would reject her offer.
  The assumption that Mary would reject her offer was made by Susan.

  John made a guess that the river was somewhere to the east.
  A guess that the river was somewhere to the east was made by John.

  Tom made the conjecture that Bill was telephoning Harry.
  The conjecture that Bill was telephoning Harry was made by Tom.

  They made the assertion that we couldn't prove Riemann's theorem.
  The assertion that we couldn't prove Riemann's theorem was made.

The same can be said for (70):

(70)   *John ridiculed the claim that the rain was causing the accidents.*
  The claim that the rain was causing the accidents was ridiculed by John.

  Susan questioned the assumption that Mary would reject her offer.
  The assumption that Mary would reject her offer was questioned by Susan.

  John relied on a guess that the river was somewhere to the east.
  A guess that the river was somewhere to the east was relied on by John.

Tom discussed the conjecture that Bill was telephoning Harry.

The conjecture that Bill was telephoning Harry was discussed by Tom.

They didn't appreciate the assertion that we couldn't prove Riemann's theorem.

The assertion that we couldn't prove Riemann's theorem wasn't appreciated.

In (69) the sentence complements of the deep structure objects can be extraposed in the passive construction, but this is not so in (70). In general, the condition for this extraposition seems to be that the main verb be a "proverb" (of minimal semantic content), such as *make* or *have*, that does not in this context have its literal meaning before such objects:

(71) *The claim was made by John that the rain was causing the accidents.*

The assumption was made by Susan that Mary would reject her offer.

A guess was made by John that the river was somewhere to the east.

The conjecture was made by Tom that Bill was telephoning Harry.

The assertion was made that we couldn't prove Riemann's theorem.

*The claim was ridiculed by John that the rain was causing the accidents.

*The assumption was questioned by Susan that Mary would reject her offer.

*A guess was relied on by John that the river was somewhere to the east.

*The conjecture was discussed by Tom that Bill was telephoning Harry.

*The assertion wasn't appreciated that we couldn't prove Riemann's theorem.

The optional structure-preserving S movement that precedes the passive transformation, making possible the acceptable passive constructions in (71), is indicated by the arrow in (72):

(72)

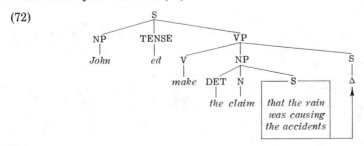

This rule provides an explanation for certain other characteristics of S complements to phrases like *make the claim, make a guess*, etc.

The introductory *that* of S complements to nouns ordinarily cannot be deleted. For example, *that* cannot be deleted in (70) or in the passive sentences in (69). However, an introductory *that* may be deleted in many S complements to verbs, as in (73):

(73)   *John claimed (that) the rain was causing the accidents.*
         Susan assumed (that) Mary would reject her offer.
         John guessed (that) the river was somewhere to the east.

It is also true that *that* may be deleted in at least some of the sentences in (69) in what are superficially S complements to nouns; the extent of the deletability of *that* seems subject to dialectal variation:

(74)   *John made the claim the rain was causing the accidents.*
         Susan made the assumption Mary would reject her offer.
         John made a guess the river was somewhere to the east.

The important point here is that *that* can be deleted in S complements to nouns only if that complement is extraposed. That is, *that* cannot be deleted in complements to nouns that may not be extraposed:

(75)   **John ridiculed the claim the rain was causing the accidents.*
       *Susan questioned the assumption Mary would reject her offer.
       *John relied on a guess the river was somewhere to the east.
       *Tom discussed the conjecture Bill was telephoning Harry.
       *They didn't appreciate the assertion we couldn't prove Riemann's
           theorem.

Thus we can preserve the generalization that *that* deletion does not occur inside noun phrases by making it contingent on complement extraposition. [In my dialect *that* deletion sometimes may not take place even when complement extraposition takes place. For example, it may not take place in the grammatical passive sentences in (71).]

According to the complex NP constraint given in Ross (1967a), the rule of WH fronting may not extract an NP from an S that is dominated by an NP that has a head noun (and place it outside the dominating NP). In particular, WH fronting may not remove an NP that is part of an S complement to a noun. This constraint predicts the ungrammaticality of the sentences in (76):

(76)   **The rain that John discussed the claim caused the accidents lasted*
           for hours.
       *Who did Susan question the assumption would reject her offer?
       *They set out for the river which John had relied on a guess was to
           the east.

What did John ridicule the claim the rain was causing?
Where did John rely on a guess the river was?
*The offer Susan is questioning the assumption Mary will reject is
    quite generous.*

Sentences in which WH fronting extracts an NP from an S complement to
phrases like *make the claim* and *make a guess*, as in (77), are more acceptable
than the corresponding sentences in (76):

(77)   *The rain that John made the claim caused the accidents lasted for
        hours.*
    ?Who did Susan make the assumption would reject her offer?
    *They set out for the river which John had made a guess was
        somewhere to the east.*
    What did John make the claim the rain was causing?
    ?Where did John make a guess the river was?
    *The offer Susan is making the assumption Mary will reject is
        quite generous.*

We can ascribe the greater acceptability of these sentences to the fact that the
S complements from which WH fronting extracts an NP are extraposed. That is,
the complex NP constraint does not prevent WH fronting from applying in
(77), since the S complements in the structures underlying (77) are not immediately dominated by an NP with a head noun when WH fronting applies.
[A dialect in which the examples in (77) are unacceptable and those in (76)
doubly so could be described by ordering WH fronting BEFORE complement
extraposition. In such a dialect these two rules would have to apply in the wrong
order to produce the somewhat unacceptable sentences in (77), but there would
be no ordering of rules that could yield the totally unacceptable sentences in (76).]

It appears therefore that the rule of complement extraposition is well
motivated, and is another example of a structure-preserving S movement rule.
Of course the more instances there are of transformations with the same output
(S's as the last constituents under a VP, in the case at hand), the more important
it is that the nonaccidental character of this be reflected by appropriate general
principles (such as the structure-preserving constraint) that limit the notion
"possible transformation."

V

Extending the Structure-Preserving Constraint to Adjectival and Prepositional Phrases

A structure-preserving constraint on movement transformations is proposed in Chapter I, and it is shown in Chapters III—IV that NP and S movement rules of English that apply in embedded sentences are subject to this constraint. In this chapter, I show how the structure-preserving constraint applies to movements of other phrase nodes, in particular those of the adjective phrase (AP) and prepositional phrase (PP) nodes.

V.1 ADJECTIVE PHRASES

By ADJECTIVE PHRASE (AP) I mean the constituent whose head is an adjective and that also dominates any of the (usually preceding) modifiers characteristic of adjectives (*very, so, how, too, as, more, most*, measure phrases like *five miles*, other adjectives like *tremendously, slowly*, etc.) and the PP and S complements of adjectives. See Bresnan (1973) and the references given there for detailed study of the internal structure of this constituent.

One important rule that moves AP's is the WH fronting rule. Some examples of constituents that it moves to the front of an S are given in (1). However, I will not discuss WH fronting in this section, since this rule and its effects are taken up in Sections V.6—V.8.

(1)   *How does the patient seem today?*
      How quickly did he finish the boat?
      How capable do you consider him?
      How long a chapter should he write?
      John wondered how important it was to return on time.

> ***How brave*** *he became when he was safe at home!*
> *I don't want to go with you, no matter **how slow** you go.*
> *I don't want to go with you, **however slow** you go.*

(The WH word in the modifier of the AP, *how*, can stand alone in questions just as the WH words in the determiner of an NP can: ***What*** *did he buy?*)

V.2   ADVERBIAL ADJECTIVE PHRASES

In this section, the positions of adverbial AP's (i.e., AP's whose head ends in the suffix *ly*) will be discussed vis-à-vis the structure-preserving constraint. We cannot at the outset focus our attention on specific adverbial AP movement rules, since there has been no general acceptance by transformationalists of any particular formulation of such rules, even though there is general agreement that such rules exist. Nor have transformationlists been able to agree on the source in the base for adverbial AP's of various sorts.

Because of the uncertainties involved in an analysis of adverbial AP's, I will restrict the discussion to the placement and meaning of these constituents in declarative clauses with finite verbs, in the hope that my conclusions can be extended so as to be valid in other clauses (infinitives, gerunds, participles, imperatives, and questions) as well.

It is well known that *ly* adverbials can appear in finite clauses in several positions. For example, in (2) the adverbs in parentheses can appear in any of the blanks:

(2)   _____, *John* _____ *could* _____ *have* ___??__ *been there by*

      six. (*probably*)

   _____, *John* _____ *has* ___??__ *been* _____ *answering*

      questions _____ *for an hour.* (*oddly*)

   John has ___??__ *been* _____ *answering questions* _____ *for*

      an hour. (*slowly*)

   _____, *John* _____ *has* _____ *been* ___??__ *answering*

      questions for an hour. (*evidently*)

   John has _____ *been* _____ *answering questions for an hour.*
      (*merely*)

At first this apparent freedom of occurrence seems to indicate that English adverbial AP's are not subject to the structure-preserving constraint. However, care must be taken in distinguishing what constitutes evidence against this constraint. If a constituent X appears in two surface structure positions, P and P' with the SAME MEANING (except perhaps for differences due to the different roles X might play in the two positions with regard to surface structure rules of interpretation), this is evidence against the structure-preserving constraint. For in this case either position, say P, can be taken as the deep structure position of X. Semantic projection rules then associate this position with appropriate meanings, and a non-structure-preserving transformation T moves X from P to P'.

In this case, in order to avoid a non-structure-preserving transformation, either X must be generated in both P and P' in deep structure—in which case two sets of projection rules operating on X, each yielding the same meanings, must be written for P and P'—or else an X that is always empty must be generated in P' by the phrase structure rules only for the (ad hoc) purpose of making T structure-preserving. In either case the generalization captured by a non-structure-preserving transformation would be lost.

(If the same projection rules can interpret X in P and in P' without recourse to additional symbols, the evidence against the structure-preserving constraint disappears, for there is no objection to accounting for distribution alone by phrase structure rules rather than by transformations.)

However, assuming that the set of meanings of X common to both P and P' is M, suppose that in at least one position, say P', X has a further set of meanings M'. (Evidence for this in a particular case might be ambiguities of X in P', a wider range of lexical entries for X in P', etc.) An obvious way to account for the discrepancy would be to associate the deep structure position P' with projection rules yielding the meanings M' for X, and to associate P with projection rules yielding M for X. The transformation T, which moves X from P to P', is now positive evidence FOR the structure-preserving constraint rather than evidence against it, since one needs an explanation for why T moves X to another deep structure position of X and not to some arbitrary position. (Of course the existence of one or two rules in the grammar of this sort could be an accident, but I am trying to show that all nonroot transformations in English that are not local transformations have this property.)

I will try to show in this section that adverbial AP's in English exhibit the behavior described in the last paragraph and, hence, are actually evidence for the structure-preserving constraint. Consider now the adverbs enclosed in braces in (3):

(3)
$$\text{John answered the questions} \begin{cases} \textit{intelligently.} \\ \textit{with intelligence.} \\ \textit{in an intelligent way.} \end{cases}$$

They called $\begin{Bmatrix} loudly \\ in\ a\ loud\ manner \end{Bmatrix}$ through the halls.

They called through the halls $\begin{Bmatrix} loudly. \\ in\ a\ loud\ manner. \end{Bmatrix}$

He puts his books away $\begin{Bmatrix} carefully \\ with\ care \\ in\ a\ careful\ way \end{Bmatrix}$ in the drawer.

He puts his books away in the drawer $\begin{Bmatrix} carefully. \\ with\ care. \\ in\ a\ careful\ way. \end{Bmatrix}$

He uses symbols in his explanations $\begin{Bmatrix} understandably. \\ in\ understandable\ fashion. \end{Bmatrix}$

He uses symbols $\begin{Bmatrix} understandably \\ in\ understandable\ fashion \end{Bmatrix}$ in his explanations.

China has industrialized $\begin{Bmatrix} rapidly. \\ in\ rapid\ fashion. \end{Bmatrix}$

The rain is cleaning our car $\begin{Bmatrix} thoroughly. \\ in\ thorough\ fashion. \end{Bmatrix}$

John took the wallpaper off $\begin{Bmatrix} efficiently \\ in\ an\ efficient\ manner \end{Bmatrix}$ first.

Adverbial AP's that can be paraphrased as in (3) are manner adverbials. For purposes of exposition I assume here that an adverbial AP that follows and modifies a verb V without an intervening breath pause (comma) is dominated by VP. (Adverbial adjectives in phrases like *barely on time* and *hardly a dozen people* are not sister constituents to verbs even when they follow them, but they do not modify the preceding verbs either; rather, they are part of the constituents PP and NP.)

Most of the adverbial AP's that follow a verb without a pause are manner adverbials. In some cases the PP paraphrases for these adverbials, of the kind given in (3), are clumsy and even ungrammatical. But if such PP paraphrases do not distort the MEANING of the adverbial AP, I assume that the adverbial in question is a manner adverbial. Examples of this kind are given in (4); nothing in what follows strictly depends on enlarging the manner adverbial class in this way:

(4)   *This business has failed completely.*
       *This business has failed in a complete way. (ungrammatical, but
          similarly interpreted)
       The sun is shining dimly through the clouds.
       *The sun is shining in dim fashion through the clouds.
          (ungrammatical, but similarly interpreted)

The adverbial AP's that follow a verb but are preceded by a comma can be shown to be derived by means of a root transformation; hence, they are immediately dominated by S, not VP. This root transformation is similar to the "right dislocation" rule that moves NP's out of sentences to the right (cf. Chapter II), so I call this rule ADVERBIAL DISLOCATION. The adverbials that undergo this rule are not manner adverbials [i.e., they do not have paraphrases similar to those in (3)] but, rather, factive adverbials. The deep structure source of such adverbials is discussed later in this section.

Examples of dislocated adverbials are given in (5), along with paraphrases:

(5)   *We aren't doing our share, actually.*
           We aren't actually doing our share.

           That man could have been replaced, possibly.
           That man could possibly have been replaced.

           John sneaked away in time, evidently.
           John evidently sneaked away in time.

           John didn't answer any questions, wisely.
           John wisely didn't answer any questions.

           John won't cooperate, supposedly.
           John supposedly won't cooperate.

           Bill took the wrong turn, fortunately.
           Bill fortunately took the wrong turn.

The examples in (6) show that adverbial dislocation is a root transformation, since an adverbial AP apparently cannot be "dislocated" out of an embedded S that is not rightmost under a root S:

(6)   **Her accusation that we aren't doing our share, actually, is groundless.*

       Her accusation that we aren't actually doing our share is groundless.

       *They gave the only man that could have been replaced, possibly, a tenured position.

       They gave the only man that could have possibly been replaced a tenured position.

       ?Even though John sneaked away in time, evidently, his wife was caught.

       ≠Even though John evidently sneaked away in time, his wife was caught.

       *The fact that Mary didn't answer any questions, wisely, allowed John to avoid prosecution.

*The fact that Mary wisely didn't answer any questions allowed
John to avoid prosecution.*

**The people saying that I don't cooperate as much as John does,
supposedly, are slanderers.*

*The people saying that I don't cooperate as much as John
supposedly does are slanderers.*

**I think that the fact that Bill took the wrong turn, fortunately, saved
our lives.*

*I think that the fact that Bill fortunately took the wrong turn saved
our lives.*

I return now to the question of finding a deep structure source for manner
adverbials. Katz and Postal (1964) have suggested that they should be derived
from an underlying PP roughly of the form *in a(n)* AP *way.* Such a derivation
would accomplish the following: (i) It would account for the meaning of (and
certain selectional restrictions on) adverbial AP's without an adverbial projection rule for interpreting the configuration

(ii) It would explain why postverbal manner adverbials can appear both before
AND after certain other postverbal PP's, as in (3), since the PP's of the type
they are derived from can also so appear. (iii) It could utilize a rule needed
independently in the grammar for deleting *in* before an object whose head is
way:

(7)   *John answered the questions (?in) the wrong way on purpose.*
       They call through the halls (?in) this loud way to get people up.
       I'll put my books away (?in) any way I want to.
       He used that lemma in his proof (?in) the understandable way.
       Russia industrialized the rapid way.
       John took the wallpaper off (?in) the efficient way first.

Sentences in which this *in* deletion rule would apply before *a(n)* are not usually
grammatical:

(8)   **John answered the questions a wrong way on purpose.*
           *They call through the halls a loud way to get people up.
           *I'll put my books away a careful way.
           *He used that lemma in his proof an understandable way.
           *Russia industrialized a rapid way.
           *John took the wallpaper off an efficient way first.

However, we can allow *in* deletion to apply before *a(n)* if we subsequently reduce the sentences in (8) to manner adverbial AP's by deleting *a(n)* and *way*, as in (9):

(9)

```
        V P                    V P
         |                      |
        NP          =====>     AP
       / | \                    |
   DET  AP  N                   XX
    |   |   |
  a (n) XX way
```

According to the pruning principle I follow here, the loss of the specifier and the head of the NP causes it to prune. This correctly predicts that manner adverbials will not appear in focus position in cleft sentences. (This is discussed in Chapter IV.) The deletion in (9) produces the examples in (10):

(10)   *John answered the questions wrongly on purpose.*
        They call through the halls loudly to get people up.
        I'll put my books away carefully.
        He used that lemma in his proof understandably.
        Russia industrialized rapidly.
        John took the wallpaper off efficiently first.

This derivation of manner adverbials is compared with an alternative analysis later in this section.

A manner adverbial often precedes rather then follows the V that it modifies. When a manner adverbial appears in this position, it does not always seem to be an EXACT paraphrase of the postverbal manner adverbial, but the differences in meaning are slight and may well be due to surface structure interpretation of what represents the "focus" or "new information" of the sentence. Thus the following pairs are near paraphrases (even though the second example in each pair may also have an alternate sense):

(11)   *John has answered the questions intelligently.*
        John has intelligently answered the questions.

        They called through the halls loudly.
        They loudly called through the halls.

        He puts his books away carefully.
        He carefully puts his books away.

        He can use symbols understandably in his explanations.
        He can understandably use symbols in his explanations.

        China has industrialized rapidly.
        China has rapidly industrialized.

        The rain is cleaning our car thoroughly.
        The rain is thoroughly cleaning our car.

> John has taken the wallpaper off efficiently.
> John has efficiently taken the wallpaper off.
>
> The sun is shining dimly through the clouds.
> The sun is dimly shining through the clouds.
>
> This business has failed completely.
> This business has completely failed.

Certain manner adverbials do not exhibit this alternation, under conditions that I will not try to specify here:

(12)   We must eat simply in this town.
                 ≠We must simply eat in this town.

                 John explained that theorem understandably.
(?) ≠John understandably explained that theorem.

Most manner adverbials cannot, however, precede the auxiliaries or the subject NP. Adverbial AP's in the latter positions have either no meaning or else a nonmanner sense in the great majority of cases:

(13)   Intelligently, John has answered the question.
                 ≠ John has answered the question intelligently.

                 ?Carefully, I will put my books away.
                 ≠ I will put my books away carefully.

                 *Thoroughly, the rain cleaned our car.
                 ≠ The rain cleaned our car thoroughly.

                 Conscientously, Bill is working under his father.
                 ≠ Bill is working under his father conscientiously.

                 *This business completely has failed.
                 ≠ This business has failed completely.

                 *The sum dimly is shining through the clouds.
                 ≠ The sun is shining dimly through the clouds.

                 The government rightly has already acted on this matter.
                 ≠ The government has already acted rightly on this matter.

                 My lawyer has actually been helping me.
                 ≠*My lawyer has been helping me actually.

                 We simply must eat in this town.
                 ≠ We must eat simply in this town.

                 They nearly were crushed by the throng.
                 ≠*They were crushed nearly by the throng.

The examples in (13) show that manner adverbials do not have freedom of occurrence in all adverbial positions in the sentence. Rather, they occur in the positions of the PP's of which they are paraphrases and also immediately before the verbs they modify. If the source of a manner adverbial AP is a PP, as suggested earlier, the second sentence in each pair in (11) must be derived from the first by means of a "manner movement" transformation. This rule would move an adverbial AP under a VP to a position just preceding the head V. Since such a rule would not be a root transformation or a local movement rule, it would be important to determine if it were structure-preserving or not.

Before we turn to this crucial question, let us see if any alternative analyses or manner adverbials could furnish evidence against the structure-preserving constraint.

If the manner movement transformation were rejected in favor of generating manner adverbials preverbally in the base, this would not in itself be evidence against the structure-preserving constraint, for if no movement rule applies to manner adverbials, such constructions obviously provide no evidence for or against any constraint on movement transformations. However, generating manner adverbials in preverbal position would entail duplicating or at least extending the interpretive mechanisms for manner adverbial PP's that follow the verb, along the lines of Jackendoff (1972).

If manner adverbial AP's were generated in the base in preverbal position AND if a "manner-postposing" rule moved such AP's into postverbal positions, this would be evidence against the structure-preserving constraint. Such a rule would not be a root transformation or a local movement rule, and it would not be structure-preserving because manner adverbial AP's can appear postverbally in positions where predicate adjective AP's cannot (namely, PP positions):

(14)   *John disappeared last night quite abruptly.*
       **John appeared last night quite abrupt.*
       John appeared quite abrupt last night.

       John answered some questions at the police station impatiently.
       **John became at the police station impatient.*
       John became impatient at the police station.

The hypothetical manner-postposing rule would be formulated roughly as in (15):

(15) $$[_{\text{VP}}\text{AP}-X-(\text{PP}) + (\text{S})] \implies \emptyset-2 + 1-3$$

Example (15) has three disadvantages that lead to its rejection. First, such a rule does not explain why manner adverbials have PP paraphrases, as in (3). Second, at least two classes of adverbial AP's can appear in preverbal position (these are discussed later) that may not appear in postverbal position. These

AP's would have to be prevented from undergoing (15) in ad hoc fashion.[1] Third, if postverbal PP's can be reduced to manner adverbial AP's, then (15) is totally redundant. Therefore if (15) is in the grammar, manner adverbial PP's should not be reduced to AP's by deletion of *in* and *a(n) way*. This, in turn, means that there is no principled explanation for the discrepancy between the sentences in (7) and (8), which are juxtaposed in (16):

(16) *John answered the questions* $\begin{Bmatrix} \text{the wrong way} \\ \text{*a wrong way} \end{Bmatrix}$ *on purpose.*

They call through the halls $\begin{Bmatrix} \text{this loud way} \\ \text{*a loud way} \end{Bmatrix}$ *to get people up.*

I'll put my books away $\begin{Bmatrix} \text{any old way.} \\ \text{*a careful way.} \end{Bmatrix}$

He used that lemma in his proof $\begin{Bmatrix} \text{the understandable way.} \\ \text{*an understandable way.} \end{Bmatrix}$

Russia industrialized $\begin{Bmatrix} \text{the rapid way.} \\ \text{*a rapid way.} \end{Bmatrix}$

John took the wallpaper off $\begin{Bmatrix} \text{the efficient way} \\ \text{*an efficient way} \end{Bmatrix}$ *first.*

[If manner adverbial AP's are derived from manner adverbial PP's as previously suggested, the starred phrases in (16) are ungrammatical because they are obligatorily transformed into manner adverbial AP's.]

Thus there are three reasons for rejecting (15) as a transformational rule of English.

If manner movement (from postverbal PP position to preverbal position) is a rule of English, we must determine whether or not it is structure-preserving. Structurally, manner movement performs the change indicated in (17):

(17)

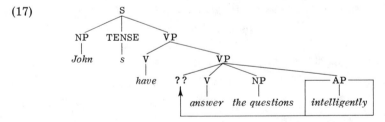

The crucial question, given such a rule, is whether there is any justification for generating AP's at the beginning of VP's (in the base) for other

---

[1] On the other hand, a CORRESPONDING restriction on the manner movement preposing rule previously suggested does not arise. The fact that certain manner adverbials such as *simply* and *understandably* must be marked as not undergoing manner movement preposing would be equivalent to their being marked as obligatorily undergoing manner movement postposing.

constructions besides manner adverbials. If there is not, then manner movement is evidence against the structure-preserving constraint. If there is, then the rule is evidence in favor of the constraint.

With this in mind, consider the class of adverbs such as *simply, merely, really, hardly, barely, scarcely, nearly*. These adverbs do not follow the V's that they modify and cannot be paraphrased (in the senses we are interested in here) by a PP; thus a postverbal source is not appropriate for them. Further, they do not alternate with adjectives; cf. *the mere way, *any near way I want to, *the bare way*. (Of interest later will be the fact that these adverbs cannot precede the subject NP either, except, in some cases, by virtue of the root transformation of negative preposing discussed in Chapter II.) Typically an adverb of the *scarcely* class can appear in ALL (and only) the blanks in an example like (18):

(18) *John* _____ *would* _____ *have* _____ *been* _____
$\left\{ \begin{array}{l} questioned \\ injured \end{array} \right\}$ *by the police.*

These adverbs indicate a necessity for a new source of adverbs, such as that given in the modified base rules (19) and (20); if each auxiliary is a verb or an M, as argued in Chapter VI, (19) and (20) account for all the positions of *scarcely* adverbs in (18):

(19)   VP → (AP)−V−. . .

(20)   S → COMP−NP−(AP)−M−. . .

The *scarcely* class is generable in any of the AP positions given by (19) and (20), as (18) shows. Manner movement, on the other hand, moves manner adverbials only to the AP position IMMEDIATELY PRECEDING the V they modify. Thus manner adverbials cannot appear in any of the blanks in (21), while members of the *scarcely* class can:

(21) *John* _____ *would* _____ *have* _____ *been questioned by the police. (*intelligently)*
      He _____ *could* _____ *have* _____ *been driving his car.*
      *(*cautiously)*
      The building _____ *was* _____ *being destroyed. (*completely)*

Since adverbs of the *scarcely* class have a different origin than manner adverbials, we also expect that they will not satisfy the requirement that verbs like *phrase* and *word* have manner adverbials:

(22)   *John has $\left\{ \begin{array}{l} merely \\ barely \\ nearly \end{array} \right\}$ $\left\{ \begin{array}{l} worded \\ phrased \end{array} \right\}$ the announcement.*

With the introduction of (19) into the grammar, manner movement is a structure-preserving rule, as shown in (23). It should be reemphasized that the basis of this argument is the existence of a class of strictly preverbal AP's that cannot be analyzed as manner adverbials and, contrary to the behavior of the latter, can precede any V or M, not just a nonauxiliary V:

(23)

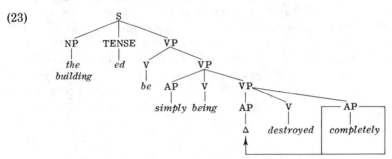

(the building was simply being completely destroyed)

Confirmation of the structure-preserving analysis of manner movement is furnished by the unacceptability of placing a manner adverbial before the V if a member of the *scarcely* class occupies that position in surface structure. [Evidence on this matter can be obscured by the possibility of manner adverbials themselves being modified by a *scarcely*-class adverb, but the examples in (24) are not easily subject to such interpretations.]

(24) *John was simply driving his car more cautiously.*
      John was (*simply) more cautiously driving his car.

      John was merely questioned by the police briefly.
      John was (*merely) briefly questioned by the police.

      John merely answered all the questions intelligently and then left.
      John (*merely) intelligently answered all the questions and then left.

      She was hardly speaking politely to her parents.
      She was (*hardly) politely speaking to her parents.

      She nearly killed her brother accidently.
      She (*nearly) accidentally killed her brother.

      I can barely speak French intelligibly.
      I can (*barely) intelligibly speak French.

A third class of *ly* adverbials may be called the "factive adverbials." Like the *scarcely* class, they cannot appear after a V and be immediately dominated by VP, and either they lack PP paraphrases or else their PP paraphrases are not the same ones (i.e., *in an* AP *manner, in* AP *fashion,* etc.) that manner adverbials have. They differ from the *scarcely* class, however, in that they can precede the subject NP, provided that a breath pause (comma) intervenes, and in that they seem increasingly unacceptable after a second, third, and fourth auxiliary, and very often after a *not* or *n't.* In (25) factive adverbials can appear in all and only the blanks indicated (factive adverbials are also the only adverbials that can undergo the previously discussed adverbial dislocation rule):

(25)   _____, *John* _____ *sneaked away in time,* _____. *(evidently)*
         _____, *John* _____ *could* _____ *have* __?? __ *been replaced,*
         _____. *(possibly)*
         _____, *we* _____ *haven't* _____ *been* __?? __ *trying too hard,*
         _____. *(actually)*
         _____, *there* _____ *was* _____ *no reason for the disturbance,*
         _____. *(truly)*
         _____, *John* _____ *didn't answer the question,* _____.
         (wisely)
         _____, *John* _____ *won't cooperate,* _____. *(supposedly)*
         _____, *the birds* _____ *have* _____ *been* __?? __ *surviving*
         the pollution, _____. *(strangely)*
         _____, *they* _____ *may* _____ *have* _____ *been taking the*
         right pills, _____. *(fortunately)*

Factive adverbials also differ from both *scarcely* adverbials and manner adverbials in that a sentence S with a factive adverbial AP can usually (not always) be paraphrased by *it is* AP *that* S. Sentences with the other two kinds of adverbial AP's never have such paraphrases. [The classes of items that may be factive and manner adverbials overlap, but in most cases there is a clear difference in meaning between the two uses; compare (13) on this point.]

The presubject position of factive adverbial AP's is possibly due to a root transformation; if so, it would not be a possible deep structure source for these adverbials. There are many types of embedded S's in which such adverbial positions are excluded:

(26)   *John bought more paper than I usually do.*
         **John bought more paper than usually I do.*

         The men you supposedly saw were my employees.
         **The men supposedly you saw were my employees.*

         I wonder whether John has truly lost his talent?
         **I wonder whether truly John has lost his talent?*

         He came to the realization that John conscientiously would work
         *   under his father.*

*He came to the realization that conscientiously John would work under his father.

I am aware that Mary unfortunately has no other home.
?I am aware that unfortunately Mary has no other home.

He answered the same questions as you wisely had skipped.
*He answered the same questions as wisely you had skipped.

It angered my employer that I might possibly quit.
?It angered my employer that possibly I might quit.

The judgments of grammaticality in sentences like those in (26) are not always clear-cut, but there does seem to be a consistent difference. There are some embedded sentences in which presubject factive adverbials are acceptable, but these S's seem to be just those in which the restrictions against other root (i.e., non-structure-preserving) transformations are sometimes relaxed. Thus presubject factive adverbials are sometimes acceptable in the S complements of subordinating conjunctions like *because, although, so that*, etc., and of verbs like *believe, say*, etc.

Either there is a root transformation of AP preposing, and the acceptable embedded S's with presubject factive adverbials are to be explained by appeal to devices of semigrammaticality, or else the presubject AP position is represented in the phrase structure rules, and the starred sentences in (26) must be explained by some other device. In order to be consistent with my treatment of similar cases in Chapter II, I prefer the first alternative.

However, even without taking a stand on this issue it is possible to argue that the existence of a third class of adverbial AP's in English (with its distribution that is different than that of manner and *scarcely* adverbials) can only strengthen the structure-preserving hypothesis. Alternative arguments can be presented as follows:

1. Suppose some of the factive adverbial AP's that appear in surface structure positions generated by (19) and (20) are moved to these positions from some other source position. (This source might be the presubject position if this is a deep structure position, or it might be a paraphrase of the type *it is* AP *that* S.) Since these sources are not appropriate for either manner or *scarcely*-class adverbials that appear in these surface positions, we need some principle that explains why the surface positions of the different classes of adverbials are the same. (For instance, why are the factive adverbials not placed between the verb and its direct object NP?) This principle is the structure-preserving hypothesis.

2. Suppose the factive adverbial AP's that appear in surface structure positions generated by (19) and (20) are in these positions in deep structure.

(That is, suppose they have the same or a subset of the deep structure sources as *scarcely* adverbials.) In this case, it would be likely that presubject factive adverbials would result from a root transformation. But more important, even though this would not give a new argument for the structure-preserving hypothesis, it would strengthen the argument given earlier based on the partially similar and partially dissimilar distribution of the manner adverbial class and the *scarcely* adverbial class, since the somewhat small class of *scarcely* adverbials would be expanded to include the large factive class. A partial similarity between the surface distribution of two such large adverb classes (manner and factive) that have different deep structures cannot be dismissed as accidental.

Thus whatever the correct analysis of factive adverbials, their distribution is such that the structure-preserving hypothesis is not weakened by it.

A final word in this section concerns adverbial AP's that can occur in all the adverbial AP positions (presubject, between subject NP and main V, and after V) with the same meaning. Frequency adverbials (*frequently, usually, occasionally, rarely*) and certain manner adverbials (*gradually, accidentally, quietly, immediately*, etc.) appear to have this property. This could be accounted for by moving them transformationally into any AP position required for the correct analysis of the other adverbial classes, or by analyzing them as both factive and manner adverbials that have the combined distribution of both classes but are synonymous in either usage. If all adverbials had this freedom of occurrence, it would be evidence against the structure-preserving hypothesis. But once it is evident that at least three other classes have partially the same and partially different distributions, the arguments for separate deep structure positions and for structure-preserving rules for adverbial AP's cannot be weakened by the existence of a class with a wider range of occurrence in these positions (i.e., the frequency adverbials and similar types).[2]

This concludes the discussion of adverbial AP movement rules. Although the evidence that adverbial AP movements are structure-preserving is not as strong as that available concerning NP movements, this lack seems attributable to the relatively small number of generally agreed-upon transformations that move such AP's. A close examination of a rule like manner movement reveals that these rules place AP's not randomly in trees but, rather, in positions that are characteristically shared by other AP's with different deep structure sources.

---

[2]The fact that neither *scarcely*-type adverbials nor manner adverbials nor factive adverbials really exhibit free movement under their immediately dominating node, as instanced by (2), (6), (24), and (26), indicates that there is no special "transportability" transformation for English adverbs, as suggested in Keyser (1968).

V.3   ADJECTIVE MOVEMENT[3]

In general, nouns can be modified by a following VP introduced by *ing*, as in (27). These VP's are called PARTICIPLES. As (27a) and (27c) show, this *ing* is not simply a reduced form of the progressive morpheme pair *be—ing*:

(27)   a.   *We picked up a box **containing some books**. (cf. *The box was containing some books.)*
      b.   *The workers **burning the boxes** were sweating.*
      c.   *The students **having seen this movie** should let us know. (cf. *The students were having seen this movie.)*

Furthermore, not any VP (i.e., not any sequence of verbs excluding TENSE and modals that can appear in sentences) can modify a noun in this way:

(28)   a.   **We were speaking to a man **being very jealous of his father**.*
        (VP = ing + be very jealous of his father)
      b.   **I loaned him a book **being important for his studies**.*
        (VP = ing + be important for his studies)
      c.   **The books **being contained in the box** were worthless.*
        (VP = ing + be contained in the box)
      d.   **The boxes **being being burned at the dump** are foul smelling. (VP = ing + be being burned at the dump)*
      e.   **The boxes **being burning at the dump** are foul smelling.*
        (VP = ing + be burning at the dump)
      f.   **The person **being being kindest to me** was my aunt.*
        (VP = ing + be being kindest to me)

Instead of the ungrammatical sequences in (28), we find a corresponding set of grammatical sentences, (29). Each example in (29) can be obtained from (28) by deleting the first *being* in boldface in each example in (28).

(29)   a.   *We were speaking to a man very jealous of his father.*
      b.   *I loaned him a book important for his studies.*
      c.   *The books contained in the box were worthless.*
      d.   *The boxes being burned at the dump are foul smelling*
      e.   *The boxes burning at the dump are foul smelling.*
      f.   *The person being kindest to me was my aunt.*

It seems therefore that the full range of *ing* + VP forms CAN appear as participles modifying nouns, provided that we postulate a rule to obligatorily

---

[3]The analysis of participles given here, except that part which deals with the relation of this construction to the structure-preserving constraint, is taken directly from my dissertation with only minor rewordings. A similar analysis has subsequently appeared in the literature (Ross, 1972a). The import of (27) was first indicated to me by E. Klima.

delete the initial *being* in a participle that is modifying a head noun. According to this analysis, (27b) and (29e) are structurally ambiguous, being derivable from an underlying participle that may or may not be in the progressive form. On the other hand, (29d) and (29f) can have only an underlying progressive source, since an underlying *ing* + *be* + *en* + *burn* would become simply *burned*. This is confirmed by the fact that verbs that cannot appear with the progressive auxiliary in full sentences are also excluded in sentences like (29d) and (29f):

(30) **The books being contained in the box are worthless.*
　　　*The person being most important to me was my aunt.

Thus in this type of participle the progressive—simple form alternation appears in surface structure only in the passive voice.

　　　Given the refinements introduced by the *being* deletion rule, these noun-modifying participles (including the adjective phrases derived from them) are otherwise generally synonymous with relative clauses whose subject is a relative pronoun and that have no modal (M). Therefore I assume that these participles are derived transformationally from relative clauses by deletion of $\left[_{NP} \left\{ \begin{array}{c} which \\ who \end{array} \right\} \right]$—TENSE and insertion of *ing*, as in Smith (1961).

　　　The rule of *being* deletion that derives (29) means that AP's can sometimes follow nouns inside NP's, as in (29a) and (29b). It is well known, however, that AP's derived from participles by *being* deletion THAT END IN THEIR HEAD A [(i.e., they contain no PP or S complements, as (29a) and (29b) do] precede rather than follow the nouns they modify in surface structure. Compare the pairs in (31):

(31) **We were speaking to a man very jealous.*
　　　We were speaking to a very jealous man.

　　　*The tourists anxious boarded the bus.
　　　The anxious tourists boarded the bus.

　　　*I loaned him a book important.
　　　I loaned him an important book.

　　　*The possibility of a decision crucial being made is minimal.
　　　The possibility of a crucial decision being made is minimal.

Similarly, it appears that certain participles can also move over the nouns they modify (the VP's that move must, like AP's, end in their heads):

(32) *The quietly sleeping children shouldn't be disturbed.*
　　　This often retold story is now being made into a movie.

　　　To account for the position of the attributive adjectives in (31), Smith (1961) proposes an "adjective movement" rule that derives the grammatical strings in (31) from structures underlying the strings of the corresponding starred examples. If this rule is to account for the sentences in (32) also, it should be formulated to move VP's as well as AP's, or else the principle of derived structure suggested in Chomsky (1957), which predicts that VP's of certain "adjective-like form" will automatically be moved by an AP movement rule, must be appropriately refined. (There are differences between the movement of VP's and AP's: VP movement is often optional and often blocked; cf. *The children quietly sleeping shouldn't be disturbed* and **The stopping cars are mostly old* versus *The cars stopping are mostly old*.)

It might be thought that adjective movement is a local movement transformation that permutes an N with a following modifying AP or VP, but the following consideration indicates that this is not correct.[4] As argued in Chomsky (1970), there appear to be certain deep structure postnominal PP's, and the adjective phrase movement rule must move constituents over them:

(33)   *The visibility at the airport, poorer than here, scares me.*
   *The visibility, poorer than here, at the airport scares me.
   The poorer visibility at the airport scares me.

   I envy any fans of Elvis (who are) younger than me.
   *I envy any fans (who are) younger than me of Elvis.
   I envy any younger fans of Elvis.

   They broadcast that tale of horrible goblins often retold at campfires.
   *They broadcast that tale often retold at campfires of horrible goblins.
   They broadcast that often retold tale of horrible goblins.

---

[4] If adjective movement is a local movement transformation, it is of course permitted by the structure-preserving constraint. There might appear to be a problem connected with the fact that there is a condition on the rule that the constituents moved by it must end in their heads, which necessitates using a variable in the statement of the rule: $A'' (= AP) = X - A$. According to the definition of local transformations given in Chapter I, the phrase node involved in such a rule must be stated without a variable. However, the condition that prenominal adjectives phrases end in their heads is almost certainly due to the surface recursion restriction informally introduced in Chapter I. If this is the case, adjective movement could be written as a local rule without using a variable in its formulation, as required.

It is well known that adjective movement does not move constituents over composite pronouns like *nobody, everything, someone, someplace*, etc. This can be explained if these pronouns are analyzed as DET's at the point when the rule applies. Independent justification for such an analysis is that the determiners from which these pronouns are formed (*no, some, every, any*) retain their syntactic characteristics in these composite forms. For example, the *some—any* distribution in negative context carries over to *something—anything*, etc., and the composite forms of *every* are definite just as *every* is. These facts indicate that composite pronouns are dominated either by a single preterminal symbol DET or by the sequence of symbols DET—N, and not by N alone. But the fact that these pronouns are spelled as single words and that their second element must be unstressed, unlike other sequences of DET—N (*each boy, that thing, any body*, etc.), indicates that they are single morphemes in surface structure, i.e., instances of DET. (Further, the form *body* in composite pronouns does not have the syntactic characteristic -ANIMATE of the noun *body*.)

Such sentences indicate that adjective movement must move phrasal constituents over N—PP sequences in English, something that cannot be accomplished by a local movement transformation. The structure-preserving constraint then requires that adjective movement be a structure-preserving rule, and this, in turn, must mean that an AP is generable in deep structure in prenominal position.

It is not difficult to find examples of prenominal adjective phrases that cannot be derived from relative clauses and are hence candidates for deep structure prenominal adjectives. Assuming that deep structures are the same as surface structures in the absence of a convincing counterargument, it appears that some or all of the classes of adjectives exemplified in (34)—(38) are prenominal in deep structure; hence, adjective movement can be formulated as structure-preserving.

Example (34) cannot be paraphrased (in one of its senses, at least) as *Students are the revolutionaries who are traditional*; rather, it means *Students are traditionally the revolutionaries*. In (35), *three possible suspects* should not be derived from **three suspects who are possible*. The adjectives in (36) cannot appear as predicate attributes (although four of them do appear as adverbs in *ly*), so it is unlikely that they are derived from underlying relative clauses:

(34) *Students are the **traditional** revolutionaries in that country.*

(35) *They have arrested three **possible** suspects.*

(36) ***Potential** criminals are hard to detect.*
      *Don't overestimate the **actual** importance of the election.*
      *The **main** purpose of these assignments has never been made
        known.*
      *We witnessed an **utter** failure.*
      *Chasing butterflies is his **favorite** pasttime.*

In (37), the prenominal adjectives have meanings that are seemingly related to the usual (predicate attribute) meanings of these adjectives. On the other hand, these meanings of the adjectives in question cannot be DIRECTLY derived from relative clauses:

(37)   *The **poor** man has more money than he can handle.*
       ≠ *The man who is poor has more money than he can handle.*

            *My **little** sister weighs 200 pounds.*
       ≠ *My sister who is little weighs 200 pounds.*

            *He is one of my **oldest** friends.*
       ≠ *He is one of my friends who is oldest.*

            *Do you have any **later** word on that flight?*
       ≠?*Do you have any word on that flight which is later?*

In (38), the second clause has a meaning (in fact the principal meaning in the context) that is not paraphrasable by a relative clause like *She is a bridge player who is eager*. This clause means something more like *She is eager to play bridge*. Similar remarks apply to the other examples in (38):

(38) *Mary is quite retiring, but she is an **eager** bridge player.*
      *A good track man should be a **slow** eater.*
      *John scolded the **most willing** hikers for not cooperating in other*
          matters.
      *John is a **very frequent** caller.*
      *A **likely early** leader is now approaching the starting gate.*

Thus there are several constructions that we may assume are a result of the deep structure expansion NP → ... (AP)–N ...; consequently adjective phrase movement is a structure-preserving movement of the node AP from an NP-final to a prenominal position.

However, with such a formulation the fact that adjective phrase movement also must move certain VP's, as in (32), means that the principle of derived structure proposed in Chomsky (1957), referred to earlier, must be assigned certain limitations and worked out in detail.

Although this might be the right track to follow, there is a competing analysis of the prenominal–postnominal alternation of English adjective phrases that utilizes structure-preserving rules but does not require such a principle of derived structure. In the remainder of this section, I will discuss this alternative.

For different reasons, Smith (1964) and Jackendoff (1968) have argued that relative clauses should originate in prenominal position. A very systematic and quite convincing case for generating restrictive relatives in this position is made in Milner (1972). (For purposes of this discussion, it is not necessary to decide whether such a prenominal source for relative clause S's is under or a sister to DET.) If this is correct, we can replace "adjective movement" with a transformation that postposes the constituents S and PP from prenominal position AFTER relative clause reduction takes place.

Such a rule could be formulated as structure-preserving if it moved relative clause S's, whether reduced or not, to the noun complement S position, and reduced relative clause PP's to the noun complement PP position. Since there can be more than one postnominal relative in English, more than one such base position would have to be available. Phrase structure rules of the form NP → NP–PP and NP → NP–S for noun complements in the base would provide such nodes. That such rules are needed at least for PP complements is indicated by sentences such as *The weather and the mode of dress in most areas are compatible*, which cannot be easily analyzed unless the deep subject NP is assigned the following internal structure:

(39) $\left[_{NP} \left[_{NP} \left[_{NP} \text{ the weather }_{NP}\right] \text{ and } \left[_{NP} \text{ the mode of dress }_{NP}\right] _{NP}\right] \left[_{PP} \text{ in} \right.\right.$
most areas $_{PP}\left._{NP}\right]$

Thus we can assume that full relatives, participial reduced relatives, and prepositional phrase reduced relatives can be postposed within their noun phrases by a structure-preserving rule with the following structural effect:

(40)

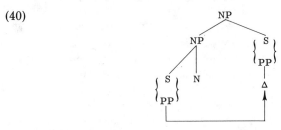

RELATIVE POSTPOSING, the transformation that would place both reduced and nonreduced relative clauses in postnominal position as in (40), is in most cases obligatory, and we can ascribe this to the surface recursion restriction tentatively put forward in Chapter I. The exceptions to this are (i) reduced participles such as in *the quietly sleeping children, the often retold story,* etc., in which case postposing appears optional, and (ii) adjective phrases without complement PP's or S's, as in (31), which NEVER postpose. For (i) the explanation would be the fact that prenominal reduced participles that lack phrase node complements do not violate the surface recursion restriction. For (ii), the same reason explains why AP's without complements MAY occur prenominally, but the fact that they MAY NOT postpose would in this analysis be explained by the structure-preserving constraint, because there is no AP node generated to the right of the head noun in the NP. However, this would immediately raise the question, How can AP's that contain complement PP's or S's postpose within the NP in structure-preserving fashion? To explain this, we would have to treat such a postposing in just the way we treat the postposing of NP's that contain S's or PP's to the end of a sentence in Chapter III (the complex NP shift rule). That is, we would have to extend the sentence boundary condition roughly as follows:

(41) **Cyclic Node Boundary Condition:** *If* A_j *is a rightmost or a leftmost constituent of an* S *or an* NP, *a transformational operation that substitutes* B *for* A_j *is structure-preserving if* B *dominates* A_i, *provided that there is no* S *such that* $B = X \left[_S Y A_i Z_S\right] W.$

(I do not know if the proviso on the sentence boundary condition should be revised in some way if the extension to a cyclic node boundary convention is correct; I have simply reproduced it unchanged.) For postposing relative clauses reduced to an AP containing an S or a PP complement, A = S or PP, B = AP.

An analysis of reduced relatives along these lines would offer the possibility of explaining various conditions on the alternation of prenominal and postnominal reduced relative clauses in terms of general conditions such as the structure-preserving constraint and the surface recursion restriction. At the same time, it would obviate the need for a principle of derived structure based on the suggestion in Chomsky (1957), which the alternative and more widely accepted analysis described earlier seems to require. However, both alternatives seem to be compatible with the requirement that the alternation in question be treated by a structure-preserving rule, so I will not attempt a definitive solution to the problem here.

V.4 THE NODE PP AND ITS DISTRIBUTION[5]

In this study, the node label PP indicates not only prepositional phrases in the traditional sense of that term (preposition with NP object) but also certain clauses introduced by subordinating conjunctions and certain other adverb phrases. Some justification for this should be given.

The prepositional phrase of traditional grammar, generable by the rule PP → P—NP, can serve as an adjunct to a noun, verb, or adjective; the extremely varied uses of PP in English are well known. Such phrases, however, are better seen not as an isolated phrase type but as part of a larger paradigm.

Among the traditional "parts of speech," only verbs and prepositions generally take (direct) "objects." But some verbs take no object, others take only sentence or infinitive (S) complements, and others take various combinations of $\emptyset$, NP, and S. If we extend these properties of verbs to prepositions, the traditional "prepositions" are TRANSITIVE prepositions, the heads of prepositional PHRASES; certain traditional "subordinating conjunctions" are prepositions with sentence complements, the heads of prepositional CLAUSES; and certain traditional simple adverbs (of those not derived from adjectives) are INTRANSITIVE prepositions. For justification of this last claim in particular, see Emonds (1972a).

In this way, the following structural parallels can be set up and can be expressed by lexical strict subcategorization features on prepositions:

---

[5] Many of the ideas of this section are due to Edward Klima, especially those that postulate similarities between verbs and prepositions. Geis (1970) derives all subordinate clauses from (traditional) PP's. This analysis is compatible with any remarks made later in this section on PP movement rules in connection with the structure-preserving hypothesis. It is these remarks, of course, and not the introductory analysis of the node PP, that are most important to the hypothesis.

(42)

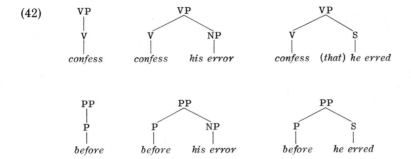

Prepositions that take different combinations of complement types are give in (43):

(43)   *John arrived before the last speech.*
           John arrived before the last speech ended.
           John arrived before (hand).

$$He\ did\ it\ \begin{Bmatrix} until \\ because \end{Bmatrix}\ his\ friend\ arrived.$$

$$He\ did\ it\ \begin{Bmatrix} until \\ because\ of \end{Bmatrix}\ his\ friend's\ arrival.$$

$$*He\ did\ it\ \begin{Bmatrix} because. \\ until. \end{Bmatrix}$$

           They were walking in (side) the house.
           They were walking in (side).
           *They were walking in (side) the people were dancing.

           I haven't seen him since the party began.
           I haven't seen him since the party.
           I haven't seen him since.

One may also want to relate the following pairs of constructions by strict subcategorization features:[6]

(44)   *They are unwise in trying to escape.*
           They are unwise in that they are trying to escape.

           What would he say now?
           What would he say now that the news is out?

In Chapter IV I discuss the cleft construction, showing why only NP's and PP's can occupy the "focus" position. This accords well with the extended notion

---

[6]Some of the features in question are these: *before*, P, + _____ ({NP, S}); *until*, P, + _____ {NP, S}; *inside*, P, + _____ (NP); *while*, + _____ S; *together*, P, + _____ ; *for*, P, + _____ NP.

of PP introduced here, since the adverbs and subordinate clauses that I am analyzing as PP's can be found in this position also:

(45)   *It was because John left that Mary cried.*
        It was after the president had finished that the disorder began.
        It was afterwards that the news broke.
        It's upstairs that we have no heat.

Certain NP's like *yesterday, every morning, last week,* etc. are used as adverbs of time. Their ability to prepose inside other NP's (cf. the possessive transformation discussed in Section III.5) indicates that they are NP's:

(46)   *yesterday's newspaper, every morning's news, last week's weather,*
        etc.

In order to regularize statements of NP distribution, I assume that these NP's are dominated by a PP in deep structure (whose head is probably *on*). The P of this PP is then deleted in surface structure [cf. *He is (at) home; He did it (in) the wrong way*].

Confirmatory evidence in favor of combining prepositions, subordinating conjunctions, and certain adverbs into the single syntactic category P is the behavior of the particle *right*. The members of the category P that express spatial or temporal location and direction (but not frequency) can all be preceded by *right*:

(47)   *He kept on drinking right until midnight.*
        She put it right into her pocket.
        The boy came right from the store.
        They kissed right after the ceremony.

        He came in right before the party started.
        He kissed her right while her boyfriend was looking.
        I know right where he is.

        Come in here right away!
        I know I put it right down.
        I should be doing it right this minute.

(Notice, for example, that *while*, which takes only S complements, can be preceded by *right*.) Before adjectives and before manner or frequency adverbials, *right* is not allowed in standard English:

(48)   **They came over right often.*
                *John drove right carefully.
                *She is right pretty.
                *Fights happen right seldom around here.

There are, as expected in this analysis, prepositional clauses containing infinitives rather than full sentences, such as those introduced by *so as* and *in order*. There is even one preposition (*lest*) that takes a present subjunctive S complement, parallel to verbs like *require*. Thus prepositions take the same range of complements as verbs; there is the difference that prepositions apparently take at most one complement, although even this is disputed in Jackendoff (1973) and Shopen (1972).

The general rule for expanding PP, then, is (49). INT (intensifier) is a grammatical formative realized as *right* before P (and as *very* before A), and cooccurs only with P's of a certain semantic class, as shown in (47):

(49)
$$PP \rightarrow (INT)-P-(\left\{ \begin{array}{l} NP \\ S \end{array} \right\})$$

Example (49) is a rule specifying the interior structure of PP's; let us now consider rules that generate PP's under other constituents. Rules of the following kind have appeared earlier in this study:

(50)
$$VP \rightarrow \ldots V \ldots (PP) \; (S)$$
$$NP \rightarrow \ldots (PP) \; (S)$$

[The S in (50) yields a full sentence or an infinitive, at least in surface structure.] Probably the rules in (50) are part of a more general rule schema, such as that given in (51), but this is not important for our purposes here:

(51)
$$\left\{ \begin{array}{l} NP \rightarrow \ldots \\ VP \rightarrow \ldots \\ AP \rightarrow \ldots \end{array} \right\} -(PP)^*-(S)$$

Rule (50) or (51) is not sufficient, however, to account for all prepositional clauses and phrases. A number of "causal" prepositions [*because (of)*, *in case (of)*, *on account of*, *in order*, *so that*, *in that*, *now that*, *if*, *unless*, *despite*, *although*, *in spite of*, etc.] are not generable inside NP, AP, or, if we judge by the position of S complements, inside VP's that immediately dominate V's [appropriate constituents are in boldface in (52)]:

(52) *****Stalin's military blunders because of his nationalism** are* *understandable.* (NP)

　　Cf. *It is understandable that Stalin blundered militarily because of his nationalism.*

　　***I had heard of **John's despair because he had lost his money**.* (NP)

　　Cf. *I had heard that John despaired because he had lost his money.*

　　***He **forbid his son because of the unrest to attend that college**.* (VP)

　　Cf. *He forbid his son to attend that college because of the unrest.*

*How rich if you are a farmer can you become? (AP)

Cf. *How rich can you become if you are a farmer?*

*Tom's cooperation despite his previous mistreatment was
surprising. (NP)

Cf. *That Tom cooperated despite his previous mistreatment was
surprising.*

**I could persuade John because he was drunk that Mary was
Canadian.* (VP)

Cf. *I could persuade John that Mary was Canadian because he was
drunk.*

*A crisis on account of widespread unemployment is sure to
come. (NP)

Cf. *On account of widespread unemployment, a crisis is sure to
come.*

"Causal" PP's in the class being discussed here characteristically appear
ONLY at the end of VP's; more precisely, they may and often must follow S
or VP complements to the main verb. All the grammatical sentences in (52)
exhibit or are consistent with limiting such PP's to a post-S position in the
VP. I will assume therefore that PP's introduced by words like *because* are
not generated by (50) but should originate at the end of sentences or infinitives
(i.e., at the end of S's or VP's), or perhaps at the end of both, by means of a
rule like (53) or (54):

(53)   S → S—PP

(54)   VP → VP—PP

For the moment whether (53) or (54) is part of the grammar is not important;
for purposes of exposition I arbitrarily choose (54).

V.5   STRUCTURE-PRESERVING MOVEMENTS OF PP

Consider now the paraphrases in (55):

(55) *John knew before he married her that she was intelligent.*
John knew that she was intelligent before he married her.

It isn't necessary on this campus to be very smart.
It isn't necessary to be very smart on this campus.

It seems sometimes that we'll never obtain peace.
It seems that we'll never obtain peace sometimes.

*Mary demonstrated in very convincing fashion last Saturday that
John shouldn't be licensed..*

*Mary demonstrated last Saturday that John shouldn't be licensed in
very convincing fashion.*

It frightened me when I was a child to be examined by a doctor.
It frightened me to be examined by a doctor when I was a child.

*It meant nothing after Einstein had devised his theory to speak of
simultaneity.*
*It meant nothing to speak of simultaneity after Einstein had devised
his theory.*

Given rule (54), the following surface structures can be assigned to a typical
pair of sentences in (55):

(56)

(57)

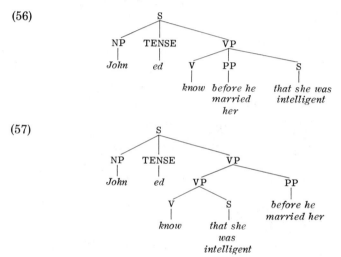

Since the phrase structure rules can generate PP's in the positions of the
PP's in both (56) and (57), independent of the constructions being considered
here (locative PP's of space and time, manner adverbial PP's, etc.), any movement transformation that relates (56) and (57) can be formulated as structure-
preserving. For example, if (56) is to be derived from (57), the rule accomplishing
this derivation has a structure-preserving effect, as indicated in (58):

(58)

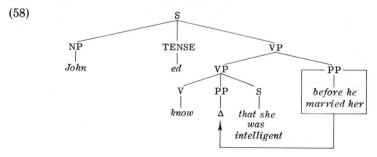

Actually the structures generated by (54) are to be preferred to those given by (53) because they allow us to extend the results in Lakoff and Ross (1966) concerning the *do so* construction. They propose that a sentence like (59) be derived from a structure like (60) by means of a rule like (61):

(59) *John told us the game was canceled before we left, and Mary did*
      so at the airport.

(60)

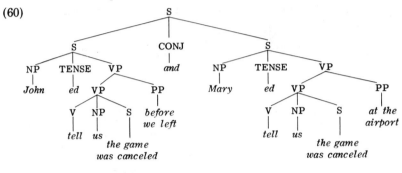

(61) $X-VP-Y-VP-Z \Rightarrow 1-2-3-do\ so-5$

where $2 = 4$ and 2 begins with a nonstative verb.

Rule (61) similarly derives (62) from a structure like (60) in which *at the airport* is replaced by *before we left* (and *too* is added as a constituent immediately dominated by the S whose subject is *Mary*):

(62) *John told us the game was canceled before we left, and Mary did*
      so before we left, too.

But (61) also (correctly) derives (63) from such a structure:

(63) *John told us the game was canceled before we left and Mary did*
      so too.

The fact that either of the VP's in the right-hand S of a structure like (60) can be deleted by (61), given identity with a VP in a left-hand S, justifies rule (54), which specifies a VP-over-VP configuration, in preference to (53).[7]

---

[7]There can be little doubt that the *do* inserted by (61) is dominated by V, since the TENSE affixes attach to this verb as to any other. This has led Ross (1972b) to claim that VP's whose heads are nonstative are complements to a deep structure *do* in underlying structure. That is, he assumes that the VP in (60) that is deletable by (61) should be replaced by the following structure, in which the lower VP is essentially transformationally replaced by *so*:

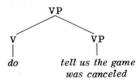

Bresnan (1971a) proposes that another rule that moves PP's in structure-preserving fashion relates the pairs of sentences in (64) by moving the PP (in boldface) from the subject NP to the VP:

(64)   *Our opinions **about war** are similar.*
        *Our opinions are similar **about war**.*

        *Her preferences and mine **in foreign foods** are incompatible.*
        *Her preferences and mine are incompatible **in foreign foods**.*

As Bresnan points out, this rule applies only if the VP contains certain "similarity predicates" such as *identical, similar, compatible*, etc.:

(65)   *Their opinions about war are stupid.*
       **Their opinions are stupid about war.*

       Her preferences and mine in foreign foods are easily describable.
       **Her preferences and mine are easily describable in foreign foods.*

Of course the fact that such a rule, if it exists, is structure-preserving is not an argument for its status as a transformation, a separate claim for which I give no evidence other than that already supplied by Bresnan.

A third structure-preserving movement rule for PP's (and S's) is that proposed in Chomsky (1970), which derives sentences like those in (66) by a movement like that in (67) (most of the examples are Chomsky's):

(66)   *The prospects are for peace.*
               Their talk was of snow and of fireplaces.
               The plan is for John to leave.
               The question is whether John should leave.

Footnote 7 continued

[Actually Ross assumes that the lower infinitival VP in this structure is immediately dominated by NP; I argue against this assumption in Chapter IV. For the purpose of this discussion, this discrepancy between Ross's analysis of (60) and mine is not important.]

Ross's hypothesis, if correct, leads to the question of whether the *so* in sentences like (59), (62), and (63) continues to occupy the S position at the end of the VP whose head is *do*. If the *so* in sentences like the following is inserted by the same rule that deletes clause complements after *do* [a modified version of (61)], evidence is available on this question:

> *John said **the play would soon start** and Bill said **so** too.*

S complements generally follow the *to* phrase after *say*:

> **John said that the play would soon start to Mary.*

Yet *so* must precede rather than follow a *to* phrase after *say*:

> *John said to Mary that the play would soon start, and Bill said* $\begin{Bmatrix} so\ to\ Joan. \\ {}^*to\ Joan\ so. \end{Bmatrix}$

Thus it seems that *so*, as inserted by (61), is a particle that immediately follows *do*, and not an S or a VP sister to *do*.

(67)

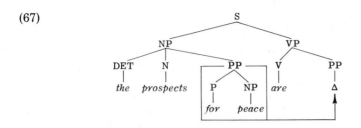

The evidence for such a derivation is provided by examples such as those in (68):

(68)   *The prospects for peace are for a long delay.
        *Their talk of vacations was of snow and of fireplaces.
        *The plan for John to leave is that Bill should stay.
        *The question whether John should leave is why Bill stayed.

    We have seen in this section that if the pairs of sentences in (55) and (64) are to be related transformationally, the PP movement rules that accomplish this are structure-preserving. This is so because the PP's that occur in noun phrases, are sisters to verbs, and are sisters to VP's are generable by at least three different independently motivated phrases structure rules, the two in (50) and the one in (54). We saw in the previous chapter that there is a focus placement rule for cleft sentences that is structure-preserving and applies to PP's. In the following section we will see that the evidence favoring a structure-preserving formulation of WH fronting involves the transformational movement of PP's in a crucial way (i.e., certain special conditions on WH fronting are inexplicable unless it is granted that the structure-preserving constraint applies to PP movement rules). Thus there is a reasonable amount of evidence that PP movement rules are, like NP, S, and AP movements, structure-preserving.

V.6   THE NATURE OF WH FRONTING

    The remainder of this chapter is devoted to the statement and effects of WH fronting in the structure-preserving framework, and to explanations of apparently exceptional data regarding the operation of this rule.
    WH fronting moves an NP, a PP, or an AP to the front of the clause if they are introduced by one of the WH words such as who, what, which, when, where, why, how, whose, whether, and a few others. (The WH word may be preceded by a preposition in many constructions.) In certain contexts the rule may not operate, and in others it moves a constituent that dominates the constituent introduced by the WH word, as in the father of whom. It is usually held that general conditions on movement rules predict these special

cases automatically, so that the statement of WH fronting itself is straight-forward; these general conditions are studied extensively in Ross (1967a).

Some typical uses of WH fronting are given in (69), along with the usual name given to the construction the WH word introduces:

(69) **Direct Questions in Full Sentence Form:**
Whose father was the President?
In which town does he reside?
How did he achieve this?
How big does this appear on a screen?

Direct Questions in Infinitive Form; Only Why Permitted:
Why buy more stock at this time?
Why knock yourself out for someone else?

Exclamations:
What big paws he has!
How brave he is!

Conditional Clauses:
Whatever measure they take, they are sure to fail.
However long you stay, you will be welcome.

Relative Clauses in Full Sentence Form:
I found a man who you can buy tickets from.
I found a man from whom you can buy tickets.
The taste of what they are serving is delicious.
The only place where I feel at home is in a city.

Relative Clauses in Infinitive Form:
I found a man from whom to buy tickets.
You have fifteen days in which to finish.
Some tools with which to work will soon arrive by mail.

Indirect Questions after Nouns in Full Sentence Form:
The problem of how often we should meet hasn't been discussed.
John's understanding of how this works is faulty.

Indirect Questions after Verbs in Full Sentence Form:
I wonder whether he will show up.
I forgot how efficient she was.
They weren't sure (of) why she left.

Indirect Questions after Nouns in Infinitive Form:
The question of who to consult in this matter is perplexing.
They have no knowledge of which routes to take.

Indirect Questions after Verbs in Infinitive Form:
They told you how to operate that.
John asked Mary when to stop.

WH fronting is clearly not a local movement transformation nor a root transformation. (It operates in embedded sentences that do not exhibit subject—auxiliary inversion; furthermore, root transformations that are fronting rules take constituents to the front of the HIGHEST S in the tree.) Thus if the structure-preserving hypothesis is to stand without major revision, WH fronting must be a structure-preserving rule.

However, it is clear that WH fronting effects the movement of the phrasal constituents NP, AP, and PP, and equally clear that such phrase nodes should not be generated by the base in sentence-initial (presubject) position. If they were, many of the root transformations discussed in Chapter II, such as topical-ization, directional adverb preposing, comparative substitution, etc., could incorrectly apply in structure-preserving fashion in dependent clauses. Further, generating empty nodes in presubject position can be allowed only if some base construction exhibits such (nonempty) nodes, according to the restriction on nodes that are generated by base rules that was set up in Chapter I, and no such construction exists.

Thus if we considered WH fronting solely as a transformational operation on phrase nodes, it would violate the structure-preserving constraint. How-ever, there is a characteristic of WH fronting that does fit the paradigm of structure-preserving rules nicely: If it is viewed as AN OPERATION ON THE SYNTACTIC ELEMENT WH, then it holds that the rule moves WH from one posi-tion in the tree to another position where this element is independently gene-rated in the base, the COMP position. This characteristic of WH fronting, in fact, differentiates it from the root transformations of Chapter II—they cannot be construed as operations on features or categories that are also generated in the COMP position in the base.

I have already proposed (in Chapter III) the formal statement of the condition that permits WH fronting to be classed as structure-preserving, which I repeat here:

(70) **The Sentence Boundary Condition:** *If A_j is a rightmost or a leftmost constituent of an S, a transformational operation that substitutes B for A_j is structure-preserving if B dominates A_i, provided that there is no S such that* $B = X \left[_s Y A_i Z _s\right] W$.

This condition does not require, incidentally, that A be mentioned in the struc-tural description of the transformation. In particular, WH fronting generally substitutes constituents for the feature complex [COMP, WH], but only COMP need (or should, as we will see subsequently) be mentioned in the structural description of the rule. It is nonetheless true in such cases that WH is the leftmost constituent of an S that undergoes WH fronting.

In the following section, I provide and justify a particular formulation of WH fronting. In subsequent sections, it will be shown how several apparently irregular restrictions on WH fronting are predicted by the structure-preserving constraint.

V.7   STATEMENT OF WH FRONTING

A formulation of WH fronting can be given as (71), where COMP is the sentence-initial grammatical formative category proposed in Bresnan (1970):

(71) **WH *Fronting:***[8] $COMP-X-\left[\begin{smallmatrix} NP \\ AP \\ PP \end{smallmatrix}\right\}$ $(P)+WH+Y]-Z \Rightarrow 3-2-\emptyset-4$

An important observation about (71) is that it does not require that WH be immediately dominated by the phrase node that is fronted [i.e., that appears in the structural description of (71)]. This is necessary not only because (71)

---

[8] Several comments are in order that do not bear directly on the development in the text but concern the validity of (71) as a statement of WH fronting.

It might at first be thought that WH fronting in questions can move AP's, whereas WH fronting in relative clauses cannot, thereby establishing a difference between the two uses of the rule (or the two rules) that necessitates crucially mentioning phrasal categories in two statements of WH fronting. However, the relevant difference seems, rather, that WH fronting in relative clauses never affects the WH word *how*, even though it introduces an NP: *The men how many I've met are polite, *I'll get the bread how much you want*, etc. Thus the difference in question seems to turn on the nature of the WH element (and not on the phrasal node involved), which is consistent with the argument in the text that WH fronting is basically a transformational operation on WH.

French and English have similar WH fronting rules, although in French WH fronting must always move a P with the following sister NP. Perhaps notational conventions should allow for different statements of the rule in the two languages. On the other hand, this difference in WH fronting seems reflected in other rules common to English and French, as noted by Ross (1967a), so perhaps the conventions for writing individual rules should prevent us from so expressing the difference. In this case, (71) could stand as the statement of WH fronting for both English and French, with the difference between the two languages being expressed by output conditions on prepositions such as those proposed in van Riemsdijk (1972) for a dialect of Swiss German.

As it stands, (71) appears to require a condition that $3 \neq (P)+S$, to prevent the rule from moving the following constituents in boldface or parentheses:

> *John is wondering (about **why she's late**).*
> *Mary questioned them (on **whether they had been home**).*
>
> **About why she's late is John wondering?*
> **Why she's late is John wondering about?*
>
> **On whether they had been home did Mary question them?*
> **Whether they had been home did Mary question them on?*

(The preceding starred examples are in fact analogous to sentences in which topicalization is incorrectly applied to a phrasal constituent in a *yes—no* question: **About books does Harry talk? *Books does Harry talk about?* If they have some marginal status, the fronting rule involved is topicalization, not WH fronting.) To my knowledge, most treatments of WH fronting neglect to state this condition. However, note that this condition follows directly from the sentence boundary condition (i.e., from the definition of structure-preserving rule that is applicable here), and so need not be stated separately in this analysis.

moves PP's, which do not immediately dominate WH, but also because of cases like those in (72):

(72)   *Whose father's store did they furnish with the most merchandise?*
        Whose father should we take this to?
        How many young people did you see there?
        How intelligent a woman is she?
        How big a bear did you capture?
        How many feet high should we make this bookcase?
        I won't go into the tunnel, no matter how many miles longer the
          other road is.[9]
        How frighteningly short life seems!
        How many feet behind the house should I put the table?

The question may be asked, What prevents the smaller phrase nodes that dominate WH in the preceding examples from being fronted by themselves, as in (73)—(74)?

(73)   **Whose father's did they furnish store with the most merchandise?*
        **Whose should we take this to father?*

(74)   **How many did you see young people there?*
        **How intelligent is she a woman?*
        **How big did you capture a bear?*
        **How many feet should we make this bookcase high?*
        **How many should we make this bookcase feet high?*
        **I won't go into the tunnel, no matter how many miles the other*
          road is longer.
        **I won't go into the tunnel, no matter how many the other road is*
          miles longer.
        **How frighteningly life seems short!*
Cf.   *How many feet should I put the table behind the house?*

Ross (1967a) answers this question by proposing the "left branch condition," a special case of the "A-over-A principle" (cf. Chomsky, 1968, Chapter 2 for discussion):

(75)   **Ross's Left Branch Condition:** *No* NP *that is the leftmost constituent of a larger* NP *can be reordered out of this* NP *by a transformational rule.*

---

[9]*No matter* is not fronted by WH fronting but resembles, rather, a subordinating conjunction: *I'm not going in there, no matter if you give me $100.* Earlier in this chapter, it was pointed out that we expect similar ranges of complements for P and for V, and *no matter* can be taken as a P which requires an indirect question.

Ross analyzes both adjective phrases and intensifier phrases as noun phrases, so that the examples in (74), as well as those in (73), are to be explained by this condition. However, I do not think these are correct analyses (cf. Schachter, 1973, for criticisms); rather, I propose that the left branch condition should be stated in more general terms as follows:

(76) ***Restated Left Branch Condition:*** *No syntactic element to the left of the head in an* NP *or an* AP *can be reordered out of this larger constituent by a major (nonlocal) transformational operation.*[10]

In studying stylistic movement of phrase nodes in certain styles of English poetry, Banfield (1973b) states Ross's condition in approximately this way. It should be noted that I have expressly excluded local transformations from (76) because of the quantifier postposition rule discussed in Section VI.3.4 that relates *all the boys will leave* to *the boys all will leave*.

The restated left branch condition correctly does not restrict WH fronting of phrase nodes to the left of the head in PP's, as in (77), whereas (75) incorrectly would, given the usual contention of Ross that a PP is an NP:

(77)   *How many feet should I put the table behind the house?*

Before we discuss the interplay of WH fronting and the structure-preserving constraint, I should explain why the convention of "Pied Piping," proposed

---

[10] Certain formal restatements of this condition suggest themselves. For example, it could be stated in terms of the notion "recursive side of a phrase node" developed in Chapter I:

> *No syntactic element on the nonrecursive side of a cyclic phrase node* H″ *can be reordered out of this larger constituent by a major transformational operation.*

Alternatively, (76) might be extended in some way to phrase nodes to the left of a lexical head of any cyclic node (INCLUDING S, whose lexical head is V), so that the constraint proposed in Bresnan (1972a), to the effect that a subject NP cannot move out of an S over the COMP node, might follow as a special case. If this were to be so, the node $\overline{S}$ proposed by Bresnan (which includes COMP and the subject NP) would be cyclic, but S would not be, and $\overline{S}$ would have to "prune" in the absence of COMP; i.e., COMP would be in this sense the "specifier" of S. None of this seems implausible, but I have not investigated the area in detail.

The statement of WH fronting in (71) is somewhat redundant in that the grammar independently specifies that WH is generated in the COMP position and in the specifiers of NP and AP, and also states in (71) that WH fronting applies to WH elements "only" in these positions. This redundancy might be eliminated by restating the left branch condition as a positive requirement on the operation of transformations:

> *If a syntactic element* C *in* N″ *or* A″ *is to the left of the head in that phrase, then any major transformational operation that reorders* C *with respect to elements exterior to* N″ *or* A″ *must also so reorder* N″ *or* A″.

Given this constraint, WH fronting could be stated as follows:

$$\text{COMP}-X-(\text{P})+\text{WH}-Z \implies 3-2-\emptyset-4$$

Such a restatement of WH fronting brings out very clearly that the rule is structure-preserving, i.e., that it moves an element WH to another position where that element is generable in the base.

in Ross (1967a), does not play a role in my discussion of WH fronting. In Ross's view the Pied Piping convention, and not the statement of WH fronting, is responsible for the fact that the "larger" constituents in (72) are fronted:

(78) **Pied Piping Convention:** *Any transformation that is stated in such a way as to effect the reordering of some specified node* NP, *where this node is preceded and followed by variables in the structural index of the rule, may apply to this* NP *or to any noncoordinate* NP *that dominates it, as long as there are no occurrences of any coordinate node, nor of the node* S, *on the branch connecting the higher node and the specified node.*

The Pied Piping convention also accounts for examples like (79), where WH fronting apparently "takes along" a larger (boldface) constituent in which WH does NOT appear to the left of its head (as required by my statement of WH fronting):

(79) *?Students* **the height of the lettering on whose jackets** *the administration prescribes almost always rebel.*
      ?Students **the lettering on whose jackets** *the administration prescribes the height of almost always rebel.*

I grant that some convention or rule must account for the marginally acceptable examples in (79); however, I claim that such a mechanism (some version or revision of Pied Piping) is not the same as that which generates (80), namely, the WH fronting rule itself:

(80) *Students* **whose jackets** *the administration prescribes the height of the lettering on almost always rebel.*
      A student **whose jacket's size and color** *the administration has prescribed is likely to rebel.*

My reasoning is that sentences like those in (80) are totally acceptable, while those in (79) seem systematically to be only marginally acceptable. This difference I think has a theoretically interesting explanation, but first let us compare more data accounted for by WH fronting itself with data for which Pied Piping is necessary:

(81) a.   *The boy whose guardian's employer we elected president ratted on us.*
      b.   *?The boy the employer of whose guardian we elected president ratted on us.*
      a.   *The boy about whose guardian's employer we were talking was absent.*

b.   **The boy about the employer of whose guardian we were talking was absent.*

a.   *They are interested in any authors who you might have books by.*

   They are interested in any authors whose books you might have.

b.   **They are interested in any authors books by whom you might have.*

a.   *The strikers are interested in the works whose authors their leftist friends have books by.*

b.   **The strikers are interested in the works books by whose authors their leftist friends have.*

a.   *The airports which we can find out the visibility at are all closed for the night.*

   The airports whose availability we can find out about are all closed for the night.

b.   *?The airports the visibility at which we can find out are all closed for the night.*

a.   *I haven't yet seen a wall which you can easily make out the pictures on.*

b.   *?I haven't yet seen a wall the pictures on which you can easily make out.*

a.   *?A strike which we shouldn't forget about the outcome of took place at Republic Steel.*

   A strike whose outcome we shouldn't forget about took place at Republic Steel.

b.   *?A strike the outcome of which we shouldn't forget about took place at Republic Steel.*

The (a) examples in (81) are generated, according to the analysis given here, by WH fronting, while the (b) sentences require some additional mechanism such as Pied Piping to generate them. As noted previously, this difference in the grammatical source of such constructions seems to be reflected consistently by differences in acceptability.

The explanation for these differences, I would claim, is that the Pied Piping convention, which accounts for the reorderings in (79) and (81b), is a device of the stylistic component of the grammar; i.e., it has the same properties as the "stylistic transformations" defined and studied in Banfield (1973b).

According to Banfield, various free word order and deletion phenomena (particularly various "gapping" patterns), which very nearly characterize a poet like Milton's departures from normal English syntax, exhibit several properties that differentiate them from the constructions produced by strictly grammatical transformations: The rules or principles that produce these free word order and gapping patterns are always optional operations; they never depend on or introduce specified morphemes; they always follow all grammatical rules in a derivation; and they generally are not a source of ambiguity (i.e., they do not apply if they produce ambiguity with strictly grammatical sentences). Moreover, Banfield notes that such rules generally resist formulation in terms of linear analyzability conditions (i.e., they cannot be properly stated in the algebra of transformations) and that they CHARACTERISTICALLY PRODUCE OUTPUTS THAT ARE LESS ACCEPTABLE THAN THEIR INPUTS AND ARE CONSIDERED BY NATIVE SPEAKERS TO BE (SUCCESSFUL OR UNSUCCESSFUL) TURNS OF PHRASES OR FIGURES.

It seems as if ALL these characteristics hold for the sentences that I claim are generated only by virtue of a device (Pied Piping) that is distinct from WH fronting. In particular, whether or not Banfield has sufficiently and correctly characterized the formal properties of the stylistic transformations, it seems that their outputs and the outputs of Pied Piping should be grouped together because of the type of intuitions one has on their marginal grammatical status. This permits WH fronting as in (70) to stand as formulated, even though it does not of itself account for the examples in (79) and (81b).

V.8   *EXAMINATION OF THE SEVERAL CASES OF WH FRONTING*

WH fronting has been stated as a substitution of a phrase node dominating WH for the sentence-initial COMP node. However, the structure-preserving constraint requires that the rule apply only if WH is present in the COMP position as either an empty or a filled node. In order to see that the constraint makes correct and interesting predictions about this rule, we will examine how the rule operates for each configuration that can appear in the COMP position.

The base rule that specifies the possibilities for COMP I take to be the following:

(82) $$S \rightarrow COMP-NP-\cdots \left(\begin{Bmatrix} WH \\ FOR \end{Bmatrix} \right)$$

The three feature complexes COMP, [COMP, WH], and [COMP, FOR] correspond, respectively, to the complementizers *that*, *whether*, and *for* studied in Bresnan (1972a). I accept Bresnan's arguments that *whether* and *for* are present in deep structure and that *that* is inserted under COMP by a rather late transformational rule; in fact I will give supplementary justification for this distinction between deep and surface complementizers.[11]

Given the possibility of empty nodes and the lack of a deep COMP that is both + WH and + FOR, rule (82) can yield five different base configurations, which we will examine separately:

(83)
$$\text{COMP}$$
$$|$$
$$\Delta$$

(84)
$$\text{COMP} \quad \text{and} \quad \text{COMP}$$
$$\text{WH} \qquad\qquad \text{WH}$$
$$| \qquad\qquad\qquad |$$
$$\textit{whether} \qquad\qquad \Delta$$

(85)
$$\text{COMP} \quad \text{and} \quad \text{COMP}$$
$$\text{FOR} \qquad\qquad \text{FOR}$$
$$| \qquad\qquad\qquad |$$
$$\textit{for} \qquad\qquad \Delta$$

1. $[_{\text{COMP}} \Delta]$. This configuration underlies *that* clause complements and relative clauses exhibiting *that*, in which WH fronting does not apply. (These are discussed at length in Section IV.3.1.) Typically a late rule of *that* insertion replaces Δ. The structure-preserving constraint prohibits WH fronting in this case because neither WH nor one of the phrasal categories dominating WH that are moved by WH fronting appears in the COMP position.

Bresnan (1972a) has argued that sentence-initial *than/as* in comparative constructions is a complementizer. Since these morphemes occur ONLY in these constructions—i.e., they introduce sentences whose deep structure position is in the specifier system of adjectives—we can assign them a deep structure $[_{\text{COMP}} \Delta]$ as well. *Than/as* is then introduced by an early rule dependent on this (underlying) context. (For our purposes this is equivalent to saying that *than/as* is a deep structure COMP but of sharply limited distribution.)

In this view, comparative clauses are never introduced by WH in deep structure, and the structure-preserving constraint predicts that such clauses never exhibit WH fronting. However, nothing in principle prohibits a deletion of *as* or *than*, in which case we would expect the *that* insertion rule to produce

[11]A careful study of exclamatory constructions in French by Milner (1974) concludes that these constructions, as well as interrogatives, must be introduced by the same complementizer (here, WH). This means that embedded as well as independent clause exclamatives can have the same transformational derivations (including WH fronting) as interrogatives, provided that French and English are sufficiently similar in the relevant respects. Examples of embedded exclamatives:

I had forgotten how wonderful he was!
Have you seen what a big car they have?

a surface *that* in a comparative construction. Thus we can expect *that*, but never a WH word, to alternate with *than/as* in some comparative constructions.

A case of this sort is the basically comparative construction that appears in relative clause positions modifying *the same* N or *a different* N:

(86)   *He bought the same type of cereal as I bought yesterday.*
        A different machine than the one you have will be needed.
        He likes the same people as you like.

In some contexts the *as* of this construction may be deleted; as expected, the late *that* insertion rule can then apply:

(87)   *He bought the same type of cereal that I bought yesterday.*
        He likes the same people that you like.

Also as expected, the absence of a deep structure WH means that WH fronting cannot apply:

(88)   **He bought the same type of cereal which I bought yesterday.*
        *He likes the same people who you like.

Other analyses could, of course, exclude WH words in comparative constructions without difficulty; I present (88) only as an interesting alternation in the COMP position that is consistent with the general framework being developed.

2. $[_{\text{COMP,WH}}$ *whether*$]$. Clauses that are direct or indirect questions $[$cf. (69) for examples$]$ are derived from underlying structures with a *whether* complementizer. An NP or an NP with a WH in the specifier position can replace this (recoverable) $[_{\text{WH}}$ *whether*$]$ when WH fronting applies in such constructions.

3. $[_{\text{COMP,WH}} \Delta]$. We recall that empty nodes play no part in subcategorization, i.e., that this COMP configuration cannot be the deep structure configuration with verbs, nouns, and adjectives that are lexically specified for indirect question (WH) complements.[12] As far as cooccurrence restrictions are concerned, an empty COMP, WH is just like the neutral COMP (i.e., the surface *that*). Just as with COMP, the Δ will block any derivation from which it is not removed, and one possibility is the replacement of Δ by the neutral complementizer *that*. Or the Δ of this configuration must be removed by some other rule— i.e., WH fronting—if the derivation is not to block.

Now WH fronting cannot take place in dependent clauses that are not questions unless some rule has inserted WH into some specifier within the clause, and only the relative clause is of this type. (The insertion of WH into the specifier of the NP in the relative that is coreferential with the NP modified

---

[12]Otherwise we would expect *that* to alternate with *whether* in indirect questions, yielding **I wondered that he would come on time.*

by the relative clause is discussed in the previous chapter.) Therefore the COMP configuration under discussion results in well-formed English surface structures in the case of relative clauses; in particular, this is the COMP configuration for relative clauses that exhibit WH words.

The fact that AP's are not fronted in relative clauses is due to the fact that WH insertion in relatives never results in the WH word *how*, as discussed earlier.

It is perhaps well to keep in mind that this use of an empty WH node for relative clauses is identical to the use of empty phrase nodes throughout the text. My usage of empty nodes is one possible formalization of the notion that certain transformations move a constituent to another position in the tree where the phrase structure rules "could" generate such a constituent; empty nodes may not be the best formalization of this idea, but my use of it is consistent here. WH can be generated in COMP position in deep structure, and WH fronting is a transformation that moves WH to the COMP position, whether or not that position exhibits a filled deep structure WH in any given construction.

What does differentiate my treatment of WH fronting from my treatment of other phrase node movements is that I invoke the sentence boundary condition to explain why this rule, and only this rule among leftward movements, can move constituents that CONTAIN, but are not identical to, the element that is moved in structure-preserving fashion. That is, the phrase nodes moved by WH fronting are moved to positions where such categories CANNOT be generated in the base.

4. $[_{\text{COMP, FOR}} \, for]$ or $[_{\text{COMP, FOR}} \, \Delta]$. The second of these configurations never results in well-formed derivations, since no transformation, to our present knowledge, moves or inserts an element with the distinguishing feature of the complementizer *for* (represented here in ad hoc fashion as FOR) into the COMP position.

As with finite clauses (clauses with TENSE), the only embedded clauses introduced by *for* in which WH fronting might apply are indirect questions and relative clauses. Let us turn first to relative clauses; the existence of infinitival relatives with the complementizer *for* and certain of their properties were first brought to my attention by Edward Klima (personal communication).

According to the definition of a structure-preserving movement, WH fronting cannot move WH into either of the COMP configurations being discussed, since the S expansion rule in (82) does not permit WH and FOR to cooccur. When we examine the occurring infinitival relatives, however, we find not total exclusion of WH fronting but, rather, some extremely limited possibilities of application quite different from the range of possibilities in finite questions and relative clauses:

(89)   *I found an usher from whom to buy tickets.*
              Some tools with which to fix the table will soon arrive.
              You have fifteen months in which to pay.

In (89) WH fronting has replaced a *for* complementizer, apparently in non-structure-preserving fashion, with a prepositional phrase.[13] But we note that a similar replacement with a noun phrase is not permitted:

(90)   **I found an usher who (for Mary) to buy tickets from.* (cf. *I found an usher who Mary can buy tickets from.*)

      *Some tools which (for you) to fix the table with will soon arrive. (cf. *Some tools which you can fix the table with will soon arrive.*)

      *John is looking on the map for a route which (for his guests) to take back. (cf. *John is looking on the map for a route which his guests can take back.*)

      *What (for you) to fix the table with will soon arrive. (cf. *What you will fix the table with will soon arrive.*)

Furthermore, WH fronting can apparently operate in clauses with a *for* complementizer as in (89) only if the sequence *for* + subject NP has been deleted:

(91)   **I found an usher from whom for Mary to buy tickets.* (cf. *I found an usher from whom Mary can buy tickets.*)

      *Some tools with which for you to fix the table will soon arrive. (cf. *Some tools with which you can fix the table will soon arrive.*)

      *You have fifteen months in which for somebody to pay. (cf. *You have fifteen months in which somebody must pay.*)

The data in (89)−(91) would all be explained by the structure-preserving hypothesis IF the structure of a sentence with a *for* complementizer is as in (92) at some point in the derivation prior to WH fronting:

(92)

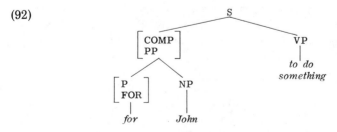

[13] Some speakers apparently reject (89) as well as (90)−(91). Such a dialect is easy to describe; we simply say that the rule particular to *for* clause subjects, to be justified later, applies after WH fronting. It is this rule that creates the structure needed for the derivation of the sentences in (89).

    I refer to the subordinate infinitive clauses in (89)−(91) as "relative clauses." Perhaps they should be derived from some other source; the only relevant point is that WH fronting operates in this construction under the conditions outlined in the text.

(It may be that the COMP node should also retain the feature FOR; nothing in what follows depends on this detail.)

Before seeing if (92) can be justified, let us see how it provides the basis of an explanation for (89)—(91). As seen earlier, WH fronting effects the substitution of a phrase node for COMP. If COMP is also dominating a subject NP as in (92), replacement of COMP results in a nonrecoverable deletion of the subject that is not permitted. (Even if some deletion were defined as recoverable, such as the deletion of *one*, the replacement of COMP with another PP by means of WH fronting would effect that deletion.) In any case the structure in (92) predicts that the COMP substitution rule, WH fronting, operates in *for* clauses only if there is no surface subject in such clauses; this explains the examples in (91).

Whatever the rules that effect the deletion of the subject in a *for* clause, including, in one common view, equi-NP deletion and a rule deleting a subject *one*, the complementizer *for* is in all such cases deleted (perhaps by a separate rule) if and only if the subject is. Thus the results of these various deletions on the structure in (92) would be (93), if the option of leaving Δ is taken.

(93)

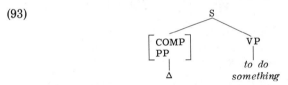

As noted earlier, WH fronting CANNOT SUBSTITUTE WH in structure-preserving fashion for a COMP that includes the feature FOR. However, if WH fronting applies to a clause with the structure of (93), it CAN SUBSTITUTE A PP BUT NOT AN NP in accordance with the structure-preserving constraint. And in fact this is exactly the condition on WH fronting in *for* clauses exemplified in (89)—(90). That is, in *for* clauses WH fronting is a structure-preserving movement of the PP node.[14]

Thus the limited possibilities for applying WH fronting in clauses with *for* complementizers is predicted exactly by the structure-preserving constraint, PROVIDED THAT justification for representing such clauses as in (92) at some stage in the transformational derivation can be found. Of course the rule that produces such a representation must itself conform to the structure-preserving constraint.[15] This rule is the subject of the following section.

---

[14]The definition of structure preserving does not require that the node substituted for be a base node; it may, as in this case, be generated by a preceding local transformation.

[15]In the analysis in the text, the rule or rules that delete the subject NP in infinitival relatives, so as to yield (93), must PRECEDE WH fronting in such a clause. If one such rule is equi-NP deletion, then WH fronting apparently would not apply in infinitival relatives during the transformational cycle of the relative clause S, but on a succeeding cycle after equi-NP deletion applies; this is because equi-NP deletion, as we usually think of it, does not apply on the cycle of the S whose subject it deletes.

The other kind of infinitive in which WH fronting can apply is an indirect question infinitive. We note first the striking contrast between these infinitives, which DO have a deep structure WH element in the COMP position, and the infinitival relatives just discussed; the deep structure WH is what permits all the usual WH fronting possibilities [fronted NP's, PP's, and AP's are in bold-face in (94)]:

(94)   *I asked John **who** to consult about this matter.*
         *They told us **what firm** to buy tickets from.*
         *The question of **how many renters** to take in is difficult.*
         *She wasn't sure about **how** to move the table.*

The fact that infinitival indirect questions exhibit behavior in (94) that indicates a deep structure *whether* means that these infinitives are NOT instances of clauses with a COMP *for*, since (82) does not permit WH and FOR together in the COMP position. And in fact these infinitives (again in contrast to infinitival relatives) never exhibit this *for*, as predicted:

Footnote 15 continued

This might be considered somewhat striking—that WH fronting does not apply on the cycle of the S in which it preposes a constituent. However, on further examination we see that this view is consistent with certain other facts, on the one hand, and, on the other, that the conclusion is necessary only given somewhat unjustified assumptions about the nature and/or existence of equi-NP deletion.

First, we saw in Chapter IV that WH fronting can be treated as a unified process only if it follows a rule that inserts WH into an NP inside the relative clause, called "WH insertion." In fact WH insertion depends on the coreference of the NP to which it applies and of the antecedent NP for the relative clause; thus WH insertion, which precedes WH fronting, takes place on a cycle of some constituent that includes both the relative clause S and its antecedent NP, i.e., a later cycle than that of the relative clause S itself. This, then, indicates independently than WH fronting does not always apply in the cycle of the S in which it preposes a constituent.

Second, there seem to be different ways of viewing the deletion of the subject NP in infinitival relatives as an operation THAT TAKES PLACE ON THE CYCLE OF THAT RELATIVE CLAUSE S. If any of these are correct, there is no reason to assume that the analysis in this chapter implies anything about which cycle WH fronting applies on.

For example, there are supporters of the view that equi-NP deletion, as a rule that deletes an NP under coreference, does not exist (cf. Jackendoff, 1972, and Brame, in preparation). If, instead, infinitives with no surface subjects are derived from deep structures with deleted dummy subjects, there is no reason to assume that this deletion is an operation ordered on a later cycle than that of the infinitive itself.

Another view might be based on the extensive literature that attempts to establish that the NP that is coreferential to the NP deleted by equi-NP deletion (i.e., the "controller" NP) is to be determined by general principles [refinements of Rosenbaum's (1967) "erasure principle"] and, hence, need not be mentioned in the structural description of equi-NP deletion at all. In such a case the relevant subcase of this rule might be written simply as follows:

Equi-NP Deletion in Infinitives: *for* $+\text{NP}-\text{VP} \Rightarrow \emptyset - 2$

Again, there is no reason to assume that this rule cannot be ordered on the cycle of the infinitive itself; that is, there is no reason to assume that it must be ordered on a cycle late enough to include every possible "controller" NP, since they do not appear in its structural description.

(95)   **I asked John who for them to consult in this matter.*
     *They told us what firm for the company to buy tickets from.
     *The question of how many renters for an older landlord to take in
          is difficult.
     *She wasn't sure about how for them to move the table.

I conclude that WH fronting is never a structure-preserving operation on WH when COMP contains FOR, as the structure-preserving constraint requires. The sole case when WH fronting applies in such clauses is to PP's, and I will now show that in this case PP is being moved to a position where the grammar independently generates PP; i.e., the movement is structure-preserving.

V.9   THE RULE OF FOR *PHRASE FORMATION*

In the previous section it was found that the structure-preserving constraint correctly predicts a number of restrictions on WH fronting, PROVIDED that some preceding transformation can be motivated such that (96) is transformed into (97):

(96)

(97)

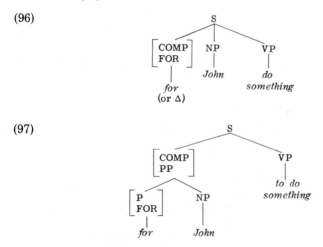

Clearly a transformation that effects this cannot be a root or structure-preserving operation. However, a LOCAL TRANSFORMATION, which produces the right dominance relations and satisfies the restrictions on this type of rule given in Chapter I, can easily be stated:

(98)   **For *Phrase Formation:*** $X - [_{\text{COMP}} \text{FOR}] - \text{NP} - Y \Rightarrow 1 - 2 + 3 - \emptyset - 4$

A condition must be placed on (98): NP cannot dominate WH. This accounts for the exclusion of examples like those in (99):

(99)   *The man for whom to realize this first was John.* (cf. *The man to*
          realize this first was John.)
       The man for whose friends to realize this is John.
       They pointed out the ones for whom they preferred to leave first.
       For whom does John prefer to leave first?
       Who does John prefer for to leave first?

(There of course remains the more general problem of accounting for the block-
ing of any relative clause structure in which the relativized WH form does not
get fronted either because of extraction constraints or because of restrictions
on particular rules.)

     We will turn later to the question of how (98) introduces the node PP
in derived structure; first, however, I present motivation for the rule that is
independent of the explanation it can provide (cf. the preceding section) for
the restrictions on infinitival relatives exemplified in (90)−(91).

     In Section II.10 (cf. especially note 20), we saw that certain adverbial PP's
can be placed between the COMP and the subject NP in various dependent
clauses. Examples of this type are as follows:

(100) *Mary asked me if, in St. Louis, John could rent a house cheap.*
       He doesn't intend that, in these circumstances, we be rehired.
       You should do that so that, when you're old, you'll be protected.
       They build machines that, during lunch hours, businessmen can
          exercise on.
       She got as many votes in the countryside as, in the last election,
          her predecessor got in Paris.

Of all the complementizers, only *for* excludes adverbs in the position in question:

(101) *Mary arranged for, in St. Louis, John to rent a house cheap.*
       He doesn't intend for, in these circumstances, us to be rehired.
       You should do that in order for, when you're old, us to be able to
          live well.
       They build machines for, during lunch hours, businessmen to
          exercise on.
       She got enough votes in the countryside for, in the next election,
          us to expect her to win.

     The structure in (97) induced by (98)──in particular, the claim that in
for clauses the surface subject is dominated by COMP──explains the contrast
between (100) and (101) in either of two alternative views of how the adverbs
in question come to occupy sentence-initial position.

If one claims that the adverbs themselves are preposed into the context COMP_____, then the structure in (97) claims that the preposed adverbs may appear AFTER the surface subject in *for* clauses (which is true, given the expected comma intonation). In conjunction with a general condition that would not allow transformations—at least nonlocal transformations—to move material INTO a PP, the structure in (97) also explains (101). Such a condition would seem, upon a little reflection, to be obviously necessary, and is no doubt an extension of Chomsky's (1965) "lower-S" constraint.

On the other hand, if one claims, as I do in Section II.10, that the sentences in (100) are generated by moving S (where $\overline{S}$ = COMP−S, as in Bresnan, 1970) over the adverbial PP's by a root transformation, then the fact that in (97), after *for* phrase formation applies, the surface subject is no longer in S but, rather, under COMP explains why the examples in (101) are ungrammatical. [In fact in (97) the subject NP and the predicate do not even form a constituent, and so could not be moved by a transformation.]

Thus in either account of how the sentences in (100) are generated, postulating that $[_{COMP} for] + NP$ is a surface constituent explains the contrast in between (100) and (101).

For phrase formation further accounts for the appearance of the infinitive marker *to* in clauses with the *for* complementizer. Generally this marker appears with verb phrases that are not specially marked by the participle morphemes (*ing* or *en*) and have lost their subject NP (for example, as a result of subject raising, equi-NP deletion, or deletion of the subject *one*); this pattern is pointed out in Kiparsky and Kiparsky (1971). If we make precise the notion "loss of subject" by a rule stating that a VP that is the head of an S loses its subject when it no longer has an NP sister constituent on its left, then this explains the appearance of *to* in surface structures corresponding to (97). Alternatively, all VP's whose verbs have no suffix after affix movement can be assigned *to* (cf. Section VI.2.5), and then *to* can be deleted in the context COMP−NP−(AUX) −_____. Such a rule correctly does not apply to the structure in (97).

For phrase formation can also explain why the pronouns in the subject NP of *for* clauses exhibit objective (not subjective) pronouns. Klima (1969) argues that in the maximally simple (easiest-learned) dialect of Modern English the subject pronouns (*I, he, she, we, they*) appear in just those NP's that are immediately dominated by S. For example, Klima points out that the most common dialect of Modern American English does not exhibit subject pronouns in predicate nominatives, which are immediately dominated by VP: *it's me, that's him*, etc.[16]

---

[16]It should be remarked that subject pronouns, though assigned near surface structure in English, are not assigned to those NP's that come to be immediately dominated by S as a result of root transformations such as topicalization and left dislocation.

Klima also remarks that children very commonly use subject pronouns in single-NP subjects (*I left, He left,* etc.) but object pronouns in conjoined-NP subjects: *Me and him left* or *Me and him, we left.* This is explained by the fact that the subject NP's in conjoined subjects are immediately dominated by another NP rather than by S. Immediate dominance by S in derived structure as the defining condition for subject pronouns also explains the dialect of Modern English in which *whom* (an object pronoun form) appears ONLY if a PP is WH fronted, whereas *who* appears in all other cases: *To whom did you write?* and *Who did you write to?* versus **To who did you write?* and **Whom did you write to?* (for this dialect).

The derived structure of the COMP—subject NP sequence given by (98) provides the intervening node between the subject NP and the dominating S that explains the occurrence of object pronouns in such subjects, according to Klima's subject pronoun condition. The invariant appearance of object pronouns in *for* clauses could not be explained in terms of the deep structure in (96) unless an ad hoc exception to Klima's principle were added to the grammar of English.[17]

Let us now consider the question of how *for* phrase formation assigns a PP node in derived structure to the FOR—NP sequence. First, nothing in the

---

[17] There is a characteristic of *for* clauses that *for* phrase formation does not account for, namely, that such clauses never exhibit TENSE or the modal auxiliaries. The following line of argument, however, shows that this fact should NOT be associated with *for* phrase formation.

In Emonds (1970) I argue that the present subjunctive in English, which also lacks TENSE and the modal auxiliaries, should be transformationally related to infinitival *for* clauses. Examples of this construction:

> They insist **that he be given more money**.
> **That she not know this before tomorrow** is crucial.

The arguments for relating *for* clauses and the present subjunctive have to do with their similar internal structure (vis-à-vis the auxiliaries, the position of *not*, etc.), with similarity of distribution, and with their identical or near-identical meanings, compared to the meaning of an ordinary *that* clause:

> It is preferable that the room be air-conditioned.
> It is preferable for the room to be air-conditioned.
> It is preferable that the room is air-conditioned.

The best way to relate these constructions within our framework is to derive present subjunctives from *for* clauses by deleting a deep structure FOR BEFORE *for* phrase formation as in (98) applies. In this way, the lack of modal auxiliaries and TENSE, and the common element of meaning shared by present subjunctives and surface *for* clauses, can be attributed to the deep structure complementizer FOR (which is perhaps to be identified with the feature SUBJUNCTIVE found in other languages), and not to *for* phrase formation.

The deletion of FOR in present subjunctive contexts means that such clauses do not meet the structural description given in (98). Consequently *to* does not appear with the verb in present subjunctives, nor do object pronouns appear in subject position. Since the COMP node is empty after FOR deletion, the late rule of *that* insertion proposed in Bresnan (1972a) also (correctly) applies in present subjunctives.

definition of local transformation in fact excludes the statement of the rule
itself from doing this, as in (102):

(102) $X-[_{\text{COMP}} \text{ FOR}]-NP-Y \Rightarrow 1-[_{\text{PP}} 2+3]-\emptyset-4$

This addition of a category symbol to an otherwise well-motivated rule is
sufficient to validate the explanations of the restrictions on WH fronting in
(89)−(91) discussed in the previous section.

It should be kept in mind that the structure-preserving constraint in large
part solves the problem of what kind of derived structure transformations assign.
The fact that it is so restrictive in the case of root and structure-preserving
transformations balances whatever variety of operations that it may be necessary to permit in the strictly local transformations.

However, it is very likely that the node PP can be assigned by (98) automatically, i.e., by general conventions that determine the categories of phrase
nodes. *For* phrase formation essentially transforms COMP into a phrase node
by bringing a phrase node under its domination. (This is the definition of
phrase node: one that can dominate an NP.) It is suggested in Chomsky (1965,
p. 116) that phrase node categories AND lexical node categories are uniquely
determined in linguistic theory according to the types of configurations they
appear in in the base. (In Chapter I I take the lexical categories as arbitrarily
given, and only propose that they, in turn, determine the phrasal categories.)
A recent proposal for how such determination is made is that of Jackendoff,
Selkirk, and Bowers (1974), which is as follows:

NP's and S's are the phrasal categories that may dominate subject (in
English, pre-lexical head) NP's, whereas AP's and PP's may not. On the other
hand, S's and PP's are the phrasal categories whose heads may have object
(in English, following sister) NP's, whereas NP's and AP's may not. With
these definitions, a PP is that phrase node in the base whose head may be
followed by an object NP but not preceded by a subject NP.

Within the structure-preserving framework only the base rules and the
local transformations are free to define dominance independent of the general
conventions on transformations and of the structures generated by other syntactic rules of the grammar. It is therefore plausible to assume that local
transformations are constrained at least by the same limitations on dominance
relations as the base rules are. Under this assumption, if a local transformation
changes a nonphrase node into a phrase node, then the label of that node is
determined in the same way as that of a base phrase node.

Given the fact that *for* phrase formation changes COMP into a phrase node
(and this characteristic of the rule was crucial in establishing its existence),
the label of this phrase node then HAS to be PP, if Jackendoff's characterizations of phrase nodes and the assumption that phrase nodes created by the

base and by local transformations are subject to the same characterizations are correct. This is because *for* phrase formation provides an object NP, but no possible subject NP, for the head of the new phrase node, COMP. In this way, the derived structure of (91) can be obtained without having recourse to an ad hoc specification of the category PP in the structural change of *for* phrase formation.

VI

Local Transformations and Movements of Nonphrase Nodes

In this chapter, movement rules that do not apply to phrase nodes are investigated. Since local transformations by definition always involve at least one nonphrase node, many transformations of this class that have not figured directly in earlier sections are discussed here. It should not be forgotten, of course, that a claim is involved—namely, after one has enumerated the root and structure-preserving transformations of English, as I have attempted to do in the previous chapters, all the remaining transformations will be local in the sense defined in Chapter I.

We have seen some cases of local transformations that involve phrase nodes: postverbal particle movement (Section III.3), indirect question adjustment (Chapter IV), and *for* phrase formation (Section V.9). In the sections where these rules are discussed, it is shown that they satisfy the conditions on local transformations, and so we will not devote space to them again here.

The principal part of the chapter is organized around various movements of nonphrase nodes. In most cases we will discuss transformations that move categories that dominate single morphemes rather than sequences of morphemes. First, we go over briefly some root transformations of this type; second, we go more deeply into certain structure-preserving movements of nonphrase nodes; third, we enumerate and briefly discuss several local transformations (which of course involve nonphrase nodes). In two final sections a further restriction is placed on local transformations (thus further strengthening the structure-preserving constraint), and a hypothesis about a possible strong extension of the constraint to deletion rules is tentatively proposed.

It may be well to repeat here the definition of a local transformation given in Chapter I:

(1)   **Local Transformation:** *A transformational operation that affects only a sequence of a single nonphrase node* C *and one adjacent constituent* C' *that is specified without a variable, such that the rule is not subject to any condition **exterior** to* C—C' *(or* C'—C*), is called a "local transformation."*

VI.1   *ROOT TRANSFORMATIONS THAT MOVE NONPHRASE NODES*

We saw in Chapter II that subject—auxiliary inversion and subject—simple verb inversion in English attach the nodes AUX and V, respectively, to root S's. It may be the case that tag question formation attaches AUX + (NEG) to a root S, although an alternative formulation that copies the S and then deletes the VP also suggests itself. I also proposed that the verb-second rule of German is a root transformation moving a nonphrase node.

Richard Kayne has pointed out to me that the two clitic inversion rules of Modern French that place clitics after the verb apply only in independent clauses. The first of these, which applies in questions, Kayne has termed SUBJECT—CLITIC INVERSION.[1] The second we may call AFFIRMATIVE IMPERATIVE INVERSION. They are exemplified in (2) and (3):

(2)   *Quand parlerez-vous à Jean?*
             Ne s'est-il pas souvenu de nous?
             Vous y ont-ils amenés à temps?
             Pourquoi les chats ont-ils une telle faim?

(3)   *Donnez-moi ces cigares!*
             Conduisez-les-y dans mon auto.
             Presentez-la-nous avant le diner.

Ordinarily clitic pronouns in French must precede the verb; cf. Section VI.2.6. However, in main clause questions the subject clitic may or must follow the first finite verb [as in (2)], and in affirmative imperatives all pronominal clitic objects follow the verb [as in (3)]. The structure-preserving constraint will predict that such rules can apply only in independent clauses if the operation each of these rules performs does not satisfy the definitions of either structure-preserving or local transformations.

---

[1] Subject—clitic inversion is not to be confused with stylistic inversion (cf. Section III.4), which applies in embedded sentences and I claim is structure-preserving. Kayne (1970) shows conclusively that the two rules are different rules; the one that concerns us here moves clitic pronouns, and stylistic inversion moves NP's.

Consider first whether these inversions "preserve structure." Subject—clitic inversion moves the clitic after the FIRST FINITE VERB, which is neither a clitic position nor even an NP position. Similarly, the postverbal position of the clitics in affirmative imperatives is not a clitic position, nor is it the object NP position: Clitics in imperatives can occur even with direct objects, as in (3), and such clitics cannot be separated from the verb, as direct objects can:

(4)   *Gardez toujours ce souvenir!*
                      Gardez-le toujours!
                    **Gardez toujours le!*

Thus these two inversions are not structure-preserving. To see that they are not local transformations, it suffices to note that both rules are subject to conditions on the string EXTERIOR to the affected clitic—verb input sequence. Subject—clitic inversion requires that a WH element or some other suitable "triggering" element (such as *aussi = therefore*) precede the subject, and affirmative imperative inversion requires that NOTHING precede the pronominal object clitics in the string (i.e., the negative *ne* blocks the rule: *Ne le mangez pas* versus **Ne mangez-le pas.*). The latter condition is also exterior to the clitic—verb sequence.[2]

Thus the structure-preserving constraint correctly predicts that subject—clitic inversion and affirmative imperative inversion are root transformations; i.e., they apply only in main clauses.[3]

VI.2   STRUCTURE-PRESERVING MOVEMENTS OF NONPHRASE NODES

VI.2.1   NEG Transportation

The rule of NEG transportation, proposed in Klima (1964), derives the second sentence (or at least one reading of the second sentence) in each pair in (5) from the first sentence.

---

[2]Actually material may precede the object clitics if it is set off by comma intonation: *À ce moment précis, mettez-vous à table!*

[3]The two root transformations discussed here that apply to French clitics indicate that it is not quite correct to require root transformations to attach clitics to the highest S. No nonroot S can dominate a clitic moved by a root transformation, but the status of a clitic as an affix somehow overrides the requirement that a root transformation attach a constituent to the root directly. I am not capable of elucidating the exact nature of the dominance relations involving clitics at this time. The main point in the text is that it is striking that the only two violations of preverbal clitic positions in French occur in nonembedded sentences. This problem in formulating these root transformations was pointed out by Richard Kayne (personal communication).

(5)   *John might believe that Mary didn't pass the course.*
           John might not believe that Mary passed the course.

           John seems not to read much.
           John doesn't seem to read much.

           We expect them not to be too happy about it.
           We don't expect them to be too happy about it.

[The TENSE movement rule and the rule that determines the distribution of the auxiliary *do* are also involved in (5); they are discussed in the next section.] The effect of NEG transportation in the first example in (5) is indicated by the arrow in (6):

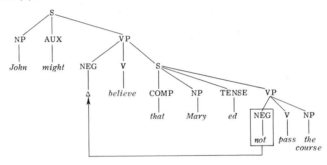

If NEG transportation exists as a transformational rule, it is clearly structure-preserving; i.e., the *not* is not moved to some arbitrary position within the higher sentence but to the very position the grammar ordinarily assigns to *not* within a single clause.

   Klima (1964) points out that the syntactic arguments favoring NEG transportation face certain difficulties due to the fact that the complement S's of predicates such as *to doubt* and *to be unlikely* share many of the "negative context" characteristics of the complements *to not believe, to not seem*, etc. (cf. *I doubt that he'll come until six*). I will not try to resolve these difficulties here, even though it might be necessary to abandon a NEG movement rule in order to do so. Until such an alternative can be definitely rejected, I can only make a conditional conclusion: If NEG transportation is a transformation, it is an example of a structure-preserving movement rule that affects a nonphrase node.[4]

---

[4] A word on a class of apparent exceptions to the usual pre-main-verb position of *not* in English is perhaps in order:

> *I think not.*
> *I think so.*
>
> *She hopes not.*
> *She hopes so.*
>
> *If so, I'll be happy to come.*
> *If not, I'll be happy to come.*

In (6) and throughout this chapter, NEG is often found just to the right of the AUX and outside the VP. I do not mean to imply that this is definitively its deep structure position; rather, there seem to be a number of (local) order interchanges with adverbial AP's of various types (cf. Section V.2) that affect the relative interpretations ("scopes") of these elements. I think we can say with more assurance that the emphatic marker is generated in the AUX_____VP position:

(7)   *John has not completely finished his task.*
          John has so completely finished his task. (so = too)
          John has certainly not finished his task.
          *John has certainly so finished his task.
          *John has certainly not either finished his task.
          John hasn't either completely finished his task.

The contracted *n't* has the same (surface) distribution as emphatic *so* and as *not either*, and can also be used to indicate AUX_____VP sequencing.

NEG transportation, formulated as a structure-preserving substitution for $[_{\text{NEG}} \Delta]$, automatically accounts for why the rule does not apply when the upper sentence in structures like (6) contains a deep structure *not*, that is, for why NEG transportation does not affect the underlying structures of the sentences in (8):

(8)   *John might not believe that Mary didn't pass the course.*
          We don't expect them not to be happy.

The presence of $[_{\text{NEG}} not]$ in the higher sentence means that the structural description of NEG transportation is not met.

VI.2.2   The English Auxiliary

Almost every analysis of the English auxiliary in a generative framework agrees that there is an "affix movement" rule, very similar to the one originally justified in Chomsky (1957), that transforms the strings in the (a) examples in (9) and (10) into those in the (b) examples:

Footnote 4 continued

A plausible explanation for this class of exceptions has been advanced by G. Lakoff (1966). He proposes that the *so* and *not* in the preceding examples are proforms for deleted (understood) sentence complements of *think*, *hope*, and *if*. Whether *so* or *not* appears in surface structure depends on whether or not the deleted sentence contains *not*. Thus when an S complement is deleted, a grammatical marker indicating whether it is asserted or denied appears in surface structure.

According to this explanation, *I think not* and *I don't think so* result from the same deep structure; the former is obtained when NEG transportation does not apply before the understood complement S is deleted, and the latter is obtained when NEG transportation does apply (moving *not* out of the complement and leaving a positive assertion). The example sentences and Lakoff's explanation of them do not constitute a definitive argument in favor of NEG transportation (over the difficulties observed by Klima), however.

(9)   a. *John—ed—have—en—take—the course.*
           b. *John—have + ed (had)—take + en—the course.*

(10)   a. *The girl—s—be—ing—play—the trumpet.*
           b. *The girl—be + s (is)—play + ing—the trumpet.*

There are many disagreements over how many kinds of surface forms have in
fact undergone this rule, but few doubts that a process of this type must be
represented as a transformation.

When we examine this rule we see that it has effects that preclude the
possibility that it is a local rule, for it can move verbal affixes over a sequence
(AP)—V, as in (11):

(11) a. *John—ed—scarcely—be—ing—merely—play—the trumpet.*
      b. *John—scarcely—be + ed (was)—merely—play + ing—the trumpet.*

In Section V.2 we saw that adverbs of the *scarcely* class are in their deep
structure position in sentences like (11b), so it is not possible to order affix
movement "before" such adverbs intervene.

This means that affix movement must be structure-preserving. Intuitively
this does not seem farfetched, since verbal affixes in English (*s, ed, ing*, and *en*)
have several different deep structure and transformational sources (to be
discussed briefly later), but they invariably appear in the same surface context,
V_____. This is the kind of behavior that the structure-preserving constraint
predicts is normal. However, a demonstration that affix movement is structure-
preserving requires that I outline in some detail an analysis of the English
auxiliary and then return to the main question afterwards. In the course of this
discussion, I will introduce a local insertion transformation and a second
structure-preserving rule (VERB RAISING) involving auxiliary verbs, which are in
themselves relevant to the concerns of this chapter.

I begin with the phrase structure rule for expanding S. I do not commit
myself to a deep structure source for NEG, although the surface position for the
contracted *n't* is characteristically AUX_____:

(12)   S → COMP—NP—AUX—(EMP)—VP[5]

AUX is defined by its role in subject—auxiliary inversion, in reducing *not* to
n't, in forming tag questions, in remaining in VP deletion contexts (*Bill came
late, but Mary didn't*), in permitting certain contractions, etc; these rules are
discussed further in the next section. For the moment AUX can be thought of

---

[5]The analysis of the auxiliary system given here does not depend on not assigning constituent status
to the sequence AUX—VP in (12). Dougherty (1970b) has convincingly argued that this must be done; I
omit the base rule required for expository purposes only.

In (12) EMP is the category for the emphatic markers *so, too,* and *either*: *John will **so** wash the dishes,
It wasn't **either** so easy,* etc.

as the syntactic category of the FIRST verbal auxiliary in a finite clause. AUX has two basic deep structure realizations—as a modal (*will, can, must, shall,* etc.) or as TENSE:

(13)
$$\text{AUX} \rightarrow \begin{bmatrix} \pm\text{TENSE} \\ \pm\text{PAST} \end{bmatrix}$$

According to (13), the modal auxiliaries are characterized by the configuration AUX, -TENSE. (Here the semantic content of TENSE is probably closer to "asserted" than to any time notion; I retain TENSE as a symbol for familiarity.) If features are permitted in expansion rules, (12) and (13) can be collapsed into one rule.

An advantage of (12)−(13) is that no further rule is needed to explain why modals do not exhibit the TENSE affix *s*. As in any analysis of the auxiliary, lexical restrictions determine that only certain modals have a past form (*could, would,* and perhaps *might* are AUX, -TENSE, +PAST).

AUX, +TENSE is the present tense ending *s* (which must be deleted except after third-person singular subjects) and the past tense ending *ed*. These two morphemes are often realized in the surface structure in combination with the auxiliary verb *do*, which rules to be discussed later will insert as an AUX. It may be that certain features further differentiate AUX, + TENSE (just as they do AUX, -TENSE = modals) so as to allow the "semimodals" *be to* and *be going to* to be generated by (13). Here I will consider *s/ed* (and the auxiliary *do*) to be characterized by AUX, +TENSE, but the rule for inserting *do* could easily be modified by adding whatever feature is necessary to distinguish *s/ed* from the semimodals.

Rules (12) and (13) for AUX do not generate any auxiliary verb that can follow a modal within a clause, i.e., various uses of *be* and *have*. For example, the progressive *be*, the passive *be*, the copular *be*, and the perfect *have*, while auxiliaries, by virtue of their being inverted in questions, attracting *n't*, etc., can also follow modals:

(14)   *Our prices should be being quoted daily.*
               These desks (may) have been cheap.

I propose to generate such auxiliaries (in my dialect, all nonmodal uses of *be* and the perfect auxiliary use of *have*) as syntactic main verbs in deep structure, very much like the verbs of temporal aspect such as *begin, start, finish, resume,* etc. These auxiliaries are subsequently assigned AUX status transformationally whenever they are first in a finite clause. Thus the sequences of "auxiliaries" given in (15)—namely, those not generated in deep structure by (12)−(13)—I contend are instances of underlying structures such as those in (16) [affix movement has not yet applied in (16)]:

(15)

$$(\textit{have}-\textit{en})-\left(\begin{matrix} \textit{be} \\ \textit{start} \\ \textit{begin} \\ \textit{keep} \\ \textit{stop} \\ \textit{etc.} \end{matrix}\right)-\textit{ing}-\left\{\begin{matrix} (\textit{be}-\textit{en})-V-\ldots \\ \textit{be}-\left\{\begin{matrix} \text{NP} \\ \text{AP} \\ \text{PP} \end{matrix}\right\} \end{matrix}\right\}$$

(16)

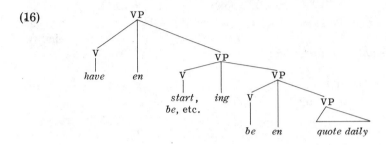

The structures in (16) underlie predicates in sentences like *Prices have started being quoted daily, Prices have been being quoted daily.*[6]

Nothing in my analysis depends on whether the structures in (16) are generated by a grammar in which VP may be a sister to V in deep structure, by one in which all such structures are due to subject raising, or by one in which both types of derivations are possible. The important point is that I claim that the auxiliaries that can follow modals (*be* and *have*) are generated by the base rule for VP:

(17) $VP \rightarrow \ldots - V - \ldots$

The relevant questions about the constituent structure proposed in (16) are these: Can we justify each auxiliary's being followed by a constituent (rather than being part of that constituent), and what category is this constituent in? We see that what are labeled as VP's in (16) cannot also be NP's:

---

[6]The base rule for generating verbal affixes and the deep structure distribution of the various verbal affixes are taken up in Section VI.2.5.

It is no doubt true that affixes are dominated by V in surface structure. There is probably a general rule or convention by which suffixal elements are attached to the preceding preterminal node as follows:

In the text I am concerned only with determining the correct positioning of various instances of affixes in surface structure, and assume that some formal device of this sort derives the correct surface structure dominance relations.

(18) *It was appreciating music that John had continued at Harvard.*
It was appreciating music that John had been at Harvard.
It was continued (been) appreciating music that John had at Harvard.
Appreciating music was continued by John at Harvard.
Appreciating music was been by John at Harvard.

Thus the principal question about (16) is whether, at some stage of a derivation, each nonlexical auxiliary after the first is the head of a VP. For example, can we justify four different VP's inside *These houses might have been being undermined for a long time?* Ross (1967a) points out that patterns as in (19) indicate that VP deletion is sensitive to different VP's (namely, *having been being undermined, been being undermined, being undermined*):

(19) *Our houses might have been being undermined for a long time, and yours might (have (been)) too.*

Patterns like (19) provide some justification for structures as in (16) independent of any consideration of the structure-preserving constraint. In Section VI.2.5 we will see that the structures in (16), in conjunction with the structure-preserving constraint, furnish certain syntactic explanations about English auxiliary and verbal affix behavior that would not otherwise be available.

The claim that the auxiliary verbs in (15) are main verbs generated by repeated application of (17) is in conflict with the proposal in Chomsky (1957) to account for the ordering among instances of *be* and the perfect auxiliary by a phrase structure rule. That is, in order to justify my analysis I must answer the following questions: Why does the auxiliary *have* never follow itself or the progressive *be*, and why does the progressive *be* never follow itself? (That is, what accounts for the ordering of these auxiliary verbs?)

Concerning the auxiliary *have*, it is a fact that verbs of temporal aspect take clause complements that (i) may not have expressed subjects in surface structure and (ii) never begin with the perfective auxiliary *have*:

(20)

$$*John \left\{ \begin{array}{l} began \\ continued \\ resumed \\ stopped \\ went\ on \end{array} \right\} \left\{ \begin{array}{l} having\ said\ something\ important. \\ having\ eaten\ dinner. \\ having\ been\ examined. \end{array} \right\}$$

$$*Harry \left\{ \begin{array}{l} tended \\ ceased \\ started \\ went\ on \end{array} \right\} \left\{ \begin{array}{l} to\ have\ written\ a\ letter. \\ to\ have\ overeaten. \\ to\ have\ spoken\ on\ politics. \end{array} \right\}$$

Since the complements to the perfective *have* and the progressive *be* are in this class (they never have expressed subjects in surface structure), I assume that they are subject to the second general restriction also:[7]

(21)
$$*\text{John was} \left\{ \begin{array}{l} \textit{having said something important.} \\ \textit{having eaten dinner.} \\ \textit{having been examined.} \end{array} \right\}$$

$$*\text{John will have} \left\{ \begin{array}{l} \textit{had eaten dinner.} \\ \textit{had overeaten.} \\ \textit{had written a letter.} \end{array} \right\}$$

The fact that the progressive *be* does not follow itself can be attributed to the general prohibition of the verb—complement sequence V—*ing*—V—*ing* in surface structure, whenever the two *ing*'s are not separated by an NP boundary (for discussion see Emonds, 1973a; Milsark, 1972; and especially Pullum, 1974):

(22)   *John regretted being eating when Mary arrived.*
         After being singing for so long, I'd like to eat.

---

[7] I would say that VP complements that never have expressed subjects are not derived from full deep structure S's, and that the perfect auxiliary *have* often cannot appear as the head of such a VP. That is, a selection restriction on the heads of certain VP complements requires that they not be the perfect auxiliary *have*. But exactly how the restriction discussed in the text is stated in the grammar is not as important for the argument here as that it must be stated.

     Consider the following potential counterexample to the restriction as stated in the text:

(i)   *John will begin to have finished his work before it is time to leave.*

By contrast, the *have—had* restriction is inviolable:

(ii)   *John will have had finished his work before it is time to leave.*
           John had had been examined before everyone else arrived.

To me the example (i) seems slightly unacceptable, although interpretable, and I would attribute the marginal character to the lack of grammaticality. On the other hand, no interpretation can be imposed on (ii) to reduce their unacceptability.

     Further, the identity of elements that render (ii) unacceptable seems to be a case of the more general fact that, given some restricted combination, the unacceptability of the combination will be greater if in fact the combined morphemes are identical. Thus the doubly starred examples in (iv) are less acceptable than the starred examples in (iii), even though the pairs of grammatical counterparts are equally acceptable:

(iii)   *John was beginning to start the dinner.*
            *John was beginning starting the dinner. (*V-ing-V-ing)*

            The two big ones you bought were tastier.
            The two ones you bought were tastier.

            For that he left to surprise you is typical.

(iv)   *John was starting to start the dinner.*
           **John was starting starting the dinner.*

           The one big one you bought was tastier.
           **The one one you bought was tastier.*

           **For for him to leave to surprise you is typical.*

*The people being telling the story are tired.
*John, being studying French, would be the person to ask.
*John was being studying French.
*The people were being telling a long story.

Thus the ordering restrictions on the auxiliaries *have* and *be* are accounted for by statements that must be added to the grammar in Chomsky (1957) in any case, which renders the specification of their order by a phrase structure rule redundant. A simpler phrase structure rule, (17), suffices. [Of course both the grammar proposed here and that in Chomsky (1957) account for the ordering of the MODAL auxiliaries by phrase structure rules.]

VI.2.3 The *Do* Insertion and Verb Raising Rules

Consider now the grammar of the auxiliary system consisting of the phrase structure rules in (12), (13), and (17), supplemented by the "double-*ing*" restriction and the exclusion of *have*—*en* in surface VP complements of temporal aspect verbs. If no transformations (other than subject—verb agreement and affix movement) were added to this grammar, it would never treat *have* and *be* as AUX (in tag questions, contractions with *n't*, VP deletion constructions, subject—auxiliary inversion, placement of NEG and EMP, etc.), and it would not generate the auxiliary *do* at all.

On the other hand, in the case of nonfinite clauses (infinitives, gerunds, participles, and present subjunctives—those clauses lacking AUX) the preceding "incorrect" results (appearance of *have* and *be* outside of AUX, placement of *not* before these elements, absence of EMP, and absence of *do*) are in fact CORRECT. Thus any rules we add to the grammar to account for finite clauses should depend crucially on the presence of AUX (or TENSE) in these clauses.[8]

The first such rule is the insertion of the "verbal" (TENSE-bearing) auxiliary *do*; this can be formulated as a local insertion transformation:

(23)   **Do Insertion:** $X + [_{\text{AUX}} \text{TENSE} - \emptyset] - Z \Rightarrow 1 - [_{\text{V}} do] - 3$ [9]

After (23) and optional NEG contraction apply, a clause lacking a deep structure modal has the following structure:

---

[8] In nonfinite clauses certain deletions of *be* and certain structure-preserving insertions of *ing* must be added to this grammar and to alternative grammars such as that in Chomsky (1957).

[9] In Emonds (1970) I erred here in not realizing that local ("minor") rules can be insertion as well as movement rules and still be in accord with the structure-preserving constraint. We might wish to restrict insertions of a lexical category C, as in (23), by requiring that a local rule can insert a lexical category C only into SPEC(C) (the specifier of C). There are certain determiners = noun specifiers, such as *lots (of)*, that may be instances of a similar process, as they have noun counterparts and noun characteristics: *a lot of bread, lots of bread.*

(24)

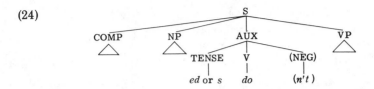

This is the correct structure for sentences with the surface auxiliary *do*, and it also provides the means for succinctly describing the auxiliary behavior of *be* and the perfect auxiliary *have*, which here are deep structure verbs. If these verbs begin the VP in (24), an obligatory structure-preserving rule can be formulated to raise them into the AUX position (this rule moves them over adverbial AP's and so must be structure-preserving). We can term this rule VERB RAISING. If the VP in (24) does not begin with *be* or the perfect auxiliary *have*, then *do* remains in the tree, subject to later deletion in affirmative declaratives.

It might be objected that once (24) is produced by a local transformation, nothing in principle stops ANY verb from being "raised" into AUX position. However, if we think of what kind of morphemes are inserted into trees by transformations, they are always those whose intrinsic lexical semantic content appears to be no more than that associated with a very few syntactic features that are otherwise needed in the transformational component. That is, if we take all the morphemes that, in various analyses, are transformationally inserted in some contexts (*there, for, not,* agentive *by, be, do, and, with, of, the,* etc.) and consider the set of features that would be necessary to uniquely specify their intrinsic lexical semantic content and their deep structure distribution, I claim that these features would all play a role in the transformational component, independent of any insertion rules.

If this observation is correct, and if we define the notion "syntactic feature" as a feature that plays a role in the grammar's transformational component (cf. Chomsky, 1965, pp. 153—154), we can require that NODES INTRODUCED BY INSERTION RULES MUST NOT ADD TO THE STORE OF SYNTACTIC FEATURES. In fact to exclude the possibility of a general verb raising rule into the V created by (23), I propose the following even stronger convention:

(25) *A node B introduced into a tree by a transformational insertion T (rather than by movement or copying) can never during the derivation dominate a feature that is not defined as syntactic independent of all transformations that move material into B (including T).*

The convention in (25) permits transformations to place morphemes under V in (24) only if every feature that characterizes these morphemes is a syntactic feature. [We probably want to exclude "rule features," if these exist, from qualifying as "independently defined syntactic features" in (25).]

We can now state verb raising, which follows *do* insertion:

(26)   ***Verb Raising:***[10] $X + \text{TENSE} - [_{\text{V}} do] - Y - \left\{ \begin{array}{c} be - \emptyset \\ have - en \end{array} \right\} + Z \Rightarrow$

$$1 - 4 - 3 - \emptyset - 5$$

where *Y* does not dominate V.

Verb raising explains many characteristics of the verbs that it moves. We now examine their behavior in several constructions, referring to *be* and the perfect auxiliary *have* as "AUX verbs."

It first of all explains why the auxiliary *do* does not precede AUX verbs as it does ordinary verbs:[11]

(27)   **Did John be helping him?*
                *Why did the boy have come?
                John **did be helping him.*
                The boy **did have come.*

The principal characteristic of AUX verbs that differentiates them from ordinary verbs is that they act like modals when they immediately follow the subject NP. For example, the subject NP is inverted around a modal (AUX) in questions, but not around a main verb (alternatively, one could say AUX moves around the subject NP):

(28)   *Will John help him?*
                Why did the boy leave?
                *Refuses John to help him?
                *Why left the boy?

But if the first verb after the subject is *be* or the perfective *have*, these also invert, as predicted by (26):

(29)   *Was John helping him?*
                Why had the boy come?

According to (12) and (13), the NEG and EMP particles appear only after AUX. Verb raising correctly predicts that these particles will follow the first

---

[10] I am certain that *do* in (26) could be replaced with just V, but I retain *do* to ensure correctness and clarity of exposition.

Need and *dare* in a negated clause are either deep structure modals or true verbs, but they are not required to appear in AUX position, as *be* and the perfect auxiliary are: **John doesn't have eaten* versus *John doesn't need to eat*. It is this requirement that (26) expresses.

In the analysis of the auxiliary system being proposed, note that modals (AUX) and verbs do not form a syntactic class, nor do they undergo any rules in common.

[11] I am not speaking here of the emphatic *do* of imperatives, which seems to be derived from a deep structure *will*: *Do come in, won't you, Do be more polite, will you*, etc.

be after a subject and any use of *have* that inverts in questions (in my dialect only the perfective *have* and *had better* have this property):

(30)   *The children mustn't play in the streets.*
             They did not get examined.
             *You could **too** take that with you.*
             *John does **so** know French.*

             **The children playn't in the streets.*
             **They got not examined.*
             He took **too that with him.*
             John knows **so French.*

             The children aren't in the streets.
             They were not examined.
             John has not followed directions.
             *Bill has **so** seen a doctor.*

             **John has not a maid come in on Saturdays.*
             Bill has **so to see a doctor.*

In contrast to the preceding, recall that in present subjunctives, in which an AUX is absent (making verb raising impossible), *not* precedes *be*, as predicted by (12), (13), and (17):

(31)   *She requests that they not be examined.*
       **She requests that they be not examined.*
       It is of great importance that the children not be in the street when
           he comes.
       **It is of great importance that the children be not in the street when*
           he comes.

We know that certain classes of adverbs can appear at the beginning of the VP, i.e., after AUX (cf. Section V.2). These adverbs cannot come between a verb and a following predicate attribute or object NP, however:

(32)   *I wonder if they could ever buy a car.*
             **I wonder if they bought ever a car.*
             *John **does** frequently visit his parents.*
             **John visits frequently his parents.*
             Mary can barely speak French.
             **Mary speaks barely French.*

             Did Mary suddenly become a radical?
             **Mary became suddenly a radical.*
             I may already look fat.
             **He looks already fat.*

The verb raising rule correctly predicts that such adverbs may follow a clause-initial *be* or auxiliary *have*, but not nonauxiliary *have* or non-clause-initial *be* before a predicate attribute. Note the difficulty of extending the analysis in Chomsky (1957) to handle these facts:

(33) *I wonder if he was ever a radical.*
He has frequently visited his parents.
Mary was suddenly a radical.
I am already tall.

*He has frequently to visit his parents.
*They have frequently a maid come in.
*I wonder if he has been ever a radical.
*He may be already tall.

In Section VI.3, I discuss a quantifier postposition rule by which the determiners *all*, *each*, and *both* may appear after the AUX. (These determiners have their deep structure source in the subject NP.) However, they may not appear after a V under the VP:

(34) *You would all enjoy a movie.*
*We enjoyed all a movie.
They didn't both enter the store.
*They entered both the store.
They should each buy lots of books.
*They buy each lots of books.

Again, verb raising predicts that these determiners can follow a *be* or an auxiliary *have* that follows the subject NP:

(35) *We were all enjoying a movie.*
They have both entered the store.
They are each avid readers.

*They had both two steaks brought in. (cf. *They both had two steaks brought in.*)

In tag S's, as exemplified in (36), the VP is deleted. This VP deletion precedes deletion of unstressed *do*, so that the latter appears in tag versions of sentences without other auxiliaries:

(36) *His son may not drive a car, may he?*
*His son doesn't drive a car, drives he?
His son doesn't drive a car, does he?

Susan sees movies as often as she can.
*Susan sees movies as often as Bill sees.
Susan sees movies as often as Bill does.

By ordering verb raising before VP deletion, we can account for the appearance of *be* and the auxiliary *have* in tags, and for the fact that *do* does not "substitute" for them as in (37):

(37)   *The reason is that he drove too fast, isn't it? (*doesn't it?)*
         Susan has seen this movie as often as Bill has. (*does.)
         Cf. *John always had to take pills, didn't he? (*hadn't he?)*

(As expected, the nonauxiliary *have* does not appear in tag S's.)

In a study of contractions of auxiliaries, Zwicky (1970) has found that the initial phonological grouping "possible consonant—vowel" of *will, would, have, has, is, am,* and *are* can be dropped after pronominal subjects. (*Has* and *is* can be contracted elsewhere as well, but this is not of interest here.) However, the contraction may apply to forms of *have*, according to Zwicky, only in those usages of *have* that can invert in questions. For example, in all dialects studied the perfective *have* and the modal *had better* invert in questions and may contract. On the other hand, the causative *have* and the *have* of obligation invert in no dialect, and also never contract:

(38)   **Have they to take lots of pills?*
                        *They've to take lots of pills.

                        *Have they a maid come in?
                        *They've a made come in.

Just in the dialects where a simple transitive *have* may invert in questions, Zwicky claims, a simple transitive *have* may contract; that is, the examples in (39) are equally grammatical in any dialect:

(39)   *?Have you many books?*
                        ?You've many good books, I know.

Given the verb raising rule, we can make the contraction depend on *have, will,* or *be* being in the AUX position (i.e., not dominated by VP) and thus explain the correlation noted by Zwicky.

It should further be noted that such contraction does not affect the perfective *have* which is not in the AUX position, even when it follows the verb: **Could they've seen him? *Will you've finished before dinner?* Compare: *They've seen him. You've finished before dinner?* This shows that a perfective *have* which is not the first auxiliary does not have AUX status. That is, it argues for the verb raising analysis here over the analysis of Chomsky (1957).

This concludes my justification of verb raising, which, as we have seen, is also a structure-preserving rule.

VI.2.4   *Do* Deletion

Since *do* insertion is obligatory into AUX position in any clause in which there is no modal, and since the only means provided so far for its removal is replacement by the "verb raising" of the auxiliaries *have* and *be*, the grammar as constructed at present generates a *do* in every clause that lacks some other auxiliary. It is true that any such clause MAY contain a contrastively stressed *do*, but an unstressed auxiliary *do* cannot immediately precede the combination (AP)—V (optional adverb plus verb). Rather, an unstressed *do* can precede such a combination only if a negative particle (*not* or *n't*), an emphatic particle (*so* or *too*), or an inverted subject NP intervenes:

(40)   John **did** faint.
              *John did faint. (did unstressed)
              *John did merely wave. (did unstressed)
              John did not faint.
              John didn't wave.
              Why did John faint?
              John did **so** faint.
              John did **too** wave.

The elements that permit an unstressed *do* to precede them, as in (40), are just those that we know are outside the VP following this *do*. NEG and EMP (the emphatic particles) are placed outside VP by (12) and (13). We also know that an inverted subject NP is outside the VP because the rule that causes the inversion is a root transformation and so could not place a constituent under a VP. This means we can formulate an obligatory *do* deletion rule as in (41) (*do* deletion follows verb raising and precedes affix movement):

(41)   **Do Deletion:** $X-[_\text{v} do]-\text{VP}+Y \Rightarrow 1-\emptyset-3$

where *do* is not contrastively stressed.[12]

Since a condition on affix movement will be that affixes can move only over the next succeeding verb, the deletion rule in (41) in effect permits the TENSE affix to move to a main verb only if *do* is deleted. That is, TENSE can move onto the main verb JUST IN CASE the latter is not preceded by an inverted subject NP, NEG, or EMP. This prediction is exactly right:

---

[12]Example (41) can easily be extended to the true verb *do* if in underlying structure it precedes activity verb phrases, as argued in Ross (1972b). (This was pointed out in Emonds, 1970.) The condition would then be that *do* is not contrastively stressed OR is not AUX.

(42)　　　　　　　　*John (merely) fainted.*
　　　　　　　　　　*John not fainted.
　　　　　　　　　　*Why John fainted?
　　　　　　　　　　John **so fainted.*
　　　　　　　　　　*John not waved.
　　　　　　　　　　John **too waved.* (where *too* $\neq$ *also*)

The sequence of transformations—*do* insertion, verb raising, subject—auxiliary inversion, and *do* deletion—that supplement the phrase structure rules in (12), (13), and (17) produce the input structures to affix movement.

VI.2.5　Affix Movement

According to the rules proposed up to this point, the TENSE affixes are generated in the AUX position in clauses without modals, and it remains for the affix movement rule to move them around the first verb on their right.

It was explained in Section VI.2.2 that, because of intervening adverbs, affix movement must be a structure-preserving rule, and of course it is also an obligatory rule. But a structure-preserving rule can be obligatory only if the category C into whose position the rule moves a constituent is itself obligatorily generated in the base, for if C is not generated in the base, the rule will not apply. This is the crux of the correct criticism in Nagahara (1974) of my previous treatment of affix movement: "And in general, we may say that a structure-preserving rule of 'must-apply' nature must not make crucial use of a node whose presence in the tree is optional [p. 33]." Therefore if the TENSE affixes are to move to the right of main verbs both obligatorily and in structure-preserving fashion, (17) must be revised as follows:

(43)　　　　　　　　VP $\rightarrow$ $\cdots$ $-$V$-$TENSE$-$ $\cdots$.[13]

The TENSE generated by (43) is the deep structure source of the *en* of the perfect (i.e., in *have*$-$*en*$-$V) and of the *ing* of the progressive (i.e., in *be*$-$*ing*$-$V).[14] In most other cases it is empty in deep structure. However, the

---

[13]The appearance of TENSE in the base rule in (43) and as a feature on the category AUX in (12) is consistent with the tentative requirement on base rules proposed in Chapter I: "Any nonphrasal category can appear but once in the base rules, except that it may COOCCUR as an optional syntactic feature on some other category without breaking the restriction." Cf. Section I.3.

[14]There are three possible reasons for considering the past participle morpheme *en* and the past tense morpheme *ed* to be instances of the same feature of PAST. The first is that the regular (productive) phonological form of both is the same: *ed*. That is, the statement "PAST is realized as *ed* for regular verbs," however it is to be stated formally, accounts automatically for past participles of verbs if we analyze *en* as TENSE, PAST.

A second reason for analyzing *en* as a realization of PAST is the often-proposed semantic analysis of the English present perfect to the effect that it is a "past relevant to the present" or "a present containing the past," etc. If this is to be expressed in the grammar, it would be facilitated if the elements carrying this meaning (*have*$-$*en*) contain the feature PAST.

restriction on base rules of Section I.1 requires that the TENSE of (43) be filled in SOME productive class of deep structures, and the restriction on empty nodes in Section III.1.2 requires that no empty node $[_{\text{TENSE}} \Delta]$ remain unfilled throughout the transformational derivation. Before we can accept (43) these two requirements of the theory must be met.

The productive class of deep structure verbs that I claim are generated with a nonempty TENSE affix (namely, *ing*) are the verbs of temporal aspect (*begin, start, continue, commence, go on, keep, keep on, finish, stop, resume,* etc.); perhaps the progressive use of *be* is just a special case of this construction:

(44) *We kept on buying comic books.*
  The rain began soaking our clothes as soon as we opened the door.
  They will probably resume speaking softly.

That is, I claim that the first example in (44) has an underlying structure *We—keep—ing—on—*VP, and that the *ing* is moved to its surface position inside the complement VP by affix movement.

Ordinarily the *ing* of VP complements marks the NP status of the complement and is inserted transformationally (cf. Section IV.2.3). But for the complements of verbs of temporal aspect it is argued in Rosenbaum (1967) and Emonds (1972b) that these VP complements are not NP's, and their *ing* there-

---

Footnote 14 continued

Third, in those clauses in which TENSE is not generated under AUX (nonfinite clauses lacking AUX and clauses with modals), or in which TENSE, PAST carries a counterfactual meaning, the auxiliary *have—en* can mean "semantic past" rather than "semantic perfect." [These two notions can be defined by possible time adverbial cooccurrences; the adverbs that ordinarily occur with *ed* are "semantic past" adverbs. For many examples and discussion, see Emonds (1974).]

While many alternatives for assigning semantic tense values to clauses can be debated, it would seem that these alternations could be accounted for by a set of interpretive rules like the following, which treat *en* and *ed* as both PAST:

1. A clause containing AUX, −PAST cannot be semantic past.
2. A clause containing PAST may be semantic past.
3. An *if* clause with AUX, PAST may be counterfactual.
4. A clause containing *have—en* (PAST, −AUX) may be semantic perfect.
5. Each instance of ±PAST in the sentence must have a unique interpretation, i.e., must choose exactly one of (1)−(4).

Item 2 claims that *en* and not *have* carries the past meaning. Anecdotal evidence for this is the following sentence, whose meaning (in context) was clearly that in the speaker's opinion it was foolish to conceive of someone's ceasing to be an artist ("once an artist, always an artist"):

  I'll answer that, since I'm supposed to have been an artist, whatever "been" means.

In contrast, the following sentence seems to me senseless:

  ?I'll answer that, since I'm supposed to have been an artist, whatever "have" means.

fore must have another source. It seems plausible that this source is the base, since there are lexical (perhaps semantic) restrictions on whether it must be present within this class of verbs:

(45)   *John began to drive fast again.*
           John began driving fast again.

           *John resumed to drive fast.
           John resumed driving fast.

           The course continued to attract philosophy students.
           The course continued attracting philosophy students.

           *The course went on to attract philosophy students.
           The course went on attracting philosophy students.

           *John began to do his work, but he never finished to do it.
           John began doing his work, but he never finished doing it.

The verbs of temporal aspect are thus a productive class of lexical verbs that may or must appear in deep structure with a following $[_{\text{TENSE}} \; ing]$, so the TENSE of (43) is not always empty in deep structure.

The problem of guaranteeing that an empty TENSE does not appear in surface structure without recourse to an ad hoc deletion can be solved by a proper formulation of the rule that introduces the infinitive marker *to*. In English surface structures the regular verbs that occur without endings fall into four classes: (i) the finite present tense verbs that are not third-person singular (*s*) forms; (ii) the verbs with the infinitive marker *to*; (iii) the verbs that follow the auxiliary *do* and the modals (including deleted modals, such as in the present subjunctive and the imperative construction); and (iv) the verbs that introduce complements after a few transitive constructions such as *make*—NP—VP, *see*—NP—VP, *have*—NP—VP, etc, and in a few constructions such as *rather than*—VP.

I assume here that finite present verbs all have the affix *s* that undergoes affix movement, and that the deletion of this ending with plural and non-third-person forms ("number agreement") follows affix movement. Furthermore, I take the verb phrases in (iv) to be irregular variants of infinitives with *to*, especially in light of related sentence types such as NP *was made* **to** VP, NP *was seen* **to** VP, and NP *tried to* VP *rather than* (**to**) VP. Finally, I assume that the verbs that follow AUX—i.e., those in (iii)—in fact also exhibit a *to* at some point in the derivation, which is regularly deleted in the context AUX_____; some exceptional cases that point to the existence of an underlying *to* in this position are the auxiliaries *ought to* and *be to*:

(46)   *John ought to leave soon.*
                         John should leave soon.
                         John is to leave soon.
                         John does leave soon.

Before these rules of number agreement and *to* deletion take place, but after affix movement, all verbs in English exhibit either a TENSE suffix (*ed, s, ing, en*) or the infinitive marker *to*, and no verb exhibits both. This means that the distribution of *to* can be accounted for quite simply: After affix movement and other affix insertion rules apply (such as those associated with NP preposing, relative clause reduction, and gerund formation), *to* is inserted before the verb whenever an empty TENSE remains after the verb. The same rule can delete the empty TENSE:

(47)   **To *Insertion:*** $X - \emptyset - V - [_{\text{TENSE}} \Delta] - Y \Rightarrow 1 - to - 3 - \emptyset - 5$

In this way, an empty TENSE never goes through an entire well-formed transformational derivation, in accordance with the requirement of the theory.

Since (43) accords with the formal requirements on base rules and empty nodes, we can now state affix movement and demonstrate its compatibility with the structure-preserving constraint:

(48)   **Affix Movement (Obligatory):** $X - \text{TENSE} - Y - V - Z \Rightarrow$

$$1 - \emptyset - 3 - 4 + 2 - 5$$

where Y does not dominate TENSE.

The structure-preserving constraint and (43) guarantee that whenever TENSE moves into a lower VP by (48) it substitutes for another TENSE node (either empty or itself vacated by the simultaneous application of affix movement to the affix it dominated).[15] In the case that the V in (48) is one of the auxiliaries moved or inserted under AUX (*be, have,* or *do*), the rule is not structure-preserving (there being but one TENSE under AUX) but is, rather, a local transformation, because the constituents interchanged are necessarily adjacent. Thus we see that the rule in question fulfills the definition of a local rule only in the case where it could not possibly be structure-preserving (because the grammar does not generate two TENSE nodes under AUX), and it fulfills the requirements of structure-preserving rules only in the case where it cannot be local (because of possible intervening adverbs in the lower VP's into which affixes may move).

---

[15] Affix movement, as has long been noted, requires a convention on the applicability of transformational rules, so that it can apply more than once in a given clause "simultaneously."

Some typical trees that illustrate affix movement follow:

(49)

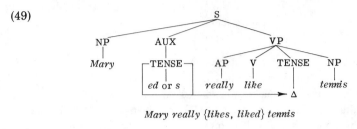

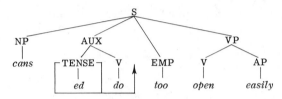

Mary really {likes, liked} tennis

Cans did too open easily

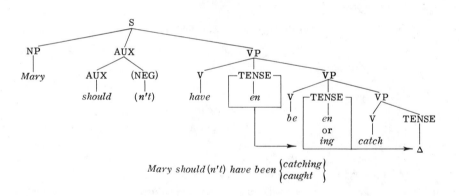

Mary should (n't) have been {*catching*} {*caught*}

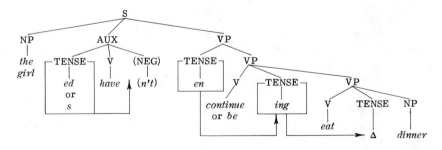

The girl {has(n't), had(n't)} {continued, been} eating dinner

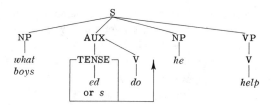

What boys {does, did} he help?

Generating TENSE by (43) means that the nonfinite as well as the finite verbal suffixes in English are of the same category, and this has several advantages. First, the finite and nonfinite affixes are in complementary distribution in deep structure in that *ed* and *s* are +TENSE, +AUX and *en* and *ing* are +TENSE, −AUX; hence, it is preferable to include them all in the same category.[16]

Second, since affix movement here applies only to TENSE, rather than to a disjunction of TENSE and the nonfinite affixes, the statement of the rule is simpler than that, say, in Chomsky (1957). (In that study, a category *Af*, which is equivalent to TENSE here, is introduced for stating affix movement, but this category is defined ad hoc as the disjunction just mentioned, and not by the base rules.)

Third, affixes in this analysis move only around the category V, and not around a disjunction of V and other auxiliary elements.

Fourth, my analysis claims that English VP's in the normal case will be introduced by various V−TENSE combinations, rather than by verbs alone. Thus the grammar ordinarily generates structures like (16) (with TENSE affixes being obligatory); this characteristic, in CONJUNCTION with the structure-preserving constraint, explains why the NP-preposing (passive) rule inserts a morpheme pair *be−en* into a position typical of such elements and not into arbitrary positions (after the main verb, before the subject, etc.). That is, NP preposing inserts this auxiliary−affix pair into the empty nodes encircled in (50), yielding *Mary was insulted by Bill*:

(50)

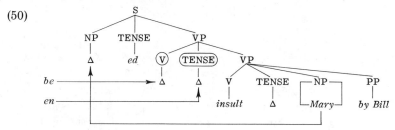

---

[16] It seems plausible that when affix movement applies to the finite affixes it moves the entire feature complex +TENSE, +AUX to the new position after the following verb. In this case, the finite and nonfinite affixes would be differentiated throughout the transformational derivation by the feature ±AUX.

Similarly, in the discussion of adjective-over-noun movement (Section V.3) we saw that the *ing* that introduces participles is not the *ing* of the progressive form. By similar reasoning, neither is the *ing* that marks the gerund. (This *ing* appears on stative verbs, on the auxiliary *have*, etc.) Now these two instances of *ing* in participles and gerunds may be directly inserted into the proper surface structure positions, or they may be moved into these positions by affix movement; but in either case the fact that these *ing*'s must occupy the same postverbal position as other TENSE affixes is predicted by (43) and the structure-preserving constraint.

In this section, we have seen that it is possible to formulate affix movement within the limits set by the structure-preserving constraint, and that when this is done a number of advantages result.

VI.2.6   Clitic Placement in French[17]

In French, pronominal objects and certain adverbial particles appear in preverbal position, in most cases obligatorily; object NP's and adverbial phrases otherwise follow the verb, as in English. Kayne (1970) shows that such pronouns and particles are "clitics" on the verb; that is, they form a constituent with the immediately following verb in surface structure, and they do not retain the NP or PP (phrasal node) status of their deep structure postverbal source.

Traditional grammars of French have long noted that these preverbal clitics do not violate the following surface ordering restriction:

$$(51) \quad \begin{bmatrix} \text{Non-third-person and all} \\ \text{reflexive pronominal object} \\ \text{clitics (direct and indirect)} \end{bmatrix} - \begin{bmatrix} \text{Third-person nonreflexive} \\ \text{direct object clitics } (le,\ la, \\ les) \end{bmatrix} -$$

$$\begin{bmatrix} \text{Third-person nonreflexive} \\ \text{indirect object clitics } (lui, \\ leur) \end{bmatrix} - \begin{bmatrix} \text{Adverbial clitic } y \text{ corres-} \\ \text{ponding to locational PP's} \\ \text{and other PP's of the form} \\ \grave{a} + \text{NP} \end{bmatrix} -$$

$$\begin{bmatrix} \text{Clitic } (en) \text{ corresponding} \\ \text{to phrase of the form} \\ de + \text{NP} \end{bmatrix} - \text{Verb}$$

Perlmutter (1970) claims that conditions on transformations cannot adequately express the ordering restrictions reflected in (51), and that therefore French clitics must be subject to an "output constraint" on the transformational component of essentially the form shown in (51). That is, he claims that motivated base rules and transformations are not sufficient grammatical devices for expressing the linguistically significant generalizations involving French pre-

---

[17] This section also appears as Emonds (1975), and appears here with permission.

verbal clitics, and that grammatical theory must be widened to incorporate a new type of device——a positively specified output constraint.[18]

The methodological weakness in Perlmutter's treatment of French clitics is that he does not state any transformations that he claims cannot in principle account for the ordering restrictions of (51). I contend that when a grammar with independently justified base rules and clitic placement transformations is explicitly presented, and a wide range of restrictions on clitic combinations accounted for, the output constraint in (51) automatically follows.

The grammar of French clitics I propose uses the various tools provided for in the structure-preserving framework in crucial ways but in no case extends them beyond their normal use. That is, "the structure-preserving constraint makes exactly the right prediction in the case of dative movement [read here, French clitic placement], and may well serve as a useful guide in research for correctly reformulating (and for discovering) other syntactic transformations [Emonds, 1972b, p. 25]."

I first propose a base rule for the verbal complex in French; it will be expanded in the course of discussion:

$$(52) \qquad V' \rightarrow \left\{ \begin{matrix} V' \\ \text{TENSE} \end{matrix} \right\} -V, \text{ where VP} \rightarrow V'. \dots$$

In turn, V' is the head of VP (i.e., V''). As is well known, there are several noncompound tenses in French; they are not of concern here.[19]

Rule (52) gives rise to structures like the following at a stage in the derivation of a sentence that follows application of rules like the passive but precedes affix movement:

(53)

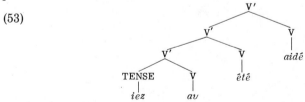

---

[18]Actually Perlmutter does not seem to make this claim for French. He first makes this claim for Spanish and argues for it, and then suggests that the apparently very similar clitic system in French must be described by a similar formal device. I will not deal with Spanish here, but will show only that no such formal device is needed for French; I am not competent to discuss the situation in Spanish. Otero (in press) and Strozer (in preparation), working independently on Spanish, have arrived at the conclusion that a positive output constraint is not needed there either.

This section owes much to fruitful discussions with Thomas Bye, who developed a sequence of transformations somewhat different from those given here that also render an output constraint on French clitics redundant.

[19]I am assuming that there is an affix movement rule in French that permutes TENSE–V; however, it may be a local rather than a structure-preserving rule in that there is no productive lexical class of verbs in French that take deep structure participial affixes (such as the English temporal aspect verbs that take *ing*). This suggests that it would be incorrect to generate TENSE in two base positions in French, as was done in the preceding sections for English.

By the general definition of "head of a phrase" given in Chapter I, the right-most V in (53) is the head of the highest V′ and, consequently, of the entire VP. We can assume that free insertion of lexical items (here, main verbs) rather than of grammatical formatives can take place only under lexical categories which are heads of phrases (heads of H″ constituents). This ensures that the two left V′s in (53) must be either empty or grammatical formatives. (It would appear that the conditioning factor for the past participle form in French in this framework is that V have V′ as a left sister.)

The first clitics I will consider are the "adverbial" clitics *y* and *en*. Kayne (1970) calls them "pro-PP" clitics, and justifies this by demonstrating that they are indifferent to the typical pronominal distinctions of number, gender, and even person. (That is, they are NOT necessarily third person: *Il a parlé beaucoup de toi, et il en parle toujours*.) They thus should be distinguished by some feature from pronoun clitics (PRO), which do exhibit these character-istics; for convenience I simply call them CL. [20]

Kayne (1970) establishes that some instances of *en* (those that do not alternate with *de* + NP, as in *s'en aller*, *en venir à* NP, *en avoir marre de* NP, etc.) appear in deep structure with the following verb. Revising (52) as (55), we could say that these uses of *en* appear in deep structure as follows:

(54)

(55) $V' \longrightarrow \left\{ \begin{matrix} V' \\ (CL) \ TENSE \end{matrix} \right\} V$

If CL is filled in deep structure, it has the realization *en*. Under certain condi-tions *de* + PRO elsewhere in the clause may be deleted and *en* inserted in CL (Gross, 1968; Ruwet, 1972). In fact Gross notes that this may take place even when there is a deep structure *en* present; as a result he postulates a rule transforming *en* + *en* into *en*. The structure-preserving formulation of this *en* insertion, however, PREDICTS that no *en* + *en* sequence can result; the facts noted by Gross can be accounted for by formulating the *en* insertion that

---

[20] It seems likely that CL is really an instance of the feature DIR (found on prepositions of direction), since the *y*—*en* distinction is basically that of *à*—*de* (*to*—*from* in English).

accompanies *de* + PRO deletion as a replacement of CL (*en* or Δ) rather than as a replacement of $[_{CL} \Delta]$ only.

Kayne (1970) points out that no transformationally inserted *y* (i.e., one that alternates with postverbal PP's) ever precedes a deep structure *en* or a transformationally inserted *en* [as would in fact be wrongly allowed by (51)]. Kayne claims that only an idiomatic *y*, such as in the impersonal expression *il y a* (*y avoir*), can precede *en*. This again can be naturally accounted for by formulating *y* insertion as a substitution for—in this case—the base-generated form $[_{CL} \Delta]$.[21]

The sentences to be excluded are of the type shown in (56):

(56) **J'ai eu beaucoup de peine à Rôme, mais je n'y en ai jamais parlé.*
   *Tu ne trouveras pas tous ces livres dans la bibliotèque, bien que tu
   y en trouveras quelques-uns.
   *A Vincennes, on met à la porte ceux qui y en ont marre.
   *Quelle histoire! La suite y en sera mal comprise!

It should be noted that in a grammar that does not formulate *en* and *y* insertion as substitutions for CL, there must be special restrictions to prevent the insertion of *y* from postverbal position if *en* is present, or the insertion of *en* if *y* is present. Such restrictions are in no way accounted for by (51). Thus I conclude that the behavior of the adverbial clitics in French supports the structure-preserving constraint in that descriptive adequacy requires that those insertions of *y* and *en* whose structural descriptions contain variables must be made into the deep structure node CL, generated by (55).[22]

Before considering the pronominal clitics we should fix our representations of the underlying forms of pronouns in NP positions. As is usual in French grammar, we take the basic pronoun forms to be the "strong forms" that appear as objects of prepositions, after *ne* V . . . *que*, in conjoined NP's, in isolated expressions, with the emphatic morpheme *même*, etc.:

---

[21]The question of how idioms like *y avoir* are to be represented does not affect the argument that all insertions of *y* and *en* by (nonlocal) transformations are into the base position whose existence is independently justified in Kayne (1970). For either *y avoir* is represented with *y* preceding the CL in the base or it is not. If it is, nothing more need be said. If not, *y* or the feature that triggers its insertion can be located on or to the left of the idiomatic V in question, and a local transformation can correctly place *y* before a surface *en*, without requiring an output constraint.

   Y avoir can perhaps best be treated analogously to obligatorily reflexive impersonal idioms (*se pouvoir*, *s'agir*, etc.) by saying that this *y* is an irregular realization of a deep structure PRO [to be introduced in (65)], whereas otherwise PRO = *se*.

[22]As pointed out to me by Lora Weinroth, Grévisse (1959, 433–434) cites literary examples acceptable to many speakers which are at odds with Kayne's restriction: *Je n'y en ai point vu. L'on me dit tant de mal de cet homme, et j'y en vois si peu.* A possible description compatible with the analysis here is given in note 31.

(57)

	Singular		Plural	
	Masculine, or unmarked gender	Feminine, or marked gender	Masculine, or unmarked gender	Feminine, or marked gender
I person	*moi*		*nous*	
II person	*toi*		*vous*	
III person, reflexive	*soi*		*soi*	
III person, nonreflexive	*lui*	*elle*	*eux*	*elles*

I take these forms to be generated by rules like the following:[23]

(58)
$$NP \rightarrow \left\{ \begin{matrix} DET{-}N \quad -\ldots \\ PRO \end{matrix} \right\}$$

$$PRO \rightarrow \begin{bmatrix} \alpha \ PLURAL \\ \beta \ FEM \\ \gamma \ III \end{bmatrix}$$

$$\begin{bmatrix} PRO \\ +III \end{bmatrix} \rightarrow \alpha \ REFL$$

$$\begin{bmatrix} PRO \\ -III \end{bmatrix} \rightarrow \begin{bmatrix} \alpha \ II \\ +REFL \end{bmatrix}$$

Let us now fix our attention on the preverbal pronominal clitics. Given the preceding arguments concerning the adverbial clitics CL, the output constraint in (51) is now somewhat reduced, to (59):

(59)
$$\left\{ \begin{matrix} me \\ te \\ se \\ nous \\ vous \end{matrix} \right\} - \left\{ \begin{matrix} le \\ la \\ les \end{matrix} \right\} - \left\{ \begin{matrix} lui \\ leur \end{matrix} \right\} \ -CL{-}V$$

This, however, is inadequate in three ways:[24] (i) In (second person) affirmative imperatives clitic sequences appear after the verb rather than before it. (ii) In such affirmative imperatives the clitic sequences permitted are those in (60)

---

[23]The arguments of Delorme and Dougherty (1972) to the effect that pronouns are not articles are very convincing for French, especially in that much of the evidence that is taken as crucial in Postal (1966) for establishing that pronouns ARE articles in English is lacking in French.

In (58), all non-third-person pronouns are assigned the syntactic feature +REFL. Nothing in the analysis crucially depends on this, although it slightly simplifies certain rules, such as (63).

[24]Problems (i)—(iii) in the text are acknowledged by Perlmutter.

rather than simply those in (59) with the V first [third-person reflexives cannot be the objects of imperatives for obvious reasons, so the *soi* in (60) is for the moment vacuous]:

(60)
$$
\left\{
\begin{array}{l}
le \\
la \\
les
\end{array}
\right\}
-
\left\{
\begin{array}{l}
soi \\
moi \\
toi \\
nous \\
vous \\
lui \\
leur
\end{array}
\right\}
-\text{CL}
$$

(61)   **N'aie pas peur; présente-toi-lui aussitôt que possible!*
          *Décrivez-nous-leur d'une manière gentille, s'il vous plaît!

(iii) In (59) we find that elements of the first and third columns cannot generally cooccur:[25]

(62)   **Jean me lui a présenté d'une manière tres gentille.*
          *Mon ami écrit à des cousins éloignés; il essaie de se leur décrire
              parce qu'ils viendront le chercher à la gare.
          *Ne nous lui avez-vous pas recommendés?
          *Quand vous leur êtes-vous adressés?

Before turning to problems (i)—(iii), it is important to note that the clitics *me* and *te* have the "strong pronoun" form of (57) when they occur postverbally in affirmative imperatives. Kayne (1970) shows that *moi* and *toi* are true clitics in these positions; some of his arguments are reproduced in section VI.1. Thus it is not clitic status that "reduces" *moi—toi* to *me—te* but, rather, (preverbal) position. This alternation must be accounted for subsequent to the positioning of the clitics in affirmative imperatives, which, in turn, must be done after the output condition in (59) applies to derivations. Hence, we can replace *me—te—se* in (59) with *moi—toi—soi*.

Perlmutter (1970) notes that problems (i)—(ii) make it "necessary to discover just what types of rules can apply after the application of surface structure constraints, constraining this class of rules as much as possible [p. 226]." One first try at imposing such a restriction might be to say that only local or root transformations can apply "after" surface structure (output) con-

---

[25] Some marginal examples are given by Perlmutter in which both elements are indirect objects; i.e., one of them is a "dative of interest," somewhat unusual in standard French. Such datives of interest characteristically—perhaps by definition—do not alternate with postverbal indirect object NP's. Their nonmarginal character in some dialects would in fact motivate a separate deep structure preverbal clitic position in the base, thus INCREASING the possible types of structure-preserving clitic placement rules. Such an approach to the datives of interest in Spanish, in fact, seems quite plausible to me.

straints. When we do this we see that the three special statements that would be required in a fully explicit grammar to account for (i)—(iii) can be reduced to two. Suppose we take (60) rather than (59) as an output constraint on clitic sequences in derivations at the point when the last rule that is not a root or local transformation applies (whether or not one agrees that such rules are all structure-preserving). Further, let the clitic sequences subject to (60) be in pre-verbal position [as are the sequences subject to (59) in Perlmutter's grammar].

A single root transformation preposing the V over such a clitic sequence (dependent on the absence of any preceding material in the string) derives the affirmative imperative construction (cf. Section VI.1). A clitic—imperative inversion of this type is clearly needed in any grammar of French. Thus (i) and (ii) are accounted for.

The assumption that (60) is the form of the output constraint also automatically accounts for why the first- and third-column forms in (59) do not cooccur as preverbal clitics. In exchange we need a local rule to interchange *le, la, les,* and those forms other than *lui—leur* in column two of (60) when these precede the verb:

$$(63)\quad \textbf{\textit{Clitic Interchange:}} \quad \begin{Bmatrix} le \\ la \\ les \end{Bmatrix} - \begin{bmatrix} \begin{bmatrix} \text{PRO} \\ +\text{REFL} \end{bmatrix}_{V'} \end{bmatrix} -(\text{CL}) + \underset{V'}{V} \Rightarrow$$

$$\emptyset - 2 + 1 - 3$$

Clitic interchange is a local rule in which the V′ is a (possibly phrasal) node specified without variables and the feature for *le, la, les* is the adjacent non-phrase node. [We will see later that the rule placing *le, la, les* at the left of V′ in an explicit grammar of clitic placement is most simply stated if the two elements are sister constituents in derived structure; the rule in question is (67)].[26]

By replacing (59) with (60) I have been able to specify what kinds of rules may apply "after" surface structure constraints more narrowly than Perlmutter (namely, only root transformations and local transformations may so apply); further, problems (i)—(iii) in Perlmutter's grammar have been reduced to two statements—the root transformation of clitic—imperative inversion and the clitic interchange rule in (63).

It will be observed that (63) is stated with PRO as its second term. The second-column forms in the new "output constraint" in (60) are in fact the SAME as the forms of PRO in NP's displayed in (57), with two exceptions: The specifically feminine-gender forms are missing in (60), and *leur* is a suppletive form for *eux.* So we are quite justified in rewriting the new output

---

[26] I assume that clitic interchange can follow affix movement, eliminating TENSE in (63). Ordinarily clitic interchange follows clitic—imperative inversion, but if not, dialect forms such as *Donnez-me-le* result.

constraint in (60) as (64); only one suppletive alternation (*eux—leur*) differentiates the clitic PRO in (64) and the PRO generated in (58) in NP position:[27]

(64)   ***Output Constraint after All Nonroot and Nonlocal Transformations:***

$$\begin{Bmatrix} le \\ la \\ les \end{Bmatrix} - \begin{bmatrix} \text{PRO} \\ -\text{FEM} \end{bmatrix} -\text{CL} - \text{V}$$

We may now pose the question concerning the need for an output constraint on preverbal clitics in French as follows: Are the configurations in trees of the form (64) (subsequent to the last nonroot, nonlocal transformation) predictable from independently motivated rules of the grammar, or must these rules be supplemented by an output constraint itself of the form (64)?

It is incumbent on one who claims that the first alternative is correct, as I do, to give the rules that yield the sequences in (64) and to justify them. The proposed analysis in what follows is divided into two parts: I first argue that the PRO position in (64) is a deep structure clitic position (like CL) that may be filled or empty, depending on the construction. Second, I show that *le, la, les* are inserted by a LOCAL transformation and that this rule has properties significantly different from the structure-preserving clitic placement rule moving a postverbal PRO into an empty preverbal PRO position.

Kayne (1970) argues that a large class of French verbs that must have reflexive pronoun objects (*s'évanouir, s'en aller*, etc.) are subcategorized in deep structure to take a preceding clitic form (i.e., they have a lexical feature such as + REFL — _____ or + PRO — _____). This claim can be accommodated in our framework by revising (55) as follows:

(65) $\text{V}' \to \begin{Bmatrix} \text{V}' \\ (\text{PRO}) - (\text{CL}) - \text{TENSE} \end{Bmatrix} - \text{V}$

We may suppose that the deep structure form of PRO in this position is, say, *soi*, if it is filled. PRO in (65) may be generated as an empty node in deep structure if the verb is not of the intrinsically reflexive class.[28]

---

[27]To further underscore the claim that the PRO of NP's and the PRO for preverbal object clitics [in (64)] are the same (save for one suppletion), one can compare PRO forms with a set of pronominal forms in French that are almost totally different from the PRO forms—the subject clitics:

> **Subject clitic pronouns:** *je, tu, on, nous, vous, il, ils, elle(s).*
> **Corresponding PRO forms:** *moi, toi, soi, nous, vous, lui, leur, elle(s).*

[28]Section I.3 suggests that a non-phrasal category such as PRO "can appear but once in the base rules, except that it may cooccur as an optional syntactic feature on some other category." It is likely that "A exhaustively dominates B" and "B is a feature that cooccurs with A" should have the same theoretical status. If so, PRO is in effect an optional syntactic feature in (58), so (65) does not violate the quoted restriction.

If not, REFL is an optional feature on PRO, and so could replace PRO in (65) and appropriately throughout the following discussion.

If Kayne's arguments are correct, both the output constraint analysis of French clitics and my analysis must generate SOME node in the position of PRO in (65), and must contain a rule that copies features of grammatical person and number from the subject NP onto this node. Such a rule can be stated as follows, if the deep structure realization of this preverbal node is taken as *soi* (or *se*):

(66) ***Intrinsic Reflexive:***

$$X - \begin{bmatrix} PRO \\ _{NP} -III \end{bmatrix} - Y - \begin{bmatrix} _{V'} [_{PRO} \ soi] - Z \end{bmatrix} + W \implies 1-2-3-2-5$$

This rule plays an important part in my argument that the structure-preserving framework is not only compatible with the facts of French clitic placement but provides explanations of it otherwise unavailable. See Section VII.2.7.

Rule (66) is one "clitic placement" rule that determines the surface form of the nodes PRO and CL generated by (65); it derives the preverbal pronominal clitics whose form depends on the subject NP. We can now state the placement rules for pronominal clitics that are transforms of pronoun objects.

When we examine the properties of preverbal object pronoun clitics, we find a series of differences that set off *le*, *la*, *les* from the others: (i) There can be two preverbal object pronouns only if one of them is *le*, *la*, *les* [as is clear from (64), whatever its status in the grammar]. (ii) *Le*, *la*, *les* are of radically different form from pronouns generated under NP, whereas (as we saw earlier) the other preverbal object pronouns are essentially of the same form as the latter. (iii) *Le*, *la*, *les* are the only preverbal object pronouns that can be marked for grammatical gender, whereas the other preverbal object pronouns can never be so marked. (iv) The contrast between *le*, *la*, *les* and *lui*, *leur* in preverbal position is the sole instance in French where one might seem to have a distinction in grammatical "case."

The last distinction, in fact, gives us the clue for accounting for the others. If there is a single generalization to be made about French, it would seem to be that French is devoid of surface case. English does have a three-way surface case division for pronouns in NP positions, but French has no possessive case for pronouns (rather, there are pronominal adjectives), nor does it have a (nonclitic) subject form for pronouns, as English does.

Thus we want to avoid any ad hoc recourse to "case" features such as "dative" in describing French. Instead, the special form of the direct object pronouns *le*, *la*, *les* (their contrast with *lui*, *leur*) should be attributed directly to the required absence of the preposition *à* in their postverbal deep structure source position. (In contrast, *lui*, *leur* derive from an *à* phrase.) For other than third-person, nonreflexive objects, whether the postverbal source phrase is a direct or indirect object makes no difference.

We can describe this formally by saying that third-person, nonreflexive DIRECT OBJECTS undergo a special placement rule different from the one that places all other pronoun objects into the preverbal PRO position generated by (65). This rule can also assign a feature that accounts for their different (non-PRO-like) form, and can preserve grammatical gender:

(67)   **Le, La, Les *Rule*:**[29]

$$X-V'-\begin{bmatrix} \text{PRO} \\ +\text{III} \\ -\text{REFL} \\ \alpha\text{PLUR} \\ _{\text{NP}}\,\beta\text{FEM} \end{bmatrix} -Y \Rightarrow 1-\begin{bmatrix} \text{DEF} \\ \alpha\text{PLUR} \\ \beta\text{FEM} \end{bmatrix} +2-\emptyset-4$$

Rule (67) is not strictly a movement rule; it is a deletion combined with an insertion of an element that agrees with the deleted element in grammatical number and gender.[30]

More important, rule (67) is a local transformation; that is, it is a "transformational operation that affects a sequence of a single nonphrase node C and one adjacent constituent C' that is specified without a variable." In this case, we can permit the phrase node to be taken as V' in the case that certain adverbial phrases (AP's) are present under V'. The fact that PRO is the only element under a phrase node NP is irrelevant; a similar situation obtains with the local transformation of English particle movement (discussed in Section II.3), in which a nonphrase node P that is the only element under a phrase node PP moves over an adjacent phrase node NP.

Rule (67) transforms the (postverbal) direct object pronouns *lui, eux, elle, elles* into the preverbal "definite article" forms, *le, la, les*. After this operation, all other preverbal object pronouns can be accounted for by a single structure-preserving pronominal clitic placement movement transformation:

(68)   ***Pronominal Clitic Placement:***

$$X-\begin{bmatrix} _{\text{V}'} \begin{bmatrix} _{\text{PRO}} \Delta \end{bmatrix} -Y \end{bmatrix} +Z-\begin{bmatrix} _{\text{NP}} (\grave{a})-\text{PRO} \end{bmatrix} -W \Rightarrow$$
$$1-\begin{bmatrix} 5 \\ -\text{FEM} \end{bmatrix} -3-\emptyset-\emptyset-6$$

It is important to note that pronominal clitic placement cannot be construed as a local transformation, because it moves elements over V' and over V'–NP sequences. I claim that it is no accident that the one object pronoun clitic place-

---

[29] We can take DEF as the feature(s) characteristic of the definite article in noun phrases (*le, la, les*). Rule (67) could assign another feature as well, but DEF serves the purpose. By (58), + III is redundant.

[30] As stated in my analysis of English auxiliaries, I am not trying to determine exactly the surface structure dominance relations of affixes and clitics. The exact derived structure produced by (67) is not at issue.

ment rule for which one CANNOT justify a deep structure empty node to the left of V' (i.e., the *le, la, les* rule) can be formulated as a local transformation, and that the object pronoun clitic placement rule that MUST contain a variable is one for which one can justify such a deep structure empty node [as Kayne (1970) did]. These "coincidences"—the import of which I return to later—are both absolute requirements on the grammar of French set by the structure-preserving constraint.

If (68) is a structure-preserving rule of a "must-apply" type, it cannot make use of the OPTIONAL PRO node, as observed in Nagahara (1974). However, Kayne (1969) argues on other grounds that in fact pronominal clitic placement is optional and is to be supplemented by negative output constraints. (I am here arguing not against negative output constraints but against positive ones.) Therefore the objection of Nagahara to a structure-preserving clitic placement rule loses its force, although his general observation remains valid.

I consider the brief discussion of Spanish and French clitics in Emonds (1970) to be inadequate (hence the completely new treatment here of the French case), and so I do not go any further in commenting on Nagahara's careful discussion of my own previous proposals.

It should be clear that the two descriptively adequate object pronoun clitic placement rules, (67) and (68), are each fairly easy to state in the algebra of transformations. On the other hand, they differ from each other strongly [so as to reflect the peculiarities of *le, la, les* placement outlined in (i)−(iv)]: (68) differs from (67) in permitting *à*, in effecting a movement rather than a deletion−insertion, in effacing rather than preserving gender marking, and in being a movement to a base position (i.e., being a substitution for an empty node).[31] It is difficult to conceive of a collapse of the two rules that would maintain descriptive adequacy or would not introduce a plethora of ad hoc conditions on the rule, even with the aid of an output constraint. But even if this were possible, an account of preverbal pronominal clitics in French that utilizes two straightforward transformations is to be preferred to one that uses one transformation and requires adding output constraints to the theory of grammar.

Clearly the three pronominal clitic placement rules in (66)−(68) yield the configurations of the "output constraint" in (64) automatically, i.e., (64) is a consequence of the correct grammar of French but not part of it. After these three rules and any rules of *y* and *en* placement produce configurations as in (64), the root transformation of clitic−imperative inversion and the local transformation of clitic interchange in (63) produce surface forms.[32]

---

[31]The dialect of those who accept *y−en* sequences as in note 22 could perhaps best be described by inserting *y* in some cases into PRO as well as into CL, for such speakers do seem to reject PRO−*y−en* sequences: **Jean nous y en a parlé beaucoup.*

[32]This analysis further solves an interesting problem raised in Kayne (1970) concerning deletion under identity without recourse either to case features or to phonological information. He notes the following:

VI.2.7   Explanatory Value of a Structure-Preserving Analysis of Clitics

The structure-preserving analysis of French clitic placement makes possible certain explanations about the behavior of this system. These explanations are not available in a system that does not use the structure-preserving constraint (which limits the class of possible transformational grammars) but uses, instead, positively stated output "constraints," which expand the class of possible transformational grammars (cf. Ruwet, 1972, pp. 22–26). For example, once we choose PRO as the clitic element that Kayne (1970) claims must be present in deep structure for intrinsic reflexives, the structure-preserving constraint requires that any movements of PRO outside of NP's [where PRO is generated by (58)] must be to this clitic position.[33] Hence, the fact that the intrinsic reflexive rule in (66) and the pronominal clitic placement rule in (68) move PRO to the same position (and that the two rules together can have a total of one application per clause) is not an accident or the result of a mysterious "conspiracy" in the structure-preserving framework—it is, rather, the behavior that is expected in a natural language.

Footnote 32 continued

The combination clitic + auxiliary verb can be deleted in the second of two conjoined verb phrases under identity with the same combination in the first conjunct, even though the clitic is an indirect object (derived from *à* + PRO) in one conjunct and a direct object in the other. He gives the following examples:

(i) *Paul nous a frappé et donné des coups de pied.*
  Paul te fera gifler par George et donner des coups de pied par Jean.

On the other hand, this deletion is excluded when the direct and indirect object clitics have different phonological forms (i.e., in the nonreflexive third person):

(ii) **Paul l'a frappé et donné des coups de pied. (cf. Paul l'a frappé et lui a donné des coups de pied.)*
  *Paul le fera gifler par George et donner des coups de pied par Jean. (cf. Paul le fera gifler par George et lui fera donner des coups de pied par Jean.)

Kayne notes that these facts indicate that the syntactic feature of case (which he assumes differentiates all indirect object clitics from all direct object clitics in French) is apparently ignored by the deletion under identity in question [cf. (i)], whereas the phonological differences in the third-person nonreflexives are not [cf. (ii)]; further, he notes that both of these characteristics, particularly the latter, are not the usual conditions under which syntactic deletion transformations apply.

In my analysis, however, there are no case features on the object pronoun clitics. In (i) it is simply then that the sequences PRO—V are deleted under (complete) syntactic identity. Further, we have seen that JUST IN THE CASE OF THIRD-PERSON NONREFLEXIVE CLITICS there is a category difference between the cliticized indirect objects (PRO) and the cliticized direct objects (termed DEF), due to the fact that the latter are placed in preverbal position not by the general (structure-preserving) clitic placement movement of PRO but, rather, by the special (local) *le, la, les* rule. That is, *l'a frappé* and *la fera gifler* in (ii) are instances not of PRO—V—V (as *lui a donné* and *lui fera donner* are) but, rather, of the SYNTACTICALLY distinct sequence DEF—V—V. Hence, there is no syntactic identity and no deletion under the usual assumptions about necessary conditions for deletion under identity (Chomsky, 1965, Chapter 4).

[33] Were another feature chosen, there could be NO clitic placements of PRO other than local transformations.

On the other hand, the surface structure or output constraints proposed by Perlmutter cannot naturally express the restriction that PRO can be moved to non-NP positions ONLY if it is moved to the clitic (base) position of PRO (or by a local transformation). For example, in a non-structure-preserving framework with an output constraint on preverbal clitics it would be as easy to describe a language in which the intrinsic reflexive clitics appeared AFTER the verb and the transforms of object pronouns appeared BEFORE the verb.

Similarly, a theory of grammar without the structure-preserving constraint but with surface structure constraints on the ordering of clitics would supposedly permit a language A identical to French except that the particle *en* is placed in preverbal position ONLY IF it originates to the left of the verb, and that *en* is placed to the right of the verb phrase if it originates to the right of the verb. Language A would then have grammatical judgments as in (69), where % indicates ungrammaticality in A:

(69) *Le dehors de cette maison est laid, mais* $\left\{ \begin{array}{l} \text{\textit{le dedans en est joli.}} \\ \text{\%\textit{le dedans est joli en.}} \end{array} \right\}$

> %*Je n'en aime pas le dehors.*
> *Je n'aime pas le dehors en.*
> %*J'en étais très fier.*
> *J'étais très fier en.*

A surface structure constraint demands that a PREVERBAL *en* follow all other clitics in French, but it does not ensure that any rule producing a clitic will move it into preverbal positions. On the other hand, analyzing surface constraints as resulting from the phrase structure rules and imposing the structure-preserving constraint on grammars excludes in principle a language like A.

Another way to look at the empirical content of the structure-preserving constraint is to ask what, in this framework, would make a preverbal pronominal clitic system impossible. We have seen that the local transformation that moves (nonreflexive third-person) direct objects over the verb does not require that a clitic node be generated in a preverbal position in French by the base rules. However, the full-blown clitic placement rule in (68), which moves both direct and indirect object pronouns over a variable, does require such a base node, and I have required that such base nodes can be generated only if there is a productive class of constructions for which they are filled in the deep structure. This means that the full clitic placement rule in (68) can exist in French only by virtue of the fact that there is a lexical class of intrinsically reflexive (more neutrally, "intrinsically pronominal") verbs. That is, the analysis given here claims that two often-noted central characteristics of the French verbal system (the predominance of reflexive constructions over intransitive constructions and the object pronoun clitic system) are crucially interdependent: The second characteristic depends on the existence of the first. This claim is of interest in reconstructing the syntactic history of the language, and is clearly falsifiable.[34]

A further advantage to a structure-preserving analysis of clitics (and a disadvantage of the output constraint theory) is that only the former automatically explains why there are no restrictions on sequences of clitics that are not (roughly) in the same "phrase." Of course the output constraint theory can add a statement to universal grammar to this effect, but there already are conventions of universal grammar governing phrase structure rules and transformations that guarantee these results.

For example, the sequences of Spanish clitics in boldface in (70), in which the clitics are in different clauses, are perfectly acceptable even though the order restrictions that hold within single clauses (whatever their source) are broken:

(70)   *El hombre que quiere lavar-**se se** fué.*
              *El hombre que quiere besar-**la me lo** dijo.*

If an analysis anything like that for French is adequate for Spanish (involving intrinsically reflexive verbs, perhaps a local transformation for direct object pronouns, and perhaps also a deep structure "dative of interest" position), then any restriction on clitics will automatically hold only for clitics that are attached to a single verb.

VI.3   SOME FURTHER CASES OF LOCAL TRANSFORMATIONS

We have already added in this chapter to the stock of local transformations for English and French. In Section VI.2 the rule inserting the auxiliary *do* in English (Section VI.2.3) and the clitic interchange and *le, la, les* rules for French (Section VI.2.6) are formulated as local transformations. In order to see what further formal restriction on the notion of "local transformation" may be appropriate, I present some additional examples of transformational operations in this class.

---

[34]There is of course no claim to the effect that clitic placements that can be effected by local or root transformations depend on the existence of lexically reflexive (pronominal) verbs. For example, in Spanish the pronoun clitics precede a finite verb but follow infinitives or participles. This does not require base clitic positions before and after the verb. Rather, the tensed verb (or nontensed verb, depending on one's analysis) can be interchanged with the clitic sequence by a local transformation. Incidentally, there is less reason to consider the verbal complex V′ to be a phrase node in Spanish than in French, as it cannot dominate adverbs in Spanish. This was pointed out to me by Carlos Otero.

VI.3.1   DEG Postposing

Adjective modifiers generally precede the head adjective of an AP. This includes not only adverbial and noun phrase modifiers, as in *surprisingly bold*, *actually stupid*, *five miles long*, *a few days* old, etc., but also the characteristically adjectival modifiers of degree (DEG) such as *very*, *quite*, *so*, *as*, *how*, *too*, *more*, and *most*. But the three adjectival modifer morphemes *enough*, *er*, and *est* (*heavy enough*, *heavier*, *heaviest*) are exceptions to this rule, since they follow the head adjectives in surface structure. Thus one postulates a permutation by which "DEG—A" becomes "A—DEG," where DEG is *er*, *est*, or *enough* only. This DEG POSTPOSING rule is a local transformation, in which DEG and A are the adjacent constituents.

VI.3.2   DET Incorporation

There is a limited class of deep structure PP's with pronominal NP objects that are transformed into adverbs (intransitive prepositions):

(71)
in this	= *herein*	*in that*	= *therein*
by this	= *hereby*	*by that*	= *thereby*
of this	= *hereof*	*of that*	= *thereof*
after this	= *hereafter*	*after that*	= *thereafter*
upon this	= *hereupon*	*upon that*	= *thereupon*

in which	= *wherein*
by which	= *whereby*
of which	= *whereof*
after which	= *whereafter*
upon which	= *whereupon*

These adverbs can be derived by a rule of DET INCORPORATION, which has the form shown in (72):

$$(72) \qquad [_{PP} \text{ P–DET}] \Rightarrow \begin{bmatrix} 2 \\ +\text{LOC} \end{bmatrix} + 1 - \emptyset$$

where DET = *which*, *this*, or *that*.

$\big[$It is probable that $2 + 1$ in (72) is dominated by P as well as by PP in derived structure, but the derived structure produced by local transformations is not at issue here.$\big]$

VI.3.3   Article Movement

Consider now the examples in (73):

(73)   *Mary wouldn't associate with a girl less fortunate than her.*
         Mary wouldn't associate with a less fortunate girl.
         Is a very young kitten able to go outside?
         That is a most depressing movie.

The indefinite article $[a(n)]$, like other determiners and numerals, precedes prenominal adjective phrases such as *most depressing, less fortunate, very young,* etc. However, if that adjective phrase is introduced by *too, as,* or *how,* this is not the case:

(74)   *A how young kitten is able to go outside?*
         How young a kitten is able to go outside?
         John is an as nice boy as you will find.
         John is as nice a boy as you will find.
         This is a too depressing movie to see a second time.
         This is too depressing a movie to see a second time.

This permutation of the indefinite article and AP (i.e., AP's introduced by *as, how,* and *too* only) can clearly be formulated as a permitted local transformation.

VI.3.4   Quantifier Postposition

Dougherty (1968) has formulated a rule by which the determiners *all, both,* and *each* can sometimes appear between the subject NP and the auxiliary. The source of these determiners in this position is an underlying subject of the form DET$-of-$NP. By this rule, QUANTIFIER POSTPOSITION, the (b) sentences in (75)$-$(76) are derived from the (a) sentences:

(75)   a.   *All of us can speak Russian.*
         b.   *We all can speak Russian.*
         c.   *All of us each can speak Russian.*

(76)   a.   *Each of the boys were playing in both the parks.*
         b.   *The boys each were playing in both the parks.*
         c.   *Each of the boys both were playing in the parks.*

It should be recalled that the auxiliaries *have* and *be* are in the AUX position when they are not preceded by other auxiliaries, owing to the verb raising rule.

It may be that the same rule that relates the sentences in (75)$-$(76) also relates the grammatical pairs in (77):

(77)   *John gave all of them some new clothes.*
             John gave them all some new clothes.
             John gave the boys all some new clothes.

> *We have been dealing with both of them.*
> *We have been dealing with them both.*
> **We have been dealing with the problems both.*

I assign a somewhat different underlying structure to NP's like *all of us* and *each of the boys* than Dougherty does:

(78)

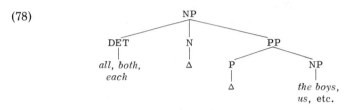

Example (78) is converted to an acceptable surface structure by a rule deleting $[_N \Delta]$ after various determiners; the same rule gives rise to NP's like those in boldface in (79):

(79) *Mary and Sue have very little education, but **both** are very clever.*
   *The bread was nice, though I didn't buy **any**.*

Of is inserted in (78) by the same rule that inserts *of* in *the destruction of the city, the length of the table, the sleep of the king, the hat of John's*, etc; the insertion of *of* may precede $[_N \Delta]$ deletion.

  The main reason for choosing an underlying representation as in (78), other than the fact that the rules that convert (78) to a surface structure are needed in the grammar anyway, is that such a structure does not conflict with the rule that assigns subjective case to pronouns in English just in case their NP's are immediately dominated by S (cf. Section V.9). That is, the subject pronoun rule works here only if the highest NP and the NP over the pronoun in *all of us, some of them*, etc. is not the same, and (78) satisfies this requirement.

  Given an underlying structure like (78) for NP's such as *all of us* and *each of the boys*, the quantifier postposition transformation must be stated thus (I assume that phrasal nodes that lose their head AND specifier "prune"):

(80) ***Quantifier Postposition:***

$$\left[_{NP} \text{DET} - [_{PP} \Delta - \text{NP}]\right] \Rightarrow \emptyset - \emptyset - 3 + 1$$

where DET = *all, both, each*.

This is a local transformation in which the nonphrase node is DET and the adjacent phrase node specified without a variable is PP.

  The determiners moved by (80) can also FOLLOW the first auxiliary (AUX); with varying degrees of acceptability, they can follow succeeding auxiliaries:

(81)　　　a.　*We can all speak Russian.*
　　　　　　　The boys were both playing in the park.
　　　　　　　My friends are each anxious to see you.

　　　　　b.　*?The kittens will be both ready tomorrow.*
　　　　　　　?Your friends should have each bought that book.
　　　　　　　?The children have been all examined thoroughly.
　　　　　　　?We may be each thinking differently tomorrow.
　　　　　　　*We should have been all packing our baggage.
　　　　　　　*Your parents must be being both severely criticized.

As Dougherty points out, assigning all such determiners a source in the subject NP explains why they do not occur when there are surface determiners of the same class inside the subject:

(82)　　　　　**All of us can each speak Russian.*
　　　　　　　*Both the boys were each playing in the park.
　　　　　　　*Each of my friends are all anxious to see you.
　　　　　　　*Any of us can all speak Russian.
　　　　　　　*Some of the kittens will all be ready tomorrow.

Ordinarily, such determiners cannot follow the verb:

(83)　　　　　**We can speak all some Russian.*
　　　　　　　*We speak all some Russian.
　　　　　　　*The boys played both in the park.
　　　　　　　*My friends like each you a lot.
　　　　　　　*The children were examined all.
　　　　　　　*We react each slowly.
　　　　　　　*The cars hit both the brick wall.

Thus a second local transformation is required for *each*, *all*, and *both* that interchanges (just those) determiners postposed by quantifier postposition with a following auxiliary:[35]

(84) ***Quantifier—Auxiliary Interchange:***
　　　　　DET—AUX $\Rightarrow$ 2—1, DET $\neq$ NP

---

[35] If (84) is integrated with my earlier analysis of the English auxiliary, then none of the examples in (81b) will be generated by it. For the majority of cases this seems correct, but it leaves a residue of unexplained cases. One possibility for some of them is that the (unstressed) perfect auxiliary *have* is contracted with the modal auxiliary into the first AUX position in the clause; I believe this suggestion is due to David Perlmutter.

VI.4 FURTHER RESTRICTIONS ON LOCAL TRANSFORMATIONS

In this study, the following local transformations have been proposed and discussed:

> postverbal particle movement
> indirect question adjustment
> *for* phrase formation
> auxiliary *do* insertion
> clitic interchange (French)
> *le, la, les* rule (French)
> DEG postposing
> DET incorporation
> article movement
> quantifier postposition
> quantifier—auxiliary interchange
> verb—clitic inversion (Spanish)

In addition, it seems plausible to assume that various contraction rules (such as the change of AUX—NEG to AUX—*n't* in English) involve syntactic rearrangements that can be described by local transformations, although I have made no attempt to work out the well-known cases in detail.

It would be remarkable if the initial attempt here to delimit a linguistically significant class of "local transformations" [by the definition in (1)] did not require modifications and even reconceptualizing when further research in this framework is carried out. I have given a fairly explicit characterization of this class of rules, not because I think it is definitive but because it can serve as the basis for explicit comparison with other definitions that (no doubt) will turn out to be superior. Nonetheless, I do strongly believe that there is an important and substantive notion of "strictly local transformation," not very far removed from that defined here, that plays a crucial role in legitimizing the structure-preserving constraint.

Before moving on to the more speculative last section, I think that a further restriction can be placed on the class of local transformations without loss of generality. To convince himself of the validity of this proposal, the reader may want to check over the various local rules already discussed.

(85) *In a local transformation the following relation must hold between the two constituents C—C' affected by the rule: There exists a node that **immediately dominates** one of these constituents that also dominates the other.*

The latter requirement can be rephrased using the notion of "in construction with" proposed in Klima (1964): Either C is in construction with C′ or C′ is in construction with C.

Perhaps when a more elegant characterization of strictly local transformation is found properties like (85) will follow directly from it.

The property in (85) can account for certain limitations on the negative output constraint excluding English $[_v V + ing] [_v V + ing]$ that have been noted in Pullum (1974). Suppose we view negative output constraints as special cases of local transformations (thereby claiming that in fact only negative output constraints of such form are permitted, as at least seems plausible). Formally this could be done by inserting Δ between the two V's in question by a local rule so as to obtain the excluded surface string, or by redefining local rule in such a way as to include surface constraints as well as mappings of input trees onto derived trees.

What, then, can be said of a tree in which an intransitive verb is followed by a participle modifying the subject, such as the following?

(86)

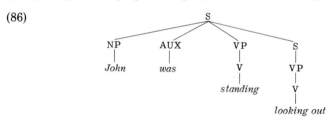

It follows from (85), since neither V is in construction with the other, that the negative output constraint will not apply, yielding a grammatical surface structure. This is in accordance with Pullum's observations.

Further, two V + *ing*'s that are in conjoined VP's (or conjoined S's) will similarly not be excluded by the double-*ing* restriction, which is correct (such facts are observed by Pullum):

The screaming, kicking professor was given the French exam.
The men fighting, knowing their cause hopeless, had started to drink.

Thus it seems reasonable to tentatively restrict negative output constraints to the class of local rules, and to impose condition (85) on the entire class of local rules.

VI.5   NON-STRUCTURE-PRESERVING DELETIONS

In this study, nothing has been said about whether transformational deletion operations should be considered as structure-preserving or not. The weakest hypothesis would be that the structure-preserving constraint does not restrict deletion, i.e., that deletion rules can operate as freely in dependent clauses as in independent clauses and can be defined in terms of nonlocal as well as local contexts.

I have not investigated deletion rules in any detail, but it seems nonetheless that the notion "possible deletion rule" can be much more severely constrained in terms of the concepts developed here, and that a few preliminary observations about plausible extensions of the structure-preserving constraint to deletion operations are in order. Since time has not allowed me to explore this question in depth, no attempt will be made here to reformulate the structure-preserving framework to make it consistent with the suggestions in this section.

The first and most general observation I would make about deletion transformations is that almost every such deletion of a SPECIFIED formative (a morpheme or Δ) that has found acceptance in generative studies of English and French is statable in terms of immediately contiguous contexts.[36] (A list of such deletions is provided later.) This suggests that such deletions may in general fall together with the class of "local transformational operations" defined in Chapter I and discussed in some detail earlier in this chapter.

It is well known that among this class of deletions of specified elements several rules, like root transformations, apply only in independent clauses. In fact such rules appear to delete just those constituents (COMP, NP, and AUX) that are immediately dominated by S; this is reminiscent of the fact that root transformations attach constituents immediately under root S's.[37] The following deletion transformations of English are of this type; that is, they delete constituents immediately dominated by a root S.

1. Deletion of the subject NP *you* and of the auxiliary *will* in subjectless imperatives:

(87)   *(You will) Please come in immediately.*
              (You will) Help me, won't you?

2. Deletion of the inverted auxiliary *should* and the subject NP *one* after a preposed *why*:

(88)   *Why (should one) buy stock at this time?*
              Why (should one) not be more prudent?

     Cf.   **How buy stock at this time?*
           *How often be extra careful on the road?

---

[36] I am not speaking here of deletion under identity and/or coreference.

[37] I mentioned earlier the observation of Kayne that root transformation (i.e., rules that apply only in independent clauses) that affect clitics are exceptions to this requirement on derived structure.

Where get badly needed drugs?
Who see for an application?

They were wondering about why buy stock at this time.
John asked me why not be more prudent.
The question of why travel to Europe hasn't been debated.

3. Deletion of the complementizers *that* and *whether* in main clauses (i.e., their appearance in dependent clauses only):

(89)   *John asked whether he could leave.*
               John asked that he be given permission.
               Whether could he leave?
               That John be given permission.

4. Deletion of the auxiliaries *be*, *have*, and *do* sentence-initially, studied in Schmerling (1973) (the following contrasts exist clearly in my speech):

(90)   *You feeling pretty lonely?*
         They been doing their share of the work?
         He come around here much any more?
         She ready to start the new job?

   Cf.   *He asked me (if) you feeling pretty lonely.*
         I don't know if they been doing their share of the work.
         I don't know if they've been doing their share of the work.
         The question of she ready to start the new job is important.

5. Deletion of the subject *you* after deletion of the auxiliary exemplified in (90):

(91) *Feeling pretty lonely?*
     Been doing their share of the work? (= Have you been doing their share of the work?)

If we attempt to assimilate the operations in 1—5 to the class of root transformations, and other specified formative deletions to the class of local transformations, the question arises as to why the operations in 1—5 are restricted to independent clauses. In 2, the reason would clearly be that the rule not only affects two adjacent constituents (AUX—NP), as in a local rule, but also requires reference to a condition in the string exterior to this sequence (the presence of *why*). In the other cases, the deletions performed are possible local transformational operations. That is, there are cases in English where COMP = *that*, NP = *one*, and AUX (in present subjunctives) are deleted in subordinate clauses. However, it must be stated for each deletion of 1 and 3—5 that the rule depends on the string variable's being empty to the left of the deleted constituent;

this doubly ensures that the rule is a root transformation—such a condition cannot be put on local rules, and the condition itself in effect limits application of the rule to independent clauses.

These considerations can be summarized as follows: Most specified formative deletions are expressible in terms of local (contiguous) contexts of the type allowed in local transformations. (However, a context of the form X_____, where X must be $\emptyset$, is not of this type.) All other specified formative deletions apply in independent clauses only. Therefore it seems plausible that the notions of local and root transformations can be extended to deletions without weakening the empirical import or the intuitive unity of these concepts. Given such definitions of root and local transformational deletion operations, the following condition can be put on grammars:

(92) **Condition on Specified Deletions:** *No deletion of a specified formative by a transformational rule is structure-preserving.*

This "condition" is more accurately considered as an extension of the definition of "structure-preserving" to operations for which the concept was not previously defined. Given the structure-preserving constraint, the resulting claim is that the deletion of a specified formative in a dependent clause must be accomplished by a local transformational operation.

At this point, it might be helpful to see what kind of rule the condition on specified deletions is meant to exclude. Consider the following two hypothetical (obligatory) rules:

(93) $$\left[\,_{\text{COMP}} \text{WH}\right] - X + \text{PP} + Y \implies \emptyset - 2$$

(94) $$\text{WH} + X + \text{V} - \text{PREP} - Y \implies 1 - \emptyset - 3$$

Rule (93), if added to the grammar of English, would delete the complementizer *whether* if a prepositional phrase followed it in the same clause, incorrectly yielding data like those in (95):

(95)   *I wonder whether Bill ate cake often.*
         **I wonder Bill ate cake often.*
         **I wonder whether Bill ate cake for breakfast often.*
         I wonder Bill ate cake for breakfast often.

Rule (94) would delete an immediately postverbal preposition only in clauses that begin with WH morphemes, as in (96):

(96)   *John asked that Bill rely on Mary.*
         **John asked that Bill rely Mary.*

         **John asked whether (why, what days) Bill could rely on Mary.*
         John asked whether (why, what days) Bill could rely Mary.

John asked whether (why, what days) Bill could assign the task to Mary.

*John asked whether (why, what days) Bill could assign the task Mary.

Upon reflection it seems clear that such specified deletions (i.e., deletions that do not depend on identity and/or coreference) "over a variable" have not been needed in grammatical descriptions. Some constraint is then needed to ensure that deletions are always defined in strictly local contexts. The condition on specified deletions is an attempt to fill this need.

It may be, of course, that the needed definition of "locally defined specified formative deletion" and the definition of "local transformation" that has been used in this study for movement and insertion rules cannot be made to dovetail in an elegant way. This would not preclude the need for the two definitions, or necessarily vitiate the claim involved in (92). For the moment it seems more probable that a unified notion of "local transformation" for all types of operations exists, but I refrain here from revising the definition of a local (movement or insertion) rule on the ground that it is premature to do so without further research.

The following list of specified formative deletions may serve as an aid in working out an appropriate generalized definition of "local transformation":

1. unstressed auxiliary *do* deletion before VP (Chapter VI)
2. deletion of certain prepositions of time (*in, on, for*)
3. deletion of the noun proform *one* or Δ after certain determiners (Section VI.3.4)
4. deletion of the "indefinite article" (a reduced form of the numeral *one*) after DET (Perlmutter, 1969)
5. deletion of the complementizer *that* in certain verb complements and restrictive relative clauses
6. deletion of *pas* from the negative *ne—V—pas* construction of French after certain verbs
7. deletion of the definite article in certain partitive construction uses in French: *Je prends de la bière* versus *Je ne prends pas de bière* and *Je prends beaucoup de bière.*
8. deletion of the complementizer *for* so as to yield present subjunctives (Section V.9)
9. deletion of introductory *to* in certain infinitives: *make him leave* versus *be made to leave*, etc.
10. many deletions of forms of *be*; for example, the *being* deletion rule of reduced relative clauses discussed in Section V.3
11. deletion of the possessive *'s* in certain gerunds: *I disapprove of John('s) leaving, I regret them (= their) knowing about this.*

12. deletion of *much* before adjectives (Bresnan, 1973)
13. deletion of *to* and *for* in indirect object movement
14. derivation of $AP + ly$ from $(in) + an + AP + way$ by successive deletions (Section V.2)
15. the number agreement rule (formulated as a deletion) of the present tense morpheme *s*
16. derivation of postverbal *not* (*I think not, I guess not*) from *not so* by *so* deletion (Lakoff, 1966)

Other rules could be added, but the point here is not to give an exhaustive list of specified formative deletions. Rather, it is to indicate that a great many of the most convincing rules of this type are specifiable in terms of local (contiguous) contexts. But there is still, no doubt, much to be done to make the condition on specified deletion work out in detail, both in sharpening and generalizing the definition of "local transformational operation" and in precisely formulating various rules of specified deletions. Whatever the problems involved, I suggest that such work would be a fruitful direction for research.[38]

---

[38] As an example of how one might be faced with both reworking previous formulations of a specified formative deletion and revising the definition of a local transformation, consider the claim in item 8 that English present subjunctives (*We prefer that he go*) are derived from deep structure clauses with a complementizer *for* (the *for* that appears before infinitives with expressed subjects, as in *We prefer for him to go*). We saw in Section V.9 that such a deletion is all that is necessary in the grammar of infinitives developed there to explain the similarity in distribution and meaning of the two constructions and the various dissimilarities in surface form.

A problem with this rule is that it appears to depend on what verb is present in the main clause, and further, it sometimes applies in embedded subject as well as object clauses:

> *That he go is important.*
> *For him to go is important.*
> *We prefer that he go.*
> *We prefer for him to go.*

However, Kayne (1969) shows, convincingly to my mind, that rules "governed" by different lexical choices of the verb in a higher clause do not necessarily exhibit a V (corresponding to the location of the governing verb in the tree undergoing the rule) in their structural description. Rather, he argues that a verb may be subcategorized lexically to take a certain complement marked as exceptional vis-à-vis a certain transformation. In such an arrangement we may say that the node label for the exceptional complement "carries" (is the location of) the exception feature; hence, only this node label, and not that of the governing verb, need appear in the structural description of the rule in question.

Let us refer to the rule deleting *for* (the present subjunctive rule) as T_s. Assume that there is a rule feature for each transformation and that the unmarked value for T_s is $-T_s$ (i.e., ordinarily the rule does not apply—the subjunctive is a "marked" syntactic construction compared to the infinitive in English). Certain verbs and adjectives (*prefer, important*, etc.) can then be subcategorized to take sentence complements marked $+T_s$, and present subjunctive formation would be given as follows:

$$T_s: [_s [_{COMP} for] - X] \Rightarrow \emptyset - 2$$

Clearly T_s as stated is intuitively "locally conditioned," as are the local movement and insertion transformations studied throughout this work. On the other hand, T_s contains a variable, and this characteristic is formally a violation of the restrictions I have put on local transformations; yet it also seems clear that the variable is "in effect" an end variable, and that the S node is rather redundant.

As a last point, let us consider the claim made in Jackendoff (1972) to the effect that transformations do not effect deletions under identity and/or co-reference. (That is, he claims that anaphora are to be accounted for by semantic rules of interpretation.) If this claim holds, and if the condition on specified deletions is correct, then we could simply define structure-preserving operations in such a way that *no* deletion would be structure-preserving.

A somewhat weaker claim about the inability of transformations to effect deletions might be made as follows: Banfield (1973b) argues persuasively that certain gapping patterns and conjunctions across constituent boundaries are accomplished by deletion operations, but that these operations fall into the class of "stylistic transformations." One might wish to maintain that the only transformational deletions under identity are stylistic in this sense, and that strictly grammatical anaphora are generated in the way suggested by Jackendoff.

Banfield in fact notes that stylistic MOVEMENT transformations do in some languages break the structure-preserving constraint. This problem is discussed in Chapter I. Therefore it would not be surprising if stylistic deletion transformations were also permitted to break the constraint (even though stylistic MOVEMENT rules in Modern English do not do this). So if we weaken Jackendoff's claim that anaphora are not effected by transformations by permitting stylistic (but not purely grammatical) transformations to delete certain surface material under identity, the following extension of the concept "structure-preserving" still suggests itself:

(97) *No purely grammatical transformational deletion is structure-preserving*

A counterexample to this extension of the condition on specified deletions would be the rule of VP DELETION. Bresnan (1971b) argues that the "identity of sense" anaphora produced by this rule are to be accounted for by a deletion transformation, and not by interpretive rules of pronominalization (which, she agrees, are the proper grammatical mechanism for "non-null" anaphora). Now VP deletion clearly takes place in dependent clauses and does not necessarily operate on adjacent constituents: *Although Bill wanted to, the rest of us decided among ourselves that we shouldn't attend the game.*

Footnote 38 continued

Thus by adopting a convention for "rule features" consistent with the arguments of Kayne (1969), I have arrived at a formulation of a rule that violates the particular definition of "local transformational operation" we have been working with, but not the intuitive notion of "strictly locally conditioned" that the definition was meant to capture. It may be that a redefinition of the notion is appropriate or that the formulation of the rule is not correct. Which alternative is correct, in this and in many other cases, cannot be decided in isolation; rather, our choice of analysis in each case must depend on the workability and restrictive power of some definition of local transformation throughout the grammar.

Further, VP deletion, if it is a transformation, is not stylistic, since two of the requirements for such rules are that they ALWAYS be optional and that they take well-formed surface structures as input. *I only ate because Bill did* cannot be derived from a well-formed surface structure by VP deletion; rather, it is derived from **I only did eat because Bill did eat*. Thus if VP deletion is a transformation, (97) does not hold.

A relevant observation by Peter Culicover is that any "deletion analysis" of the pseudo-cleft construction, along the lines of Bach and Peters (1968), is inconsistent with (97). If a deletion transformation is involved, it cannot be stylistic, because there are many pseudo-cleft forms that cannot be derived by an optional rule from a well-formed surface structure, e.g., *What John has done is eat the cake*. Hence, such an analysis is wrong, or else (97) is too strong.

Finally, as mentioned earlier, the conclusions of this section are meant to be tentative and suggestive of further research, as they have not been accompanied by thorough empirical investigation and explicit statements of rules of the grammar.

References

Aissen, Judith, & Hankamer, Jorge. Shifty subjects: A conspiracy in syntax. *Linguistic Inquiry*, 1972, *3*, 501—504.

Akmajian, Adrian. On deriving cleft sentences from pseudo-cleft sentences. *Linguistic Inquiry*, 1970, *1*, 149—168.

Akmajian, Adrian. *The two rules of raising in English*. Preliminary version, University of Massachusetts, 1973.

Anderson, Stephen, & Kiparsky, Paul. *A festschrift for Morris Halle*. New York: Holt, Rinehart & Winston, 1973.

Bach, Emmon. The order of elements in a transformational grammar of German. *Language*, 1962, *38*, 263—269.

Bach, Emmon. *Have* and *be* in English syntax. *Language*, 1967, *43*, 462—485.

Bach, Emmon & Peters, Stanley. *English pseudo-cleft sentences*. Unpublished manuscript, University of Texas, 1968.

Baker, Leroy. Notes on the description of English questions: The role of an abstract question morpheme. *Foundations of Language*, 1969, *6*, 197—219.

Baker, Leroy, & Brame, Michael. "Global rules": A rejoinder. *Language*, 1972, *48*, 51—75.

Banfield, Ann. Narrative style and the grammar of direct and indirect speech. *Foundations of Language*, 1973, *10*, 1—39. (a)

Banfield, Ann. Stylistic transformations in "Paradise Lost." Unpublished dissertation, University of Wisconsin, 1973. (b)

Berman, Arlene. On the VSO hypothesis. *Linguistic Inquiry*, 1974, *5*, 1—38.

Bierwisch, Manfred. Grammatick des deutschen Verbs. *Studia Grammatica*, II. Berlin: Academie Verlag, 1963.

Bierwisch, Manfred, & Heidolph, K. Progress in linguistics. The Hague: Mouton, 1970.

Binnick, Robert, Davidson, Alice, Green, Georgia, & Morgen, Jerry. *Papers from the Fifth Regional Meeting*. Chicago: Chicago Linguistics Society, 1969.

Blom, Alied. Konjunktie-reduktie en "gapping". Unpublished manuscript, University of Amsterdam, 1972.

Bowers, John. *Adjectives and adverbs in English*. Bloomington, Indiana: Indiana University Linguistics Club, 1969.

Brame, Michael. Conjectures and refutations in syntax and semantics. (In preparation.)

Bresnan, Joan. On complementizers: Towards a syntactic theory of complement types. *Foundations of Language*, 1970, *6*, 297—321.

Bresnan, Joan. Sentence stress and syntactic transformations. *Language*, 1971, *47*, 257—281. (a)

Bresnan, Joan. A note on the notion "identity of sense anaphora." *Linguistic Inquiry*, 1971, *2*, 589—597. (b)

Bresnan, Joan. *Theory of complementation in English syntax*. Unpublished dissertation, Massachusetts Institute of Technology, 1972. (a)

Bresnan, Joan. Stress and syntax: A reply. *Language*, 1972, *48*, 326—342. (b)

Bresnan, Joan. Syntax of the comparative clause. *Linguistic Inquiry*, 1973, *4*, 275—345.

Chiba, Shuji. On the movement of post-copular NP's in English. *Studies in English Linguistics*, 1974, *2*, 1—17.

Chomsky, Noam. *Syntactic structures*. The Hague: Mouton, 1957.

Chomsky, Noam. On the notion "rule of grammar." (1961) In J. Fodor & J. Katz (Eds.), *The structure of language: Readings in the philosophy of language*. Englewood Cliffs, N.J.: Prentice-Hall, 1964. Pp. 119—136.

Chomsky, Noam. A transformational approach to syntax. (1962) In J. Fodor & J. Katz (Eds.), *The structure of language: Readings in the philosophy of language*. Englewood Cliffs, N.J.: Prentice-Hall, 1964. Pp. 211—245.

Chomsky, Noam. *Current issues in linguistic theory*. The Hague: Mouton, 1964.

Chomsky, Noam. *Aspects of the theory of syntax*. Cambridge, Massachusetts: M.I.T. Press, 1965.

Chomsky, Noam. *Language and mind*. New York: Harcourt Brace Jovanovich, 1968.

Chomsky, Noam. Remarks on nominalization. In R. Jacobs & P. Rosenbaum (Eds.), *Readings in transformational grammar*. Waltham, Massachusetts: Blaisdell, 1970.

Chomsky, Noam. Deep structure, surface structure, and semantic interpretation. In D. Steinberg & L. Jacobovits (Eds.), *Semantics*. Cambridge: Cambridge University Press, 1971.

Chomsky, Noam. Some empirical issues in the theory of transformational grammar. In S. Peters (Ed.), *Goals in linguistic theory*. Englewood Cliffs, N.J.: Prentice-Hall, 1972.

Chomsky, Noam. Conditions on transformations. In S. Anderson & P. Kiparsky (Eds.), *A festschrift for Morris Halle*. New York: Holt, Rinehart & Winston, 1973.

Corum, Claudia, Smith-Stark, Thomas, & Weiser, Ann, *You take the high node and I'll take the low node*. Chicago: Chicago Linguistics Society, 1973.

Culicover, Peter. OM Sentences. *Foundations of Language*, 1972, *8*, 199—236.

Culicover, Peter. Introduction to J. Kurylowicz, ergativeness and the stadial theory of linguistic development. *The study of man*, 2. Irvine ,California: University of California School of Social Sciences, 1973.

Culicover, Peter, & Wexler, Kenneth. *Two applications of the freezing principle in English*. Social Sciences Working Papers, 38 (also 39 and 48). Irvine California: University of California, 1973.

Delorme, Evelyn, & Dougherty, Ray. Appositive NP constructions. *Foundations of Language*, 1972, *8*, 2—29.

Dougherty, Ray. *A transformational grammar of coordinates conjoined structures*. Unpublished dissertation, Massachusetts Institute of Technology, 1968.

Dougherty, Ray. A grammar of coordinate conjoined structures: I. *Language*, 1970, *46*, 850—898. (a)

Dougherty, Ray. Recent studies on language universals. *Foundations of Language*, 1970, *6*, 505—561. (b)

Downing, Bruce. Parenthetical rules and obligatory phrasing. *Papers in Linguistics*, 1973, *6*, 108—128.

Emonds, Joseph. Root and structure-preserving transformations. Unpublished dissertation, Massachusetts Institute of Technology, 1970.

Emonds, Joseph. Evidence that indirect object movement is a structure-preserving rule. *Foundations of Language*, 1972, *8*, 546—561. (a) [Reprinted in M. Gross, M. Halle, & M. P. Schützenberger (Eds.), *The formal analysis of natural languages*. The Hague: Mouton, 1973. Pp. 73—87.]

Emonds, Joseph. A reformulation of certain syntactic transformations. In S. Peters (Ed.), *Goals in linguistic theory*. Englewood Cliffs, N.J.: Prentice-Hall, 1972. (b)

Emonds, Joseph. Alternatives to global derivational constraints. *Glossa*, 1973, *7*, 39—62. (a)

Emonds, Joseph. Constraints on phrase structure configurations. In *Papers from the Third Annual California Linguistics Conference*. Stanford Occasional Papers in Linguistics, No. 3. Stanford University, Committee on Linguistics, 1973. (b)

Emonds, Joseph. Parenthetical clauses. In C. Corum, T. Smith-Stark, & A. Weiser (Eds.), *You take the high node and I'll take the low node*. Chicago: Chicago Linguistic Society, 1973. (c)

[Reprinted in C. Rohrer & N. Ruwet (Eds.), *Actes du colloque franco-allemand de grammaire transformationelle*. Tübingen, Germany: Niemeyer Verlag, 1974.]

Emonds, Joseph. Arguments for assigning tense meanings after certain syntactic transformations apply. In E. Keenan (Ed.), *Formal semantics*. Cambridge: Cambridge University Press, 1974.

Emonds, Joseph. An analysis of French clitics without positive output constraints. *Linguistic Analysis*, 1975, *1*, 1–32.

Emonds-Banfield, Peter. English syntactic competence. Seattle, Washington: Temple Day Care Center. (In preparation.)

Fillmore, Charles. *Indirect object constructions in English and the ordering of transformations*. The Hague: Mouton, 1965.

Fischer, Susan. The acquisition of verb-particle and dative constructions. Unpublished dissertation, Massachusetts Institute of Technology, 1971.

Fodor, Jerry, & Katz, Jerold. *The structure of language: Readings in the philosophy of language*. Englewood Cliffs, N.J.: Prentice-Hall, 1964.

Fraser, Bruce. *The verb-particle construction of English*. Cambridge, Massachusetts: M.I.T. Press, 1968.

Geis, Michael. Adverbial subordinate clauses in English. Unpublished dissertation, Massachusetts Institute of Technology, 1970.

Gleitman, Lila. Coordinating conjunctions in English (1965). In D. Reibel & S. Schane (Eds.), *Modern studies in English: Readings in transformational grammar*. Englewood Cliffs, N.J.: Prentice-Hall, 1969. Pp. 80–112.

Green, Georgia. A syntactic syncretism in English and French. In B. Kachru, R. Lees, Y. Malkiel, A. Pietrangeli, & S. Saporta (Eds.), *Issues in linguistics*. Urbana: Illinois: University of Illinois Press, 1972.

Grévisse, Maurice. *Le bon usage*. Septième édition Paris: Librairie Orientaliste Paul Geuthner, 1959.

Gross, Maurice. *Grammaire transformationelle du français: Syntaxe du verbe*. Paris: LaRousse, 1968.

Gross, Maurice, Halle, Morris, & Schützenberger, Marcel-Paul. *The formal analysis of natural languages*. The Hague: Mouton, 1973.

de Haan, G. J. On extraposition. Unpublished manuscript, Instituut A.W. de Groot voor Algemene Taalwetenschap (Utrecht), 1974.

Hamburger, Henry, & Wexler, Kenneth. *A mathematical theory of learning transformational grammar*. Social Sciences Working Papers, 47. Irvine, California: University of California, 1973.

Harris, Zellig. *Methods in structural linguistics*. Chicago: University of Chicago Press, 1951.

Harris, Zellig. Co-occurrence and transformation in linguistic structure. *Language*, 1957, *33*, 293–340.

Harris, Zellig. *Mathematical structures of language*. New York: Interscience Publishers, 1968.

Helke, Michael. On reflexives in English. *Linguistics*, 1973, *106*, 5–23.

Higgins, F. R. On J. Emonds' analysis of extraposition. In J. Kimball (Ed.), *Syntax and semantics*, vol. 2. New York: Seminar Press, 1973.

Higgins, F. R. The pseudo-cleft construction. Unpublished dissertation, Massachusetts Institute of Technology, 1974.

Hirschbühler, Paul. La dislocation à gauche comme construction basique en français. In C. Rohrer & N. Ruwet (Eds.), *Actes du colloque franco-allemand de grammaire transformationelle* Tübingen, Germany: Niemeyer Verlag, 1974.

Hooper, Joan. A critical look at the structure-preserving constraint. In P. Schachter & G. Bedell (Eds.), *Critiques of syntactic studies*, II. Los Angeles, California: University of California Linguistics Department, 1973.

Hooper, Joan, & Thompson, Sandra. On the applicability of root transformations. *Linguistic Inquiry*, 1973, *4*.

Jackendoff, Ray. Possessives in English. In S. Anderson, R. Jackendoff, & S. Keyser (Eds.), *Studies in transformational grammar and related topics.* Waltham, Massachusetts: Brandeis University English Department, 1968.

Jackendoff, Ray. Gapping and related rules. *Linguistic Inquiry,* 1971, *2,* 21—36.

Jackendoff, Ray. *Semantic interpretation in generative grammar.* Cambridge, Massachusetts: M.I.T. Press, 1972.

Jackendoff, Ray. The base rules for prepositional phrases. In S. Anderson & P. Kiparsky (Eds.), *A festschrift for Morris Halle.* New York: Holt, Rinehart & Winston, 1973.

Jackendoff, Ray, Selkirk, Elizabeth, & Bowers, John. *Lexicalist grammar.* Unpublished manuscript, 1974. [Discussed in Otero, C.-P., Introduction to N. Chomsky, *Estructuras sintácticas.* México: Siglo XXI, 1974.]

Jenkins, Lyle. Cleft reduction. In C. Rohrer & N. Ruwet (Eds.), *Actes du colloque franco-allemand de grammaire transformationelle.* Tubingen, Germany: Niemeyer Verlag, 1974.

Kajita, Masaru. *A generative-transformational study of semi-auxiliaries in present-day American English.* Tokyo: Sanseido, 1967.

Katz, Jerold, & Postal, Paul. *An integrated theory of linguistic descriptions.* Cambridge, Massachusetts: M.I.T. Press, 1964.

Kayne, Richard. *On the inappropriateness of rule features.* Quarterly Progress Report, 95. Cambridge, Massachusetts: M.I.T. Research Laboratory of Electronics, 1969.

Kayne, Richard. *French syntax: The transformational cycle* Unpublished dissertation, Massachusetts Institute of Technology, 1970.

Kayne, Richard. Subject inversion in French interrogatives. In J. Casagrande & B. Saciuk (Eds.), *Generative studies in romance languages.* Rowley, Massachusetts: Newbury House, 1972.

Kayne, Richard. *The transformational cycle in French syntax.* Cambridge, Massachusetts: M.I.T. Press, 1975.

Keyser, Samuel. Review of Sven Jacobson, "Adverbial Positions in English." *Language,* 1968, *44,* 357—374.

Kiparsky, Paul, & Kiparsky, Carol. Fact. In D. Steinberg & L. Jacobovits (Eds.), *Semantics.* Cambridge: Cambridge University Press, 1971.

Klima, Edward. Negation in English. In J. Fodor & J. Katz (Eds.), *The structure of language: Readings in the philosophy of language.* Englewood Cliffs, N.J.: Prentice-Hall, 1964.

Klima, Edward. Relatedness between grammatical systems. In D. Reibel & S. Schane (Eds.), *Modern studies in English: Readings in transformational grammar.* Englewood Cliffs, N.J.: Prentice-Hall, 1969.

Koster, Jan. Dutch as an SOV language. (1974). In A. Kraak (Ed.), *Linguistics in the Netherlands.* The Hague: Mouton. (In press.)

Kuiper, Koenraad. *A grammar of English noun compounds.* Unpublished dissertation, Simon Fraser University (Vancouver), 1972.

Kuno, Susumu. Some properties of non-referential noun phrases. In R. Jakobson & S. Kawamoto (Eds.), *Studies in general and oriental linguistics.* Tokyo: TEC Corp., 1970. Pp. 348—373.

Kuroda, S. Y. English relativization and certain related problems. In D. Reibel & S. Schane (Eds.), *Modern studies in English: Readings in transformational grammar.* Englewood Cliffs, N.J.: Prentice-Hall, 1969. Pp. 264—287.

Labov, William, Cohen, Paul, Robbins, Clarence, & Lewis, John. A study of non-standard English of Negro and Puerto-Rican speakers in New York City, vol. I: *Phonological and grammatical analyses.* New York: Columbia University, 1968.

Lakoff, George. *A note on negation.* Report NSF-16. Cambridge, Massachusetts: Harvard University Computation Laboratory, 1966.

Lakoff, George, & Peters, Stanley. Phrasal conjunction and symmetric predicates. (1966) In D. Reibel & S. Schane (Eds.), *Modern studies in English: Readings in transformational grammar.* Englewood Cliffs, N.J.: Prentice-Hall, 1969. Pp. 113—142.

Lakoff, George, & Ross, John. *A criterion for verb phrase constituency.* Report NSF-17. Cambridge, Massachusetts: Harvard University Computation Laboratory, 1966.

Lakoff, Robin. A syntactic argument for negative transportation. In R. Binnick, A. Davidson, G. Green, & J. Morgan (Eds.), *Papers from the Fifth Regional Meeting.* Chicago: Chicago Linguistics Society, 1969. Pp. 140—147.

Lasnik, Howard. *Analyses of negation in English.* Unpublished dissertation, Massachusetts Institute of Technology, 1972.

Lasnik, Howard, & Fiengo, Robert. Complement object deletion. *Linguistic Inquiry,* 1974, 5.

Maling, Joan. On "gapping and the order of constituents." *Linguistic Inquiry,* 1972, 3, 101—108.

Milner, Jean-Claude. Comparatives et relatives. (1972) In J.-C. Milner (Ed.), *Arguments linguistiques.* Paris: Editions Mame, 1973.

Milner, Jean-Claude. *Arguments linguistiques.* Paris: Editions Mame, 1973.

Milner, Jean-Claude. Les exclamatives et le complementizer. In C. Rohrer & N. Ruwet (Eds.), *Actes du colloque franco-allemand de grammaire transformationelle.* Tübingen, Germany: Niemeyer Verlag, 1974.

Milsark, Gary. Re: Doubl-ing. *Linguistic Inquiry,* 1972, 3, 542—549.

Nagahara, Yukio. Critique of Emonds' structure-preserving hypothesis. *Studies in English Linguistics,* 1974, 2, 28—60.

Newmeyer, Frederick. *English aspectual verbs.* Studies in Linguistics and Language Learning, VI. Seattle, Washington: University of Washington Linguistics Department, 1969.

Newmeyer, Frederick. The source of derived nominals in English. *Language,* 1971, 47, 786—796.

Newmeyer, Frederick. The precyclic nature of predicate raising. Paper presented at the University of Southern California Causative Festival, 1974.

Newmeyer, Frederick, & Emonds, Joseph. The linguist in American Society. In *Papers from the Seventh Regional Meeting.* Chicago: Chicago Linguistics Society, 1971.

Ogle, Richard. Natural order and dislocated syntax. Unpublished dissertation, University of California at Los Angeles, 1974.

Otero, Carlos-Peregrín. Acceptable ungrammatical [utterances] in Spanish. *Linguistic Inquiry,* 1972, 3, 233—242.

Otero, Carlos-Peregrín. Agrammaticality in performance. *Linguistic Inquiry,* 1973, 4, 551—562.

Otero, Carlos-Peregrín. *Grammar's definition vs. speaker's judgment: From the psychology to the sociology of language,* 1974 [French translation to appear in a volume edited by Mitsou Ronat. Paris: Galilée]. (a)

Otero, Carlos-Peregrín. Introduction to N. Chomsky, *Estructuras sintácticas.* México: Siglo XXI, 1974. (b)

Otero, Carlos-Peregrín. *Evolución y revolucion en romance* (2nd ed.). Barcelona: Seix Barral. (In press.)

Partee, Barbara. The syntax and semantics of quotation. In S. Anderson & P. Kiparsky (Eds.), *A festschrift for Morris Halle.* New York: Holt, Rinehart & Winston, 1973.

Perlmutter, David. Les pronoms objets in espagnol: Un exemple de la nécessité de contraintes de surface en syntaxe. *Langages,* 1969, 14, 81—133. (a)

Perlmutter, David. On the article in English. (1969) In M. Bierwisch & K. Heidolph (Eds.), *Progress in linguistics.* The Hague: Mouton, 1970. (b)

Perlmutter, David. Surface structure constraints in syntax. *Linguistic Inquiry,* 1970, 1, 187—256.

Perlmutter, David. *Deep and surface structure constraints in syntax.* New York: Holt, Rinehart & Winston, 1971.

Peters, Stanley. *Goals in linguistic theory.* Englewood Cliffs, N.J.: Prentice-Hall, 1972.

Picabia, Lelia. *Etudes transformationelles de constructions adjectivales.* Paris: C.N.R.S., Laboratoire d'Automatique Documentaire et Linguistique, 1970.

Postal, Paul. On so-called "pronouns" in English. (1966) In D. Reibel & S. Schane (Eds.), *Modern studies in English: Readings in transformational grammar*. Englewood Cliffs, N.J.: Prentice-Hall, 1969. Pp. 201—224.

Pullum, Geoffrey. Restating doubl-ing. *Glossa*, 1974, *8*, 109—120.

Quang Phuc Dong. Phrases anglaises sans sujet grammatical apparent. *Langages*, 1969, *14*, 44—51.

Rardin, Robert. *Sentence raising and sentence shift*. Unpublished manuscript, Massachusetts Institute of Technology, 1968.

Reibel, David, & Schane, Sanford. *Modern studies in English: Readings in transformational grammar*. Englewood Cliffs, N.J.: Prentice-Hall, 1969.

van Riemsdijk, Henk. A case for a trace. Unpublished manuscript, Instituut voor Algemene Taalwetenschap (Amsterdam), 1972.

van Riemsdijk, Henk. The Dutch P-soup. Unpublished manuscript, Instituut voor Algemene Taalwetenschap (Amsterdam), 1973.

van Riemsdijk, Henk, & Zwarts, Frans. Left dislocation in Dutch and the status of copying rules. Unpublished manuscript, Instituut voor Algemene Taalwetenschap (Amsterdam), 1974.

Roeper, Thomas. Approaches to a theory of language acquisition with examples from German children. Unpublished dissertation, Harvard University, 1972.

Rohrer, C., & Ruwet, N. *Actes du colloque franco-allemand de grammaire transformationelle*. Tübingen, Germany: Niemeyer Verlag, 1974.

Ronat, Mitsou. *Echelles de bases et mutations syntaxiques*. Unpublished dissertation, Université de Paris VIII (Vincennes), 1973.

Rosenbaum, Peter. *The grammar of English predicate complement constructions*. Cambridge, Massachusetts: M.I.T. Press, 1967.

Ross, John. Constraints on variables in syntax. Unpublished dissertation, Massachusetts Institute of Technology, 1967. (a)

Ross, John. Gapping and the order of constituents. (1967) In M. Bierwisch & K. Heidolph (Eds.), *Progress in linguistics*. The Hague: Mouton, 1970. (b)

Ross, John. A proposed rule of tree-pruning. (1968) In D. Reibel & S. Schane (Eds.), *Modern studies in English: Readings in transformational grammar*. Englewood Cliffs, N.J.: Prentice-Hall, 1969. Pp. 288—300.

Ross, John. Doubl-ing. *Linguistic Inquiry*, 1972, *3*, 61—86. (a)

Ross, John. Act. In D. Bairdson & G. Harman (Eds.), *Semantics of natural languages*. Dordrecht: Holland, 1972. (b)

Roos, John. Slifting. In M. Gross, M. Halle, & M.-P. Schützenberger (Eds.), *The formal analysis of natural languages*. The Hague: Mouton, 1973. Pp. 133—169.

Ruwet, Nicolas. A propos des prépositions de lieu en français. In C. Hyart (Ed.), *Mélanges Fohalle*. Liège: Université de Liège, 1969.

Ruwet, Nicolas. *Théorie syntaxique et syntaxe du français*. Paris: Editions du Seuil, 1972.

Saib, Jilali. On underlying word order in Modern Standard Arabic. Unpublished manuscript, University of California at Los Angeles, 1972.

Schacter, Paul. On syntactic categories: A critique of Lakoff's "adjectives and verbs," Ross's "adjectives as noun phrases," and Bach's "nouns and noun phrases." In P. Schachter & G. Bedell (Eds.), *Critiques of syntactic studies*, II. Los Angeles: University of California Linguistics Department, 1973.

Schachter, Paul, & Bedell, George. *Critiques of syntactic studies*, II. Los Angeles: University of California Linguistics Department, 1973.

Schlyter, Suzanne. Une hierarchie d'adverbes en français. *Recherches Linguistiques*, 1973, *1*, 139—158.

Schmerling, Susan. Subjectless sentences and the notion of surface structure. In C. Corum, T. Smith-Stark, & A. Weiser (Eds.), *Papers from the Ninth Regional Meeting.* Chicago: Chicago Linguistic Society, 1973.

Schwartz, Arthur. Constraints on transformations. *Journal of Linguistics,* 1972, *8,* 35—86.

Selkirk, Elisabeth. *On the determiner system of noun phrase and adjective phrase.* Unpublished manuscript, Massachusetts Institute of Technology, 1970.

Selkirk, Elisabeth. *The phrase phonology of English and French.* Unpublished dissertation, Massachusetts Institute of Technology, 1972.

Shopen, Timothy. *A generative theory of ellipsis.* Unpublished dissertation, University of California at Los Angeles, 1972.

Smith, Carlotta. A class of complex modifiers in English. *Language,* 1961, *37,* 342—365.

Smith, Carlotta. Determiners and relative clauses in a generative grammar of English. (1964) In D. Reibel & S. Schane (Eds.), *Modern studied in English: Readings in transformational grammar.* Englewood Cliffs, N.J.: Prentice-Hall, 1969, Pp. 247—263.

Stockwell, Robert, Schachter, Paul, & Partee, Barbara. *Major syntactic structures of English* New York: Holt, Rinehart & Winston, 1973.

Strozer, Judith. *Clitics in Spanish.* Ph.D. dissertation, University of California at Los Angeles. (In preparation).

Williams, Edwin. *Small clauses in English.* Unpublished manuscript, Massachusetts Institute of Technology, 1972.

Zwarts, Frans. *On restricting base structure recursion in Dutch.* Unpublished manuscript. Amsterdam: Instituut voor Algemene Taalwetenschap, 1974.

Zwicky, Arnold. Auxiliary reduction in English. *Linguistic Inquiry,* 1970, *1,* 321—336.

Zwicky, Arnold. In a manner of speaking. *Linguistic Inquiry,* 1971, *2,* 223—233.

Index